MEDIA AND LEFT

Studies in Critical Social Sciences Book Series

Haymarket Books is proud to be working with Brill Academic Publishers (www.brill.nl) to republish the *Studies in Critical Social Sciences* book series in paperback editions. This peer-reviewed book series offers insights into our current reality by exploring the content and consequences of power relationships under capitalism, and by considering the spaces of opposition and resistance to these changes that have been defining our new age. Our full catalog of *SCSS* volumes can be viewed at www.haymarketbooks.org/category/scss-series.

MEDIA AND LEFT

EDITED BY
SAVAŞ ÇOBAN

Haymarket
Books
Chicago, IL

First published in 2014 by Brill Academic Publishers, The Netherlands.
© 2014 Koninklijke Brill NV, Leiden, The Netherlands

Published in paperback in 2015 by
Haymarket Books
P.O. Box 180165
Chicago, IL 60618
773-583-7884
www.haymarketbooks.org

ISBN: 978-1-60846-559-0

Trade distribution:
In the U.S. through Consortium Book Sales, www.cbsd.com
In the UK, Turnaround Publisher Services, www.turnaround-uk.com
In all other countries by Publishers Group Worldwide, www.pgw.com

Cover design by Ragina Johnson.

This book was published with the generous support of Lannan Foundation
and the Wallace Action Fund.

Printed in Canada by union labor.

10 9 8 7 6 5 4 3 2 1

Library of Congress Cataloging-in-Publication Data is available.

Contents

Foreword   VII
List of Tables and Figures   IX
List of Contributors   X

Introduction   1

1   The Spectre of Marx   5
      Michael Wayne

2   Culture, Communication, & Ideology = Forms of Work   15
      Christian Fuchs

3   Media Power and Class Power
      Overplaying Ideology   44
      David Miller

4   The Cultural Apparatus of Monopoly Capital
      An Introduction   67
      John Bellamy Foster and Robert W. McChesney

5   The War Against Democracy in the UK   104
      Nick Stevenson

6   Infamy and Indoctrination in American Media and Politics   115
      Arthur Asa Berger

7   U.S. Media and the World   132
      Gerald Sussman

8   The Evolving Business Models of Network News?   139
      Oliver Boyd-Barrett

9   Corporate Social (Ir)Responsibility in Media and Communication
      Industries   166
      Marisol Sandoval

10   Media Spectacle and the North African Arab Uprisings
      Some Critical Reflections   190
         Douglas Kellner

11   Turkey's 'War and Peace'
      The Kurdish Question and the Media   232
         Savaş Çoban

      Epilogue   249
      Index   254

Foreword

Since 2007 or 2008 a few striking developments have occurred, most of which are not yet fully understood or appreciated. One is the global crisis of capitalism. In most places and by most accounts capitalism is stagnant with little prospect of sufficient growth to provide for rising real incomes and the capacity to dramatically improve the quality of life. Indeed, the present trend of global capitalism is toward ever increasing economic inequality and a persistent dire poverty for a large portion of the human race.

Second, the ecological situation has moved from grim to grimmer. More than a few scientists warn that unless there is a dramatic shift in the way people organize the economy, the prospects for human life surviving in any acceptable manner is remote. The crisis of capitalism transcends stagnation, inequality and poverty to the very issue of the survival of our species, not to mention many other species.

Third, democratic governance worldwide is straining under the pressures of capitalism. Almost everywhere the power of wealth and privilege to dominate policymaking and governance is on the rise. In my home, the United States, governance is scarcely democratic; corporate power and u.s. militarism are effectively beyond debate regardless of public opinion or who wins an election. Transnational trade agreements like the Trans Pacific Partnership effectively terminate sovereignty over core economic functions and lock-in the ability of corporations and investors to act with impunity.

That's the bad news. The good news is that across the world, to varying degrees, people are organizing to address these crises and help push humanity toward some form of post-capitalist democracy. Some of the most exciting developments are in Latin America, but there are glimmers of hope everywhere. Periodic mass uprisings, like those in 2011 stretching from the Middle East to Occupy in the USA, remind us that the people are open to a very different world.

Another set of good news is the increasing recognition of the centrality of a credible open and democratic communication system to democracy, post-capitalist or otherwise. For much of the 20th century the political left paid too little attention to issues of media. Communication was seemingly a dependent variable that would work itself out as the more important issues of the political economy were addressed. That approach clearly was a clunker. Indeed, it is not too extreme to say that the democratic quality of a post-capitalist society will be demonstrated as much as anything by how open, uncensored, vibrant and diverse its media system is.

Moreover, as communication is now central to investment and profitmaking in capitalism – 12 of the 30 most valuable corporations in the United States are primarily Internet-oriented firms – it is not an abstract or ephemeral matter; when one considers rethinking the structure of communication, one is by necessity considering the replacement of existing capitalism with something substantially different.

This book addresses the importance of communication in the current crisis and going forward to a post-capitalist democracy. It compiles the work of some of the finest communication scholars in the world and covers a broad range of issues. Several of the essays take a fresh look at the work of Karl Marx, and find that there is much of value there concerning communication. Others address the media situation in various nations in the world. In combination, this book provides an *entre* to some of the most important communication research being done, on pressing issues. For the next generation of critical scholars worldwide, this book is mandatory reading.

But it is more than that. If there is radical social change for the better in our future, toward a post-capitalist democracy, it will be led by the political left. Much of the left desperately needs to get smarter and more sophisticated about media and communication issues. It needs to dispense with banalities about technology and take communication as seriously as any other issue it addresses. This book explains why, and explains how to do it.

Robert W. McChesney

List of Tables and Figures

Tables

2.1   The subject, object and subject-object of cognitive, communicative and
       co-operative work   30
2.2   Workers, ideologies and worldviews in various fields of society   38
2.3   A typology of subjective reactions to ideology   40
6.1   Top 10 media conglomerates, 2010   121
6.2   Lifestyles, group boundaries and rules and prescriptions   126
6.3   Nature of lifestyles   127

Figures

2.1   A stage model of cultural work   23
2.2   The tripleC model of semiosis/information   28
2.3   The information process as work process   31
11.1   Perceptions of the Kurdish question   241
11.2   Perceptions of the Kurdish question, by ethnic distribution   241

List of Contributors

Arthur Asa Berger (MA, 1956)
is Professor Emeritus of Broadcast and Electronic Communication Arts at San Francisco State University where he taught from 1965 to 2003. Berger has published more than 60 books on the mass media, popular culture, humor, tourism and everyday life. Among his books are *Media Analysis Techniques* 5/E (Sage, 2014), *Media & Society: A Critical Perspective* 3/E (Roman & Littlefield, 2012), *Seeing is Believing: An Introduction to Visual Communication* 3/E (McGraw Hill, 2008), *Ads, Fads and Consumer Culture: Advertising's Impact on American Character and Society* 2/E (Roman and Littlefield, 2004), *Media and Communication Research Methods: An Introduction to Qualitative and Quantitative Approaches* 2/E (Sage, 2014), *The Art of Comedy Writing* (Transaction Publishers, 2007), *Shop 'Til You Drop: Consumer Behavior and American Culture* (Roman and Littlefield, 2004), and *Vietnam Tourism* (Haworth Hospitality Press. 2005).

John Bellamy Foster
is editor of *Monthly Review* and professor of sociology at the University of Oregon. His latest book, written with Robert W. McChesney, is *The Endless Crisis: How Monopoly-Finance Capital Creates Stagnation and Upheaval from the USA to China* (Monthly Review Press, 2012).

Oliver Boyd-Barrett
joined the School of Communication Studies as Director in 2005, a position he held for three years before deciding to return to faculty in the Department of Journalism. His current research interests include international and national news agencies, news media and the 'war on terror', and Hollywood representations of the intelligence community. He was previously Professor of Communication at California State Polytechnic University in Pomona, California, and has held various appointments at universities in the United Kingdom. Dr Boyd-Barrett has published extensively on educational and management communications, international news media, and the political economy of mass communication. He is founding chair of the division for Global Communication and Social Change in the International Communication Association.

Savaş Çoban
is an independent researcher. His university education focussed on English Teaching. His MSc degree dealt with Turkish as a Foreign Language. For his PhD he studied Radio-TV. His publications include *Azınlıklar ve Dil* (Su Yayınları,

2005), *Hegemonya Aracı ve İdeolojik Aygıt Olarak Medya* (Parşömen Yayinlari, 2013), *Media's Role in the Socialist Era* (Amani International Publishers, 2013), *Azınlıklar, Ötekiler ve Medya* (Ayrıntı Yayinlari, 2014), and *Medya ve İktidar* (Evrensel Basin Yayin, 2014).

Christian Fuchs

is Professor at the University of Westminster's Communication and Media Research Institute. He is editor of *tripleC: Communication, Capitalism & Critique* and author of books such as *Social Media: A Critical Introduction* (Sage, 2013), *Digital Labour and Karl Marx* (Routlege, 2014), *Foundations of Critical Media and Information Studies* (Routlege, 2011), *Internet and Society: Social Theory in the Information Age* (Routledge, 2008).

Douglas Kellner

is a 'third generation' critical theorist in the tradition of the Frankfurt Institute for Social Research. Kellner was an early theorist of critical media literacy and has since become a leading theorist and critic of media culture. In his recent work he has increasingly argued that media culture has become dominated by spectacle and mega-spectacle. He has contributed important studies on the processes of globalization, counter-hegemonic movements, and alternative cultural expressions for a more radically democratic society. Kellner has written extensively on the postmodern turn in philosophy, the arts, science, and technology. His more recent work explores the politically oppositional potential of new media with an emphasis on what he has termed 'multiple technoliteracies'. Previously Kellner served as the literary executor of the famed documentary film maker Emile de Antonio. Currently he is overseeing the publication of six volumes of the collected papers of the Critical Theorist, Herbert Marcuse. Kellner currently holds the George F. Kneller Philosophy of Education Chair at the Graduate School of Education & Information Studies, UCLA. His recent publications include *Cinema Wars: Hollywood Film and Politics in the Bush-Cheney Era* (Wiley-Blackwell, 2009), *Media/Cultural Studies: Critical Approaches*, edited with Rhonda Hammer (Peter Lang, 2009), *Marcuse's Challenge to Education* (Roman & Littlefield, 2009), *On Marcuse: Critique, Liberation, and Reschooling in the Radical Pedagogy of Herbert Marcuse* (Sense Publishers, 2008), *Guys and Guns Amok: Domestic Terrorism and School Shootings From the Oklahoma City Bombings to the Virginia Tech Massacre* (Paradigm Publishers, 2008).

Marisol Sandoval

is a Lecturer at the Department of Culture and Creative Industries at City University, London. Her research critically assesses questions of power, responsibility, exploitation, ideology and resistance in the global culture industries. Marisol is author of *From Corporate to Social Media: Critical Perspectives on Corporate Social Responsibility in Media and Communication Industries* (Routledge, 2014). She is the Managing Editor of the open access journal *tripleC: Communication, Capitalism & Critique*.

Robert W. McChesney
is the Gutgsell Endowed Professor in the Department of Communication at the University of Illinois. He is the author of *Digital Disconnect: How Capitalism Is Turning the Internet Against Democracy* (New Press, 2013).

Nick Stevenson
completed his PhD in SPS at Cambridge University in 1991 on the links between the New Left and culture, ideology, and politics. Between 1991 and 2001 he was lecturer in the Department of Sociological Studies at Sheffield University. During that time he published *Culture, Ideology and Socialism: Raymond Williams and E.P. Thompson* (Avebury, 1995), *Understanding Media Cultures: Social Theory and Mass Communication* (Sage, 1995), *The Transformation of the Media: Globalisation, Morality, and Ethics* (Addison-Wesley Longman, 1999), *Making Sense of Men's Magazines* (Polity, 2001) and an edited collection *Culture and Citizenship* (Sage, 2001). He was appointed Senior Lecturer in Sociology in Nottingham in 2001. He has also published *Cultural Citizenship* (McGraw-Hill, 2003), and *David Bowie: Fame, Sound and Vision* (Polity, 2006). He is currently on the editorial board of the BSA journal *Cultural Sociology and Keywords*. His most recent publications are *Education* and *Cultural Citizenship* (Sage, 2011) and *Freedom* (Routledge, 2012). His recent research topics include European modernity and culture, the future of social democracy, jazz music, and human rights.

Gerald Sussman
is Professor of Urban Studies and International Studies at Portland State University. He is the author or editor of several books including *The Propaganda Society: Promotional Culture and Politics in Global Context* (Peter Lang, 2011), *Branding Democracy: U.S. Regime Change in Post-Soviet Eastern Europe* (Peter Lang, 2010), and *Global Electioneering: Campaign Consulting, Communications, and Corporate Financing* (Rowman & Littlefield, 2005).

Michael Wayne
is a Professor in Film and Television Studies at Brunel University where he convenes the MA in Documentary Practice. He is the author of *Marxism and Media Studies: Key Concepts and Contemporary Trends* (Pluto, 2003), and *Political*

Film: The Dialectics of Third Cinema (Pluto, 2001). Both books have been trans-lated into Turkish. His most recent publication is *Marx's Das Kapital For Beginners* (For Beginners, 2012). He is also the co-director of a feature length documentary film *The Condition of the Working Class* (ThreePenny Kino, 2013). His forthcoming book *Red Kant: Aesthetics, Marxism and the Third Critique* will be published by Bloomsbury in 2014.

Introduction

Savaş Çoban

Capitalism uses the media to establish its hegemony and to mend the cracks caused by its many crises and contradictions. The chapters in this book examine the media with a critical eye from the left. All the contributors have a common point of departure: that the media must be understood as key organs within the global capitalist system. The capitalist system uses the media at every turn to promote this dominant ideology, with the result that individuals in society are unable to think, learn or question in the process of absorbing this readily available information. As Marx stated in 'The German Ideology':

> The ideas of the ruling class are in every epoch the ruling ideas, i.e. the class which is the ruling material force of society, is at the same time its ruling intellectual force. The class which has the means of material production at its disposal has control at the same time over the means of mental production, so that thereby, generally speaking, the ideas of those who lack the means of mental production are subject to it. The ruling ideas are nothing more than the ideal expression of the dominant material relationships, the dominant material relationships grasped as ideas; hence of the relationships which make the one class the ruling one, therefore, the ideas of its dominance.
> MARX and ENGELS, 2004:64

Media provides the average person with information, and in so doing shapes our understanding of power relationship in society. In capitalist countries, corporate media control filters information to convey a desired virtuality rather than reality itself. Information presents lies as truth as it passes through many channels which provide access to the public's mind. The result is that real problems are hidden, and what is normal gets turned into problems, all in support of the capitalist mode of production. As Raymond Williams states, hegemony and ideology are the very phenomena that shapes and redirects our lives.

> Hegemony is then not only the articulate upper level of 'ideology,' nor are its forms of control only those ordinarily seen as "manipulation" or "indoctrination." It is a whole body of practices and expectations, over the whole of our living: our senses, our assignments of energy, our

shaping perceptions of ourselves and our world. It is a lived system of meaning and values—constitutive and constituting—which as they are experienced as practices appear as reciprocally confirming. It thus constitutes a sense of reality for most people in the society, a sense of the absolute because experienced reality beyond which it is very difficult for most members of the society to move, in most areas of their lives.

WILLIAMS, 1977:110

Williams regards ideology as a relatively formal and articulated system of values and beliefs, which can be abstracted as a world vision or perspective of a social class. One of the uses of ideology is the process of generating ideas and meanings. Williams tries to shed more light on the definition of the media, which was a relatively new term at the time, characterizing it as an intermediary power:

In the twentieth century, the description of a newspaper as a 'medium' for advertising became common, and the extended description of the press and broadcasting 'the media' was affected by this. 'A medium' or 'the media' is then, on the one hand, a term for a social organ or institution of general communication-a relatively neutral use- and, on the other hand, a term for a secondary or derived use (as in advertising) of an organ or institution with another apparently primary purpose. Yet in either case the 'medium' is a form of social organization, something essentially different from the idea of an intermediate communicative substance.

WILLIAMS, 1977:159

Media is a device that shapes the public's consent for capitalist hegemony and facilitates the spread of its ideology. Capitalism uses media to mend cracks in the system as they emerge, and in the process reproduce the dominant ideology. The bourgeoisie not only forms the consciousness of the society via the media, more recently and with great effect using television, but through the media it keeps control over society. Hundreds of television channels blast information into our homes through the news, programs, films, music and many more venues all reflecting the ideology and hegemony of the bourgeoisie. In this respect, increasingly and to an extent greater than any time in the past, media takes on the important role of carring and spreading the discourse of this dominant ideology and ensuring hegemony in the global economy.

Mosco juxtaposes Marx's writings in the *Grundrisse* and as a journalist to argue that he represents himself both as a political economist and a cultural theorist. He concludes by arguing that "[w]hereas the *Grundrisse* suggested ways to theorize knowledge and communication labour, his journalism demonstrated how to practice it with passion and intelligence. These are lessons that communication students, and not just Marxist scholars, would do well to learn. (Mosco, 2012)"

Michael Wayne discusses how essential Marx's analysis of capitalism is for an understanding of the media. He demonstrates how Marx's methodology and categories of analysis illuminate the political economy of the media, its culture and politics. Christian Fuchs argues that media theory has ignored the relationship of work on the one hand and culture/communication/ideology on the other hand. While these two realms have been routinely separated in the work of Raymond Williams, Ferruccio Rossi-Landi and Marxist semiotics, we can overcome this separation by taking a cultural-materialist approach that interprets culture, communicaiton and ideology as specific forms of work.

David Miller is questioning the role of the media in the reproduction of class power. To put this in perspective, John Bellamy Foster and Robert W. McChesney address these emerging concerns, over the past four decades the "political economy of communication" has emerged as a dynamic field of study, and one where considerable radical scholarship has taken place. Marisol Sandoval adds to this discussion by taking a critical look at Corporate Social Responsibility in media and communication industries.

Nick Stevenson, in his essay, explores the importance of democracy for critical thinking and questions the assumption that the media and democracy are synonymous. Arthur Asa Berger provides a case study on the pseudo spectacle of democratic politcs by analysing the US Presidential elections of 2012. Gerald Sussman analyses the political economy of the US media and its domination of the public sphere. Oliver Boyd-Barrett offers a historical account of the evolution of the US television networks between 1940–2010 and investigates their complicity with the US military industrial complex.

The North African Arab Uprisings and the contradictory dynamics of globalisation is the focus of Douglas Kellner's contribution, arguing that the media turns these revolts into a spectacle, but at the same time generate a challenge to capitalist hegemony as it circulates images of revolution, insurrection and the demand for social justice and human rights around the global public sphere. Savaş Çoban's concluding chapter focuses on the Kurdish Question and the media in Turkey, arguing that the mainstream Turkish media has played a substantial role in the 'securitisation' of the Kurdish issue in public discourse. In his closing epilogue, Mandy Tröger brings the arguments laid out in this volume together.

References

Marx, K. and F. Engels. 2004. *The German Ideology*, New York, NY: International Publishers.

Mosco, V 2012. Marx is Back, But Which One? On Knowledge Labour and Media Practice, *tripleC-Open Access Journal for a Global Sustainable Information Society*, 10:2:570–576 Available at (accessed March 12, 2014) www.triple-c.at.

Williams, Raymond. 1977. *Marxism and Literature,* Oxford: Oxford University Press.

CHAPTER 1

The Spectre of Marx

Michael Wayne

The Political Crisis

If there was one characteristic that marked the interregnum between the collapse of the Soviet Union in 1991, the opening up of China to international capitalism and the economic crisis that exploded in 2008, it was an extraordinary lack of historical consciousness. How else to explain the hubris and complacency of the period, when the political and economic elites really seemed to believe their own propaganda? They declared that a new economic paradigm had arrived, bringing with it undreamt promises of wealth and consumer bliss as long as the market was left to do its own thing. Only a supreme historical blindness could have convinced the political and economic elites to forget an elementary truth, simple enough to enunciate and borne out by nearly 400 years of history: namely that the capitalist system remains structurally prone to major economic crises. Even the elites today cannot escape this uncomfortable truth.

But they are still fleeing from another closely interconnected one and it is this: that when economic crises happen on a large scale they produce a political crisis which we may call in academic terms a 'paradigm shift', but on the streets it looks more like revolt and even sometimes, whisper it, revolution. So little have the political elites learned that on the right – a term that now covers most of the mainstream political spectrum – the crises is seen as an opportunity to drive the neoliberal agenda further and complete what in the UK started as the Thatcher revolution using a political script that sounds, as with the first endeavors to privatize the police, like a Hollywood science fiction film.

Capitalism has never been particularly good at dealing with history. It would rather forget that it was born, it resists awareness of where social wealth comes from and shudders at any intimations that it may just be mortal. Marx spent a good deal of *Das Kapital* decoding the categories of bourgeois political economy and showing how they repressed the inconvenient historical and social foundations of bourgeois society. If he thought classical political economy was bad then the arid and abstract doctrines of the neo-classical paradigm, which has dominated university economics departments, corporate boardrooms and Government meetings, would have made his beard fall out.

Neo-classical economics seems to be completely blind to any sense that there are political consequences to be paid when driving through neo-liberal policies that are profoundly destructive. The surprise and the indignation on the collective face of the European political and economic elites that the Greeks have had the temerity to reject the pro-austerity policies imposed on them, is palpable. Yet the artillery of economic austerity raining down on Greece from the EU Central Bank, the IMF and international finance capital, has laid waste to public use values on a scale that makes Bashar Assad's mortar attacks on Homs look puny by comparison. But such economic violence – which has torn families apart and sent the suicide rate skywards – remains invisible to much of the western media, for whom capital is the very embodiment of rationality. Marx understood how the apparent freedom of contractual exchange in the market masked unequal power relations and violence. A good deal of *Das Kapital* was devoted to deconstructing the appearance of consent and showing that there was nothing free and equal when one side own the means of production (including financial resources) and the other side have only their labour power to sell. The 'proletarianisation' and immiseration of an entire country by outside forces, in the case of Greece, has rarely been this rapid or brutal. If this is rational, then it is rationality devoid of reason.

The political crisis now gripping Europe predates 2008. The hollowing out of democracy took the form of the elimination of ideological choices at the ballot box, the massive increase in perception management (spin), the hemorrhaging of trust in politicians, rising levels of abstention from the political process, and a gradual blurring of the boundaries between the political and economic elites. In the past Marxists – perhaps not without reason – would have been lambasted for crass economicism and neglect of the 'autonomy' of the political if they portrayed politicians as corporate glove puppets. But the autonomy of the political is a construct, not a fact of nature. And the last three decades of neo-liberalism has been spent dismantling that autonomy. Not only has the sophisticated Marxist critique come to pass, but capitalism seems determined to prove that even the crude Marxist brush strokes paint a picture closely resembling reality.

The Media Crisis

A great scandal has unfolded in the UK, involving Rupert Murdoch's media empire, the political class and the police. It is a scandal that illuminates the neo-liberal landscape and its contradictions. Murdoch sought to take full control of the revenues generated from the satellite television company British Sky

Broadcasting which it currently owns 40% of. The new Coalition government made up of the Conservatives and the Liberal Democrats looked to be waving through the take-over. Concerns were raised about giving more resources and power to Murdoch's News International and its parent company News Corporation. But the government was clearly not listening. Yet with days to go before the expected announcement that the take-over would proceed, a story about Murdoch owned newspapers' involvement in phone hacking, which had had growing momentum in the weeks and months before, exploded into the wider public consciousness, producing widespread revulsion which killed the take-over bid stone dead. It transpired that the Murdoch owned paper *News of the World* had hacked into the phone of a teenage school- girl who had been murdered in 2002. The fall-out of the scandal has been impressive. Senior police officers were forced to resign over questions that they had tried to cover up evidence that the newspaper had engaged in widespread and illegal phone hacking for years. Then the Sunday edition of the *New of the World* was shut down. Shortly afterwards, Rebekah Brookes, News International's chief executive officer, responsible for the UK press operation also resigned. Then an even bigger scalp fell. Rupert's son, James Murdoch resigned as chairman of BSkyB, even as the media regulator, OFCOM, was beginning to look into whether the Murdoch family were 'fit and proper' people to own broadcasting licenses. The scandal broke the 'political' power of Murdoch and his clan over the political class in the UK, who were now rapidly distancing themselves from him. An inquiry, the Leveson inquiry, is now underway, into the media and their links with the police and the political class as well as their general practices and ethics. The inquiry is laying bare, in an extraordinarily public way, a nexus of political and economic power that is institutional and deeply self-serving.

The question we should ask is how a media empire as powerful as Murdoch's could have been brought to this point within a matter of a few months? The answer is that there are some key contradictions within capitalism that can produce earthquakes for even the most powerful organizations and institutions. One of the crucial tasks which the state undertakes is to provide the legal framework in which relations between capitalist and workers and relations between capitalist and capitalist, takes place. It is the intra-capitalist competition and what it is doing to that legal framework which has been highlighted by a number of recent cases. Without the law which is supposed to provide the universal grounds on which business activity takes place, capitalism would quickly descend into a form of commercial warlordism.

But there is a problem. Bourgeois law is supposed to be universal. But bourgeois economics knows no universal interest – only the self-interest of the corporation and only the profit motif. And intra-capitalist competition is putting immense pressure on the law. For as capital becomes bigger, wealthier and more powerful, as it makes more and more connections with the state and seeks influence within it, so it becomes possible to conduct its intra-capitalist competition in terms that crosses the line and breaks the law. They have the weapons to do that and very, very often they can use their political influence to get away with it. And intra-capitalist competition does not go away as capital gets larger – its gets more ferocious. Everyone knows that industrial sabotage is part of the game of capitalist competition for example.

Back in 2002 I remember writing, in my book *Marxism and Media Studies* about a company called NDS controlled by News International which, it was alleged, had cracked the codes of smart cards used by digital TV channels in competition with BSKYB. NDS, it was said, circulated the codes on the internet, thus causing considerable financial problems for News International competitors such as ITV Digital and Canal Plus. It was a small story back then that few people were taking much notice of but recent events have put the case back in the spotlight. What is very likely however is that we only see the tip of the corporate iceberg in terms of industrial sabotage. Now, in the era of neoliberalism which seeks to cut back on the regulations that govern the day to day activities of capitalist business, the likelihood of capitalist economic interests infringing, subverting and breaking capitalist law, must grow, will grow and has grown.

Intra-capitalist competition also means that as powerful as Murdoch's empire was (and remains of course, especially economically), there were other media players who feared Murdoch achieving even more power within the UK media scene. The *Guardian* newspaper for example played a leading role in uncovering the hacking scandal and pushing it to the fore of public consciousness. So too did a Parliamentary committee on culture, media and sport which has been investigating the hacking scandal and which concluded in a recent report that Rupert Murdoch was indeed 'not a fit person' to exercise stewardship of a major international company. Although the Murdoch empire had cowed and bullied and bought off many MPs, they clearly were not able to render everyone impotent. As events proceeded, as News International became wounded, so individuals and groups became emboldened – and the long festering wound of Murdoch's influence over the body politic was now seen as something that could be addressed.

But all this rested on another contradiction. The contradiction that goes to the heart of social relations – namely the question of private property. Marx noted in *Das Kapital* how the turning of labour-power into a commodity meant that two conflicting property rights inevitably clashed. The purchaser of labour power maintains their right to squeeze as much value out of the commodity labour power as possible, because for the period of the working day, it has become their private property. On the other hand, because of the peculiar nature of this commodity, namely because it is inseparable from the person who sells it, the seller maintains their private property rights in wanting limits as to how far their own labour power can be squeezed. There is therefore an antinomy, Marx observes between two conflicting property rights – which is settled by the law and the balance of class forces. Now, in the case of the hacking scandal we have an antinomy between the power of private capital and the legal rights of the private person which private monopoly capital has violated by hacking into personal phone calls and answer phone messages. As evidence emerged of what the *News of the World* had been up to, a queue of celebrities and personalities went to court to find out if they had been victims. These court cases really drove the investigations of the *Guardian* and the Parliamentary select committee.

However, to understand why the *News of the World* had been driven into illegal practices in its search for stories, you have to understand the stratified nature of news journalism in the UK. There are broadly three types. Investigative journalism is one form of journalism we have every reason to be grateful for and must defend and encourage. But no-one can pretend that this form of journalism constitutes the normal activity of the corporate media or reflects the fundamental institutional relations between the media and the state. The vast majority of what the media produces falls into two other kinds of media output.

One type of news journalism is all about the networks of ties between the media and the state, the networks of collusion. Let us call it network journalism or embedded journalism. It is there in the daily briefings that the Prime Minister and his spokespeople give, along with all the political parties, to hacks who recycle their agendas without any critical thinking whatsoever. Some of these people fondly think of themselves as champions of the Fourth Estate, holding power to account. In reality the media routinely accept the neo-liberal policy agendas that flow ceaselessly from the political parties. Words like reform, modernization, choice, efficiency savings, innovation and others that are part of the vocabulary of neo-liberalism, are never questioned and are never linked to their real effects and intentions, namely privatization, social stratification, cuts and profiteering. The vast bulk of the middlebrow and liberal media output on news falls into this type of network journalism that involves recycling without critical comment what is effectively the agenda of a tiny elite within the UK.

This means that with the social strains inevitable with the emergence of the post-social democratic state, the media simply reproduce without question, the authoritarian law and order agenda of successive governments, as we saw only too clearly in the mass media coverage of the street riots in the UK in 2011. Or in relation to the Coalition government's cuts agenda, the media cultivate mass amnesia and wish us to forget that small matter of having to bail out the banking system with public money – the same system that we were told was too important to regulate properly because it was the engine of growth and the God to which we must all bow down too. Here again, you could hardly put a cigarette paper between the mass output of the media and the consensus across all the political parties that there must be cuts in public services. That consensus amongst political elites is of course incredibly damaging to democracy and the media's reproduction of that consensus is also incredibly damaging to democracy as both political and media elites move ever further apart from the majority of the people in the UK.

However, there is a third type of journalism that is also massively damaging to democracy. This is the tabloid school of journalism – the voyeuristic intrusion into the private lives and sex-ploits of mostly famous people, but also the private lives and tragedies of ordinary people as well. This type of journalism, which is very largely to be found in the tabloid press spectrum of the media – is of course what drove the hacking of phones at the *News of the World*. This type of journalism, which has grown tremendously in the last few decades is also symptomatic of the emergence of the post-social democratic state. What it marks is the stratification in our public sphere between those who have access to information and debate so that they can think of themselves as citizens who participate in the political process, and those, the majority, who do not have access to good quality information and debate, because they are addressed as consumers for whom politics is at best a ridiculous spectacle. This is necessary for the post-social democratic state, which neither wishes nor needs to have an informed and participatory mass of citizens – at best it needs only an elite of citizens informed by the consensus journalism discussed above.

So the relationship between the media, the politicians and the state more broadly is contradictory. The investigative journalism is the only type of journalism that does a service to a democratic polity but it is in conflict with the principles and the practices of the post-social democratic state and it goes against the grain of most media journalism. The routine recycling of government agendas is clearly the most collusive and constitutes the majority of what the quality and middlebrow media do in the UK. The tabloid type of journalism is more contradictory in its relations with governments. When ex-Prime Minister Tony Blair called the media a 'feral beast' it was this type of journalism that he no doubt had in mind. But while it may end ministerial careers in scandals, this type of journalism in no way breaks with the media collusion with the neo-liberal policy agenda. Indeed tabloid journalism (which mainly dominates the print media in the UK) is an important engine for pushing consumer values into the lives of its readership.

The Economic Crisis

The economic crisis now gripping Europe also of course predates 2008. I recall in the late 1980s, a common discussion on the UK left. After Thatcher deregulated the London stock exchange in 1986, we pondered how long finance capital, now uncoupled from the real economy, could keep going without crashing and burning? Twenty years might seem like a long time in the answering, and indeed many on the left during that time abandoned the conversation altogether and resigned themselves to the so called 'new paradigm'. Yet the tick tock of history goes at a different rhythm from the biographical life of the individual. But the signs of the coming fall were in fact there, beneath the euphoria of the market, floating occasionally into the consciousness of western capitalism like a bad nightmare.

At the beginning of the 1990s, Japan, which in 1970 had touched rates of profit as high as 40% and which as recently as the 80s was still seen as the poster boy of advanced capitalism, entered a decade long recession. The 1997 South East Asian crisis came and went with relatively shot term effects but politically the most important events were in Latin America where the Washington Consensus was rolled out through out the 1990s. From the 1994 North American Free Trade Agreement into which Mexico was incorporated– and what a bright future as a narco-gangster-society that helped to create – all the way down to Argentina at the tip of the continent – whose banking crisis in 2000 was an eerie premonition of things to come. In Venezuela and Bolivia, the collapsing support for the traditional political parties that pursued the neo-liberal model, is a prelude to the public de-legitimisation of Pasok and New Democracy in Greece.

The economic crisis of neo-liberalism was in truth inevitable for it was a return to the *laissez-faire* model that preceeded the crisis of capitalism in the early part of the twentieth century. Prior to the 1929 Wall Street Crash, the nineteenth century model of unregulated capitalism had been modified by light regulation in its core heartlands of Western Europe and America. Marx for example charted in *Das Kapital* the struggle for a reduction in the working day which took legislative form in the UK between 1833 to 1864. What the 1929 Crash exposed was the fundamental contradiction between the production of value and the unequal distribution of the power to consume use values that results in the unequal exchange between the worker and the capitalist at the point of production. As Marx argued, the cost of labour for the capitalist is the cost of producing and maintaining labour power on a daily, weekly and yearly basis. But the value of labour power to the capitalist is that the worker produces *more value* than they get in the wage – the wage representing the cost of labour and its reproduction. This *more*, or surplus value is essentially unpaid labour and is the basis of the profit which the capitalist stands to make. However, the capitalist can only make a profit, can only realise a profit if the surplus value which they legally own, but which is fixed in the goods or services provided by the labour power they have temporally purchased, are bought. Only by turning value congealed in goods or services into the liquid form of money can profit become real and flow back into capital accumulation. But here is the major contradiction and the inevitability of crisis. How can workers buy all the goods and services they have produced when all the goods and services they have produced embody a substantial amount of unpaid labour? Only paid labour can realise, via the wage, the portion of unpaid labour embodied in the goods and services which constitutes the basis of profit. If that sounds like a contradiction in Marx's argument – it is not. It is a contradiction within capitalism itself that plays out via competition between capitalists and the deep stratification of exploitation amongst the workers. Stratification has had an important geographical dimension, with colonial and economic imperialism submitting workers in the developing world to super exploitation. The transfer of value from workers in the factories of China today, or coffee workers on the plantations of Latin America has propped up standards of living for western workers as much as profit margins for corporate capitalism. At the same time, the internationalisation of capitalism is producing a downward pressure on the standard of living for workers in the west as they are forced to compete to attract capital investment. Such are the paradoxes, waste and absurdity of capitalism.

During the so called Keynesian phase of capitalism that began to win the hearts and minds of policy makers in the West after the 1929 Crash, social obligations imposed on capitalism by the state tried to close the gap between the real value of wages and all the accumulated values produced by the workers. Arguably it was the Second World War rather than Keynesian policy instruments that kick-started capitalism in the mid-twentieth century and established the basis for the long post-war boom. When international competition intensified and the downward pressure on profits rates returned, Keynesianism was gradually abandoned as a formal policy paradigm and instead credit was liberalised for both businesses and importantly for consumers. Henceforth private debt became a way of making up for the fact that real wages were falling as capital, liberated from its social obligations, took more and more of the available value produced by workers. Because this short-term fix was orientated around individualised solutions and consumption (such as leveraging value tied up in homes which people had yet to actually pay off), this new mode of development within capitalism, encouraged and required huge levels of media propaganda designed to cultivate, celebrate and rationalise a new subjectivity. The culture and subjectivity which this new political economy produced was often broadly celebrated by various disciplines of enquiry which really ought to have known better. However, it is perhaps not too much to hope that the 2008 Crash may yet concentrate minds and persuade academics in film, media and cultural studies to re-couple their subjects with a critique of political economy that returns once again to Marx's analysis.

Every generation must rediscover Marx's *Das Kapital*. For one thing, as the title of the book makes clear: it names the beast. Without a name, we cannot really begin to define what the problems are – in their deep fundamentals; without naming this system of social and economic arrangements, the deep structural causes elude us. The scale of the economic and political crisis demands bold political leadership and vision. In the last twenty years traditional vehicles for political action – the party in particular – have been criticized for their bureaucracy, lack of democracy and responsiveness to urgent problems and demands. New social movements have developed a range of alternative models within civil society that have stressed participation and action. These movements have included community-based groups running services and addressing local problems in the context of economic crisis. It also includes the rejuvenation of older forms of left organisation such as workers' co-operatives. Yet the traditional model of bringing about social change by acquiring political power through party-type structures remains indispensable. In Latin America, the articulation of political parties with a diverse range of social movements has been a feature of left politics. A genuine articulation between parties and civil society groups recognizes that the bottom up, participatory and democratic practices of the social movements require resources and legal frameworks to flourish in the context of co-operation rather than competition. In the social movements there are the seeds of a more substantive democracy to compliment and rejuvenate a withered formal democracy and reconnect shrinking parties with civil society.

Marx did not see it as his job in *Das Kapital* to write what he called 'recipes for the cookshops of the future'. He was usually adverse to speculating in any detail what a future society that had advanced beyond capitalism would look like. Nevertheless we can glean from his work, at least three broad principles that would need to be institutionalised in order to move beyond capitalism.

The first principle would be to shrink the working day for individuals – and use all the productive power built up by the productive forces to increase leisure time for all. A new post-capitalist society would have a different measure of wealth from the old one. Under capitalism, labour time is the measure of wealth. After capitalism, 'disposable' leisure time outside labour would be the measure of wealth. Capitalism can never deliver on that.

The second principle of a society that was truly social, a society that admitted that there was no need for artificial scarcity, is that production would be geared around use and need, not private exchange. Marx begins *Das Kapital* by saying that: "Use values...constitute the substance of all wealth, whatever may be the social form of that wealth" (Marx 1983: 44). He then goes on to spend the rest of *Das Kapital* showing how the social form of wealth that is capitalism, perverts, degrades, distorts, blocks and destroys use values. Use values, the substance of all wealth and the social form of that wealth have never been in more contradiction than they are under capitalism.

The free association of the direct producers of society is the third great principle of a society that has gone beyond the primitive, backward social relations of capitalism. Of course such a notion is an abomination to capital; it does everything it can to discredit the idea. But consider this. According to the Office of National Statistics, in 2011 UK companies were sitting on a cash pile of £752 billion. At the same time corporations want to pay less tax while the political class, the media and of course the bosses are united in insisting on the need for austerity. Is this private hoarding of social wealth not the true abomination when unemployent is so high, a new house building programme so desperate, the conversion to a post-fossil fuel economy so urgent and where the public infrastructure of education, health and culture needs substantial investment? It is certainly in flat contradiction with democracy in any meaningful sense of the term as well as social justice, let alone the free association of the producers.

References

Marx, Karl. 1983. *Capital, A Critique of Political Economy*. London: Lawrence and Wishart.

CHAPTER 2

Culture, Communication, & Ideology = Forms of Work

Christian Fuchs

Introduction

The relationship of work and ideology is a largely unclarified issue in Marxist theory. There are on the one hand Critical Discourse Analysts who analyse ideology as texts, without thinking about the circumstance that ideology is produced by people working in specific contexts under specific conditions (in marketing and PR agencies, consultancies, media organisations, press agencies, etc). On the other hand, the sociology of cultural labour tends to analyse working conditions of cultural workers without thinking about the ideological effects that many cultural products tend to have under capitalist conditions and how ideology influences work and the economy in general. It is therefore important to theorise the relationship of work on the one hand and culture and ideology on the other hand. This chapter wants to contribute to this task.

In Critical Discourse Analysis, the discussion of the relationship of work/ labour and language/ideology is conspicuous by its absence. So for example in Norman Fairclough's (2010) 592 page long book *Critical Discourse Analysis,* the terms labour and work are hardly used and if so then predominantly not for signifying work processes, but New Labour. There are no chapters dedicated to the relationship of labour and ideology, work and language. A similar assessment can be made of Fairclough's (1995) book *Media Discourse,* Teun van Dijk's *Ideology: A Multidisciplinary Approach* (1998), *Discourse & Power* (2008), *Society and Discourse* (2009), the collection *Discourse Studies: A Multidisciplinary Introduction* (2011), or the methods book *Methods of Critical Discourse Analysis* (Wodak and Meyer 2009). Questions relating to the labour of producing ideologies, the role and relationship of language/ideology and work/labour in society, is largely absent in and a blindspot of Critical Discourse Analysis. It tends to neglect basic assumptions of cultural materialism (Williams 1977). Although it is materialist in its basic critique of capitalism, it has thus far not much engaged with the relationship of language and work.

Section 2 discusses examples of a work/culture-dualism (Habermas, Holzkamp). Section 3 introduces some foundations of Raymond Williams cultural materialism that are used in section 4 for conceptualising culture as a form of work. Based on a reading of Ferruccio Rossi-Landi's semiotics, section 5 argues for understanding communication as work. Section 6 based on these foundations draws a distinction between ideological labour and critical work.

Work/Communication-Dualism: Jürgen Habermas and Klaus Holzkamp on Communication and Work

Habermas' theory of communicative action makes a sharp distinction between, on the one, hand purposive (instrumental, strategic) action that is orientated on success and, on the other hand, communicative action that is orientated on reaching understanding (Habermas 1984, 285f). Work is for Habermas always an instrumental, strategic and purposive form of action, whereas communication's goal is understanding. Habermas, just like Holzkamp, therefore separates work and communication.

   In the article *Arbeit und Interaction* (*Work and Interaction*), Habermas (1968) argues that Hegel (1803/1804, 1805/1806) in his Jena lectures on the philosophy of spirit argued that work and interaction are two ways how human beings relate to the world, organize the relationship between subject and object, and thereby constitute their self-conscious minds. Consciousness and the mind would be media of communication. The difference between work and interaction would be that the first is a form of strategic action and the second oriented on understanding. Strategic action would make decisions without trying to reach understanding with others (Habermas 1968, 22). Both work and interaction would constitute the external nature of humans, their relational being. In work, there is a relation to nature organized by tools. In communication, there is a relation to other humans organized by language and its symbols. Work and interaction could not be reduced to each other (Habermas 1968, 3), but they would be dialectically connected: "But now also instrumental action, as soon as it enters the category of the actual spirit in the form of societal work, is embedded into a network of interactions and is therefore itself dependent on the communicative boundary conditions of every possible cooperation" (Habermas 1968, 32, translation from German). Habermas argues that Hegel would have after his Jena time (1801–1807) given up the concept of the dialectic of work and interaction because he became convinced that nature and work are just attributes of spirit and can therefore be reduced to the dialectical development of spirit. Marx in contrast would have reduced communicative action to instrumental action (Habermas 1968, 45).

   In the *Theory of Communicative Action*, Habermas (1984, 1987) formalized the earlier drawn distinction between work and interaction in his own theory in the form of a distinction between instrumental-strategic rationality and communicative rationality. Habermas understands rationality as "problem-solving action" (Habermas 1984, 12). He introduces a typology of action, in which he differentiates action types based on action situations (non-social or social) and action orientation (oriented to success, oriented to reaching understanding). This results in the distinction between instrumental action, strategic action and communicative action. Instrumental and strategic action are oriented on success and driven by "egocentric calculations of success" (Habermas 1984, 286). Instrumental action means that an actor identifies and uses means in order to achieve ends and maximize his/her benefits (Habermas 1984, 285, 85). Strategic action is instrumental action in a social situation with rational opponents so that the task is to beat the opponent or be more successful than him/her (Habermas 1984, 285). In contrast, communicative action the action situation is social and the orientation is "reaching understanding" (Habermas 1984, 286). "In communicative action participants are not primarily oriented to their own individual successes; they pursue their individual goals under the condition that they can harmonize their plans of action on the basic of common situation definitions" (Habermas 1984, 286).

> The actors seek to reach an understanding about the action situation and their plans of action in order to coordinate their actions by way of agreement. The central concept of *interpretation* refers in the first instance to negotiating definitions of the situation which admit of consensus. [...] language is given a prominent place in this model.
> HABERMAS 1984, 86

Reaching understanding in communicative action would require the three validity claims of truth, rightness and truthfulness (Habermas 1984, 99). Habermas' distinction between instrumental and communicative action is reflected in his distinction between systems and the lifeword. He locates work/labour in the interchange relationship between the economic system and the private sphere that is part of the lifeworld (Habermas 1987, 320). This relationship would be a determined by the systemic steering media of money and power (exchange of money in the form of the wage for the control of labour power). Habermas (1976, 151) argues that work and language were necessary preconditions for the emergence of humans and society. Reconstructing Historical Materialism would require separating "the level of communicative action from the level of instrumental and strategic actions that are united in societal cooperation" (Habermas 1976, 160, translation from German to

English). Historical progress would only be possible by developing the forms of social integration and the productive forces (Habermas 1976, 194).

Habermas consistently used the distinction between communication and work that he took from Hegel's Jena philosophy for creating a theory of modern society. Communication and work represent for him two different logics of society, an emancipatory and an instrumental one. He is critical of money and power's colonization of lifeworld communication (Habermas 1987) and so stresses the importance of defending communication against instrumental logic. Habermas' political imperative is definitely laudable because it helps is to stress that there is a society beyond capitalism and that a true society is not steered by capital and domination. But the question is if it is feasible to dualistically separate communication and work – an approach that Habermas characterizes as media dualism (Habermas 1987, 281). There are several theoretical limits of Habermas' work/communication dualism:

- In a general sense, we can say that reaching communicative understanding and any form of communication is a form of instrumental action: the means of language is used for achieving the goal of relating oneself to other humans and reaching a joint understanding of the world.
- Communication in modern society is not an immune sphere: Ideologies are forms of communication and language that are highly instrumental. Ideologies instrumentalize language and meanings for justifying exploitation and domination. Communication thereby becomes an instrument of domination. Within communication studies, a specific field called strategic communication has developed. It studies how communication can be used for influencing and persuading specific audiences of particular purposes, especially in marketing and politics (see Hülsmann and Pfeffermann 2011, Paul 2011). Strategic communication is just another term for propaganda that serves capitalist and bureaucratic purposes. So communication is not immune from the logic of instrumentalizing humans and speech for domination, but can serve quite different purposes.
- Work not only serves strategic-instrumental purposes, but can be quite altruistic and motivated by helping others and fostering the common good that benefits all. Marx was convinced that an entire society can be built on the logic of common goods. Limiting the notion of work to strategic-instrumental action deprives theory of a vocabulary for conceptualizing social activities that produce use-values in a society based on solidarity, common goods and voluntary work.

What distinguishes humans from animals is that they have a complex form of verbal language and communication, have self-consciousness, morals and anticipatory thought. But how did these capacities historically emerge? Klaus Holzkamp's (1985) *Critical Psychology* has engaged thoroughly with this question. Holzkamp (1985, 113f) argues that communication is an optical and acoustical bidirectional/dialogical/reciprocal relationship between organism, in which information is exchanged and social meaning is given to signals and symbols. Understood in this way, communication is not specific for humans, but can also be found in the animal world, where animals communicate for purposes such as procreation, breeding, hunting, defending their territory, warning each other, etc.

Historically, practical knowledge of how to manage reality had to be fixed and organised in some form, which required cooperative work between humans on the one hand and the need to communicate and store experiences on the other hand (Holzkamp 1985, 177, 211f). Holzkamp (1985, 224) assumes that verbal communication emerged in the development between the first qualitative dominance shift (the reversal of means and ends) and the second one (the emergence of societal-historical development): cooperative work in close range would have required coordination activities and as the eyes and vision would have been used for constantly monitoring the work process and the hands and the body for changing the objects of work, the use of the mouth for coordinating work would have been a logical step (Holzkamp 1985, 224). The development of speech that uses categories for signifying specific parts of reality would have been a practical requirement of the cooperative work process (Holzkamp 1985, 226–229). Concept formation would have been practical and the emerging phonetic concepts would have been practical concepts that described tools, objects and products. So for example "the planning and coordination of activities in the production of horizontally standing and flat boards, i.e. 'tables', requires a concept of 'horizontal' and one of 'flat'" (Holzkamp 1985, 227).

The development of learning capacities and anticipatory thinking together with verbal communication would have enabled humans to speak about relations and circumstances even if they were not immediately present (Holzkamp 1985, 228). As cooperative work became ever more complex and ever more transcended spatial and temporal distances, it was necessary to find trans-individual forms of communication and information transmission. So whereas the organization of cooperative work required the development of human speech, the increasing spatio-temporal distanciation of the cooperative work process required forms of mediated communication, which historically resulted in the development of writing and painting as means for preserving, storing and communicating information (Holzkamp 1985, 230f).

Holzkamp explains in a logically consistent and convincing manner how the development of society, work, speech and communication co-evolved in a dialectical manner. He grounds his approach in Marx's theory. Marx argued that the mind is "'burdened' with matter, which here makes its appearance in the form of agitated layers of air, sounds, in short, of language" (Marx and Engels 1845/1846, 49). Marx stresses the material dimensions of the mind and language: the human being, the brain, the air that transports sound. "Language is as old as consciousness, language *is* practical, real consciousnes that exists for other men as well, and only therefore does it also exist for me; language, like conscious-ness, only arises from the need, the necessity of intercourse with other men. Where there exists a relationship, it exists for me; the animal does not 'relate' itself to anything, it does not 'relate' itself at all" (Marx and Engels 1845/1846, 49). For Marx, language and consciousness are "a social production" and remain so "as long as men exist at all" (Marx and Engels 1845/1846, 50). By saying that language is practical and social, Marx means that it has historically arisen in the course of the organisation of economic production that became a social pro-cess. Holzkamp reflects this insight by arguing that communication and lan-guage emerged from the need of practical knowledge in the work process that became ever more complex and thereby a cooperative and social process.

Work is for Holzkamp a category of the theory of society that captures "the objective-economic aspects of the production and reproduction of societal life" (Holzkamp 1985, 234, translation from German to English). Work is "collec-tive objectified transformation of nature and the control of natural forces for the precautionary disposal over the common living conditions" (Holzkamp 1985, 176f, translation from German to English). He uses in contrast the notion of activity for characterising individual behaviour, "individual life activities" of humans that organise the "maintenance/development of his/her individual existence" (Holzkamp 1985, 234, translation from German to English). Activities would include psychological processes and the individual contributions to societal production and reproduction by work – "the work activities as psycho-logical aspect of societal work" (Holzkamp 1985, 234, translation from German). Meanings would be developed in society and influence individual activities (Holzkamp 1985, 234).

Holzkamp argues that individual behaviour and psychological processes are human activities, whereas the cooperative organisation of the production of goods and services that sustain human existence, processes that are never pos-sible by single individuals, by changing, transforming and organising nature are work processes. He sees a dialectic between human individuals and collec-tive cooperation in work processes.

Holzkamp in drawing the distinction between work and activity makes the basic mistake to assume that work is only a human collaborative transfor-mation of natural resources so that goods and services (use-values) emerge that satisfy human needs. Holzkamp's approach here resembles Habermas' theory of communicative action that makes a sharp distinction between on the one hand purposive (instrumental, strategic) action that is orientated on success and on the other hand communicative action that is orientated on reaching understanding (Habermas 1984, 285f). Work is for Habermas always an instrumental, strategic and purposive form of action, whereas communication's goal is to create understanding. Both Habermas and Holzkamp separate work and communication.

Raymond Williams' Cultural Materialism

In *Marxism and Literature,* Raymond Williams questions the Marxism's historical tendency to see culture as "dependent, secondary, 'superstructural': a realm of 'mere' ideas, beliefs, arts, customs, determined by the basic material history" (Williams 1977, 19). He discusses various Marxist concepts that Marxist theories have used for discussing the relationship of the economy and culture: determination, reflection, reproduction, mediation, homology. These approaches would all assume a relationship between the economy and culture with a varying degree of causal determination or mutual causality. But all of them would share the assumption of "the separation of 'culture' from material social life" (Williams 1977, 19) that Williams (1977, 59) considers to be "idealist." The problem of these approaches would be that they are not "materialist enough" (Williams 1977, 92).

Raymond Williams (1977, 111) formulates as an important postulate of Cultural Materialism that "[c]ultural work and activity are not [...] a superstructure" because people would use physical resources for leisure, entertainment and art. Combining Williams' assumptions that cultural work is material and economic and that the physical and ideational activities underlying the existence of culture are interconnected means that culture is a totality that connects all physical and ideational production processes that are connected and required for the existence of culture.

Williams (1977, 139) concludes that Cultural Materialism needs to see "the complex unity of the elements" required for the existence of culture: ideas, institutions, formations, distribution, technology, audiences, forms of communication and interpretation, worldviews (138f). A sign system would involve the social relations that produce it, the institutions in which it is formed and its role as a cultural technology (Williams 1977, 140). In order to avoid the "real danger of separating human thought, imagination and concepts from 'men's material life-process'" (Williams 1989, 203), one needs like Marx to focus on the "totality of human activity" (Williams 1989, 203) when discussing culture. We "have to emphasise cultural practice as from the beginning social and material" (Williams 1989, 206). The "productive forces of 'mental labour' have, in themselves, an inescapable material and thus social history" (Williams 1989, 211). Marx expressed the basic assumption of Cultural Materialism well by saying that the "production of ideas, of conceptions, of consciousness, is at first directly interwoven with the material activity and the material intercourse of men" (Marx and Engels 1845/1846, 42). The production of ideas is therefore the "language of real life" (Marx and Engels 1845/1846, 42). "Men are the producers of their conceptions, ideas, etc., that is, real, active men, as they are conditioned by a definite development of their productive forces and of the intercourse corresponding to these, up to its furthest forms" (Marx and Engels 1845/1846, 42). Thinking and communication are for Marx processes of production that are embedded into humans' everyday life and work. They produce their own capacities and realities of thinking and communication in work and social relations.

Cultural Production as a Form of Work

Inspired by Raymond Williams' cultural materialism, it is feasible to argue for a broad understanding of digital labour that transcends the cultural idealism of the early digital labour debate and some works in the cultural industries school. On the one hand Williams refuses the separation of culture and the economy as well as base and superstructure. On the other hand he maintains that culture as a signifying system is a distinct system of society. How can we make sense of these claims that at a first sight seem to be mutually exclusive? If one thinks dialectically, then a concept of culture as material and necessarily economic and at the same time distinct from the economy is feasible: culture and politics are dialectical sublations (Aufhebung) of the economy. Sublation means in Hegelian philosophy that a system or phenomenon is preserved, eliminated and lifted up. Culture is not the same as the economy, it is more than the sum of various acts of labour, it has emergent qualities – it communicates meanings in society – that cannot be found in the economy alone. But at the same time, the economy is preserved in culture: culture is not independent from labour, production and physicality, but requires and incorporates all of them.

The Austrian philosopher of information Wolfgang Hofkirchner has introduced stage models as a way for philosophically conceptualising the logic connections between different levels of organization. In a stage model, "one step taken by a system in question – that produces a layer – depends on the stage

taken prior to that but cannot be reversed! [...] layers – that are produced by
steps – build upon layers below them but cannot be reduced to them!"
(Hofkirchner 2013, 123f). Emergence is the foundational principle of stage
model (Hofkirchner 2013, 115): a specific level of organisation of matter has
emergent qualities so that the systems organized on this level are more than
the sum of their parts, to which they cannot be reduced. An organisation level
has new qualities that are grounded in the underlying systems and levels that
are preserved on the upper level and through synergies produce new qualities
of the upper level. In the language of dialectical philosophy this means that the
emergent quality of an organisation level is a sublation (Aufhebung) of the
underlying level.

Applying a stage model allows to identify and relate different levels of cultural and digital work (see Figure 2.1). Cultural work is a term that encompasses
organisational levels of work that are at the same time distinct and dialectically connected: cultural work has an emergent quality, namely information
work that creates content, that is based on and grounded in physical cultural
work that creates information technologies in agricultural and industrial work
processes. Physical work takes place inside and outside of culture: it creates
information technologies and its components (cultural physical work) as well
as other products (non-cultural physical work) that do not primarily have symbolic functions in society (such as cars, tooth brushes and cups). Cars, tooth
brushes and cups do not primarily have the role of informing others or communicating with others, but rather help humans achieve the tasks of transport,
cleanliness and nutrition. Culture and information work however have feed-
back on these products and create symbolic meanings used by companies for
marketing these products. Cultural work is a unity of physical cultural work

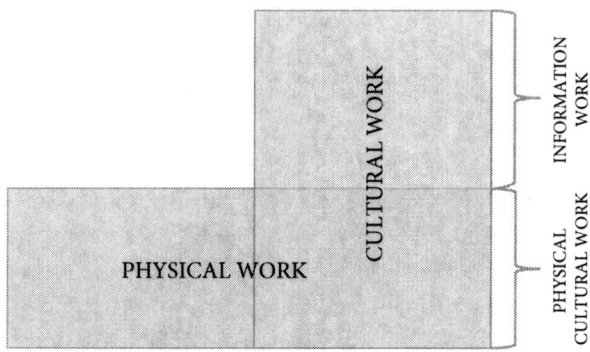

FIGURE 2.1 *A stage model of cultural work*

and information work that interact with each other, are connected and at the same time distinct.

The production of meaning, social norms, morals and the communication of meanings, norms and morals in social processes taking place in the cultural system is a work process: it creates cultural use-values. Culture requires on the one hand human creativity for creating cultural content and on the other hand specific forms and media for storage and communication. Work that creates information and communication through language is specific for work conducted in the cultural system: informational and communication work. For having social effects in society, information and communication are organised (stored, processed, transported, analysed, transformed, created) with the help of information and communication technologies, such as computers, TV, radio, newspapers, books, recorded films, recorded music, language, etc. These technologies are produced by physical cultural work. Culture encompasses a) physical and informational work that create cultural technologies (information and communication technologies) and b) information work that creates information and communication. These two types of work act together in order to produce and reproduce culture. *Meanings and judgements are emergent qualities of culture that are created by informational work, but take on relative autonomy that has effects inside but also outside the economic system. This means that specific forms of work create culture, but culture cannot be reduced to the economy – it has emergent qualities.*

Communication is the "passing of ideas, information, and attitudes from person to person," whereas communications means the "institutions and forms in which ideas, information, and attitudes are transmitted and received" (Williams 1962, 9). Information and communication are meaning-making activities created by informational work. Physical cultural work creates communications as institutions and forms that organise the creation and passing of information in social processes.

Marx identified two forms of information work: The first results in cultural goods that "exist separately from the producer, i.e. they can circulate in the interval between production and consumption as commodities, e.g. books, paintings and all products of art as distinct from the artistic achievement of the practising artist." In the second, "the product is not separable from the act of producing" (Marx 1867, 1047f). The first requires a form, institution or technology that stores and transports information, as in the case of computer-mediated communication, the second uses language as main medium (e.g. theatre). The first requires physical cultural work for organising storage, organisation and transport of information, the second is possible based only on information work.

If culture were merely symbolic, mind, spirit, 'immaterial', superstructural, informational, a world of ideas, then digital labour as expression of culture clearly would exclude the concrete works of mining and hardware assemblage that are required for producing digital media. Based on Williams' Cultural Materialism it is in contrast to the position of Cultural Idealism feasible to argue that digital labour includes both the creation of physical products and information that are required for the existence and usage of digital technologies. Some digital workers create hardware, others hardware components, minerals, software or content that are all objectified in or the outcome of the application of digital technologies.

In order to illustrate his point that culture is material, Williams mentions a passage from Marx's *Grundrisse*:

> Productive labour is only that which produces capital. Is it not crazy, asks e.g. (or at least something similar) Mr Senior, that the piano maker is a productive worker, but not the piano player, although obviously the piano would be absurd without the piano player? But this is exactly the case. The piano maker reproduces capital; the pianist only exchanges his labour for revenue. But doesn't the pianist produce music and satisfy our musical ear, does he not even to a certain extent produce the latter? He does indeed: his labour produces something; but that does not make it productive labour in the economic sense; no more than the labour of the madman who produces delusions is productive. Labour becomes productive only by producing its own opposite.
>
> MARX 1857/1858, 305

Williams remarks that today, other than in Marx's time, "the production of music (and not just its instruments) is an important branch of capitalist production" (Williams 1977, 93).

If the economy and culture are two separate realms, then building the piano is work and part of the economy and playing it is not work, but culture. Marx leaves however no doubt that playing the piano produces a use-value that satisfies human ears and is therefore a form of work. As a consequence, the production of music must just like the production of the piano be an economic activity. Williams (1977, 94) stresses that cultural materialism means to see the material character of art, ideas, aesthetics and ideology and that when considering piano making and piano playing it is important to discover and describe "relations between all these practices" and to not assume "that only some of them are material."

Besides the piano maker and the piano player there is also the composer of music. All three works are needed and necessarily related in order to guarantee the existence of piano music. Fixing one of these three productive activities categorically as culture and excluding the others from it limits the concept of culture and does not see that one cannot exist without the other. Along with this separation come political assessments of the separated entities. A frequent procedure is to include the work of the composer and player and to exclude the work of the piano maker. Cultural elitists then argue that only the composer and player are truly creative, whereas vulgar materialists hold that only the piano maker can be a productive worker because he works with his hands and produces an artefact. Both judgments are isolationist and politically problematic.

Communication as a Form of Work

Most Marxist approaches that have given attention to the communication process at a theoretical level have focused on the communicative character of work, but have neglected the question if communication is work. A few exceptions can be found in the political economy of communication-approach, such as the works by Wulf Hund (1976), Hund/Kirchhoff-Hund (1980) and Dan Schiller (1996) have stressed the importance of not separating work and communication.

If cultural production in specific work processes creates symbols that have meaning in society, then the communication of such meanings via language and media must also be a work process. An approach that helps to conceptualise communication as work is Ferruccio Rossi-Landi's (1977, 1983) Marxist semiotics. For him, language and communication are work that produce words, sentences, interconnected sentences, arguments, speeches, essays, lectures, books, codes, artworks, literature, science, groups, civilisation and the linguistic world as totality (Rossi-Landi 1983, 133–136). As "words and messages do not exist in nature" (Rossi-Landi 1983, 36), they must be the products of human work that generates use-values. They are use-values because they satisfy the human needs of expression, communication and social relations (Rossi-Landi 1983, 37). "Like the other products of human work, words, expressions and messages have a use-value or utility insofar as they satisfy needs, in this case, the basic needs for expression and communication with all the changing stratifications that have historically grown up around them" (Rossi-Landi 1983, 50).

Rossi-Landi (1983, 47) argues that language is a material instrument that is constant capital and that linguistic labour power is variable capital. A linguistic community would be a "huge market in which words, expressions and messages circulate as commodities" (Rossi-Landi 1983, 49). Words would have exchange value because in language they stand in relations to others words, whereas messages would have exchange value in the exchange of messages between humans (Rossi-Landi 1983, 49). Rossi-Landi (1983) conceptualises the linguistic value and exchange-value of expressions by saying that Marx's logic of x commodity A = y commodity B has in language a homology when one expression's meaning is compared to another, for example: "art is an institution" and art "is a particular theoretical moment of the Spirit" (Rossi-Landi 1983, 61).

Rossi-Landi's approach is important, especially because he interprets human communication processes as work and in this context uses Marx's general notion of work. But it has limits in that it uses the terms linguistic capital, linguistic market and linguistic value just like linguistic work as anthropological concepts. Whereas work is for Marx a general concept characteristic for all societies, capital, markets and value are not anthropological features of humans and society, but rather historical features of specific class societies. A homology of language with capital, markets and value therefore naturalises and essentialises historical categories. The logical consequence is that capital, markets and values appear to be characteristics of all societies in Rossi-Landi's approach. Rossi-Landi's approach is feasible, where he argues that language is work, but it fails when he argues that language is a form of trade, in which we can find capital, exchange-value and markets.

Although linguistic products in capitalist societies or other societies that use markets as economic distribution mechanisms can be traded as commodities, this does not imply that language is always a commodity that is exchanged on markets. A market is a mechanism of exclusion in that it gives you only access to a good or service if you in return provide a good or service that is considered to have equal value. In everyday life, many communications do not assume the logic of getting something in return whose value can be quantified. Mothers and fathers talk a lot to their babies out of altruism and love, but do not expect the babies to return words and sentences that are equally meaningful. In fact, the babies would not be able to learn to spoke if their parents would apply the logic of markets, commodities and exchange-value because they then would not much speak to them. Language and our brains are in general not constant capital, but rather a means of linguistic production – instruments of linguistic work. Human beings and their languaging-capacity and -activity are not variable capital, but rather they are the subjects of linguistic work. It is only in capitalism and other market-based societies that linguistic products can turn into capital and commodities, brains and language into constant capital and linguistic work capacity into variable capital. Under such circumstances, linguistic products such as books are the expenditure of specific hours of labour power. When the book is sold, one can only read it if one pays a specific price for it (except if illegal copies are distributed).

An information process is according to Peirce a triadic relationship, in which an object is represented as a sign and produces certain mental effects that we term interpretation. Semiosis is the process O – S – M, in which objects O are signified by signs S that are interpreted in the form of meanings M. Semiosis is not a static process, but continuous and dynamic because existing meanings are the starting point for new thought and communication processes through which meanings are produced and differentiated. Semiosis as dialectical process takes place both in individual cognition and communication and thereby connects individual and social human existence. It operates as a threefold, nested, emergent and interconnected process (see Figure 2.2):

1. 'Individual semiosis' is a mental thought process – cognition – in which an individual interprets the world by mentally representing parts of reality by signs in his/her imagination and creating meanings that interpret the objects and signs.

2. Individual semiosis enables and constrains and is enabled and constrained, i.e. conditions and is conditioned, by 'social semiosis': human social relations are communicative relationships, in which humans use language, i.e. systems of grammatically connected signs that form words and sentences and are expressed in spoken, written, bodily or visual

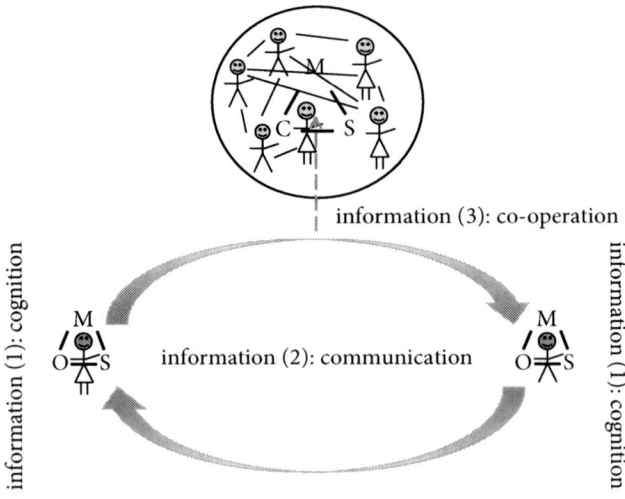

FIGURE 2.2 *The tripleC model of semiosis/information*

forms, so that meaning is mutually communicated. One individual A communicates parts of the meanings s/he gives to the world to another individual B who communicates meanings that s/he gives to the world back to A. Social semiosis means that the meanings of at least two humans are changed by communication processes. These changes of meanings can be more or less substantial. In some cases qualitatively new interpretations, values or knowledge are created, in other cases the communicated information is recognised and interpreted, but makes no profound changes. Individual semiosis emerges from humans' interactions with the natural and social environment and enables social semiosis. Cognition is conditioned by communication, which in turn conditions cognition.

3.   Many communications are ephemeral and do not bring about more substantial structural changes in society. Some communications and social relations however are transformative, i.e. they result in changes in society, such as the formation of a new social system, the differentiation of an existing social system, the emergence of new rules or resources. In such cases, social semiosis becomes *structural/societal semiosis*: communication turns in co-operation/collaboration, in which several humans act together in such a way that new structures emerge or existing ones are transformed. Communication conditions co-operation and co-operation conditions communication.

In the tripleC model of information (Fuchs and Hofkirchner 2005, Hofkirchner 2013), cognition conditions and is conditioned by communication that conditions and is conditioned by co-operation. Semiosis has an individual, a social and a societal level. It is a dialectical information process that is organised as a dialectic of dialectics: the semiosis of cognition mutually interacts with the semiosis of communication in human practices and relations, from which the semiosis of society that transforms social structures can emerge.

Information processes do not stand outside of matter and do not form a second substance besides or related to matter. Information – the semiosis of semi-os*es* and the dialectic of dialecti*cs* of cognition, communication and co-operation) – is material itself, it has the potential to transform structures. On the cognitive and communicative level of the individual and social relations, semiosis transforms cognitive structures, i.e. patterns of established meanings of individuals, to which new meanings are added. On the co-operative level of society, semiosis reproduces and/or transforms structures of society, such as rules, resources, dominant and hegemonic social values, organisations, institutions, etc. Reproduction and transformation take place within the economic, the political and the cultural system through communicative and collaborative work processes. Semiosis and structuration cannot be opposed because individual and social semiosis reproduces and changes individual autopoietic structures of human cognition, whereas societal semiosis reproduces and changes structures in the economic, the political and the cultural systems of society.

How is semiosis (the information dialectic of cognition, communication and co-operation) related to work? Rossi-Landi conceptualised the work process that he parallelised with the communication process as a dialectic of material, operations (instruments, worker, working operations) and product (see Withalm 2006). He thereby however relates two objects and not the human subject (its work mental and physical work capacity and labour power) and the objects of work to each other so that his system is not a subject-object-dialectic. Language is the result of human activities over many generations. Words are not natural objects, but produced by humans together in their culture. As being produced by humans, information is the product of human work. Hands, head, ears, mouth – body and brain – work together in order to enable speech. Work has a dual character, it has physical and social dimensions. Thinking and speaking that result in the production of information and symbols form the physical aspect, human relations the social dimension of communication.

Information can be conceived as a threefold process of cognition, communication and co-operation (Fuchs and Hofkirchner 2005). Table 2.1 below gives an overview of the dimensions of the cognitive, communicative and cooperative dimensions of information work (Fuchs and Sevignani 2013).

TABLE 2.1   *The subject, object and subject-object of cognitive, communicative and co-operative work*

	Subject	Object of work	Instruments of work	Product of work
Cognition = human brain work	Human being	Experiences	Brain	Thoughts, cognitive patterns, ideas
Communication = human group work	Group of humans	Thoughts	Brain, mouth, ears	Meaning
Co-operation = collaborative human group work	Group of humans	Meaning	Brain, mouth, ears, body	Information product with shared and co-created meaning

Figure 2.3 below shows that these three processes are connected dialectically and form together the process of information work. Each of the three behaviours – cognition, communication and co-operation – is a work process: cognition is work of the human brain, communication work of human groups and co-operative collaborative work of human groups. Communication is based on cognition and uses the products of cognition – ideas – as its object of work. Co-operation is based on communication and uses the products of communication – meanings – as object of work. Information is a work process, in which cognitive work creates ideas, communicative work creates meanings and co-operative work co-creates information products that have shared and co-created meaning. Information is a dialectical process of human work, in which cognition, communication and cooperation are dialectically connected. Each of these three processes forms a work process that has its own subject-object-dialectic in itself.

Using the Hegel-Marxist triangle model of the work process, one can argue that the development that Marx points out on behalf of the notion of the general intellect can be formalised as follows: S-O>SO...S-SO>SSO...S-SSO>SSSO and so forth. The object position of a dialectical work triangle starts with the result, the subject-object of a previous triangle and so on. The advantage of this kind of thinking is that the reference to an object and ultimately nature never gets completely lost in the theory. Hence a dualism between subject and object, e.g. communication and work is prevented. Dialectical thinking is capable of providing an integrative theory of human activity.

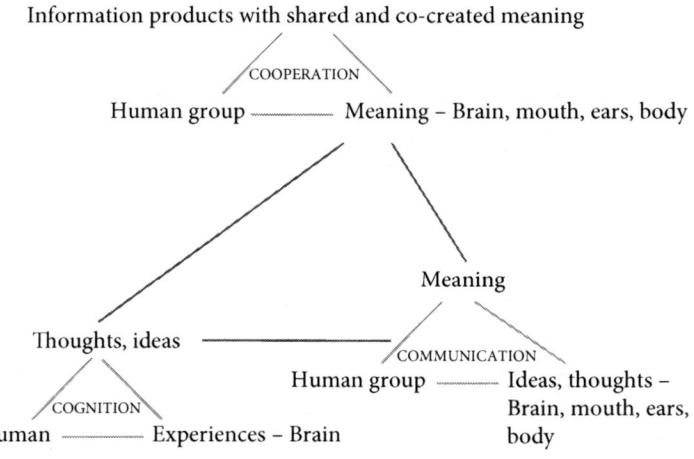

FIGURE 2.3   *The information process as work process*

An example: A person likes reading books about gardening and builds up a sophisticated knowledge of how to create and maintain a good-looking garden by reading more and more books and applying this knowledge in his/her garden. The created knowledge is a use-value in the sense that it helps him/her organise her/his own garden in a nice-looking manner. S/he meets another person, who has comparable knowledge. They start exchanging ideas on gardening. In this communication process, the shared knowledge of one person forms an object that is interpreted by the other person so that meaning, i.e. an interpretation of parts of the world, is formed. The process also works vice-versa. As a result, meanings are created as use-values on both sides; each person understands something about the other. After continuous conversations and mutual learning, the two hobby gardeners decide to write a book about gardening. They develop new ideas by discussing and bring their experiences together, whereby synergies, new experiences and new gardening methods emerge. In the book, they describe these new methods that they have tried in practice in a jointly run garden. The representations of the joint experiences and of the co-created methods in the form of a book are a use-value not just for the two, but for others too.

Work requires information processes and information creation is itself a work process. This model allows a non-dualistic solution to the question of how work and information/interaction are connected. It avoids separations between nature/culture, work/interaction, base/superstructure, but rather argues that information has its own economy – it is work that creates specific use-values. These use-values are individual in character only at the level of cognition – the human thinks and develops new ideas –, whereas they have a direct social character at the level of communication and co-operation. But humans do not exist as monads, the objects of cognitive work stem to a large degree from society itself. To interpret the information creation process as work is not philosophical idealism because idealism sees spirit as independently existing entity that is not connected to human labour. Ideas, meanings and co-created information products are objects of labour that reflect society in complex ways.

Every work process requires cognition, communication and cooperation as tools of production. Therefore the physical production of goods in manufacturing as well as agricultural work and mining are never separate from information processes. This aspect has been stressed in many Marxist analysis of the connection of communication and work. In these production forms, information is not a product, but a means of production. Work requires information. The other way round, information is also work: there is an informational mode of production that has grown in size in the 20th century (in terms of the population active in it and share of the overall created value in the economy):

it focuses on the production of informational goods and services. It is this kind of production that is the main focus of our attention in this paper. Work requires information and communication. But at the same time, it is important to give attention to information and communication as forms of work.

The production of information is work. But society and the economy cannot be reduced to information, language and communication. Pan-informational concepts of society that reduce all human existence to information are just like approaches that ignore information and culture reductionist. Work is always an economic process that produces physical and/or informational results. Information is grounded in work and the economy, but at the same time has emergent qualities in that it communicates meanings in society, which makes it a specifically cultural resource.

Ideological Labour and Critical Work

Ferruccio Rossi-Landi (1977) questions the assumption that language is always a common good that cannot be a private property. He introduces in this context the notion of linguistic private property, by which he means that a ruling class possesses "control over the emission and circulation of the verbal and non-verbal messages which are constitutive of a given community" (Rossi-Landi 1977, 191). Rossi-Landi (1983, 170f) argues that the ruling class has linguistic private property over a) codes, modalities of codification, b) channels uses for the circulation of messages, c) modalities of decoding and interpretation. "The ruling class increases the redundancy of the messages which confirm its own position and attacks with noise, or if necessary with disturbance, the codification and circulation of messages which could instead invalidate it" (Rossi-Landi 1983, 171). Communications are means for making information public and giving humans a voice that is heard by others and has the potential to influence what is happening in society. Communication power means the capacity to communicate information in society in a public manner so that it is recognised by others and has transformative effects on society. Communications can have different ownership forms.

A critical concept of ideology requires a normative distinction between true and false believes and practices. A critical concept of ideology means thoughts, practices, ideas, words, concepts, phrases, sentences, texts, belief systems, meanings, representations, artefacts, institutions, systems or combinations thereof that represent and justify one group's or individual's domination or exploitation of other groups or individuals. Domination means in this context that there is a system that enables one human side to gain advantages at the

expense of others and to sustain this condition. It is a routinised and institutionalised form of asymmetric power, in which one side has the opportunity to
shape and control societal structures (such as the production and control of
wealth, political decision-making, public discussions, ideas, norms, rules, values), whereas others do not have these opportunities and are facing disadvan-
tages or exclusion from the opportunities of others. Exploitation is a specific
form of domination, in which an exploiting class derives wealth advantages at
the expense of an exploiting class by controlling economic resources and
means of coercion in such a way that the exploited class is forced to produce
new use-values that the exploiting class controls. Ideology presupposes "societal structures, in which different groups and conflicting interests act and
strive to impose their interest onto the total of society as its general interest. To
put it shortly: The emergence and diffusion of ideologies appears as the general
characteristic of class societies" (Lukács 1986, 405, translation from German).

Terry Eagleton (1991) has noted six core understandings of the concept of
ideology:

1.   The general material process of production of ideas, beliefs and values in
     social life.
2.   Ideas coherently symbolize the conditions and life-experiences of a spe-
     cific group or class.
3.   The promotion and legitimatization of the interests of a group or class in
     the face of opposing interests.
4.   The promotion and legitimatization of the interests of a dominant social
     group in order to unify a social formation.
5.   Ideas and beliefs that help to legitimate the interests of a ruling group/
     class by distortion and dissimulation.
6.   False and deceptive beliefs arising from the material structure of society
     as a whole.

We can think about Eagleton's (1991) six concepts of ideology as variously
interlinked levels of ideology. The differentiation between levels allows us also
to see that false consciousness is not a necessary element of ideology; it may be
just one outcome of ideological strategies, but can also be resisted (although
there is no automatism of resistance and the means for producing hegemonic
ideology and counter-hegemony are unequally distributed). Ideology is not
necessarily a state of consciousness of dominated groups. It can be, but it is
more a process, in which dominant groups communicate dominant ideas, to
which others react in certain ways or do not react. Dominant ideas impact the
culture of the dominant itself (e.g. neoliberal work norms – the new spirit of

networked capitalism – that impact not only what is expected of the behaviour of workers, but also managers).

Ideology is a semiotic level of domination and exploitation – it practices the production and spread of information and meanings in the form of ideas, belief systems, artefacts, systems and institutions so that domination and exploitation are justified or naturalised. Ideology is a special form of individual, social and societal semiosis that is embedded into structures of domination and aims at justifying, naturalising, upholding, defending and containing actual or potential resistance against specific forms of domination. It aims at making a broader public believe that society or a social system in its dominative or exploitative status should remain unchanged and is good, fair, free, or just the way it is. This goal is associated with the task of spreading information that tries to convince subordinated individuals and groups not to work for transformations or to support forces and ideas that question the status quo.

If language use and communication are work processes, then a specific subset of language use and communication is ideological in character and a specific other subset is critical in character. Ideologies are the outcome of ideological work, critical knowledge the outcome of critical cultural work.

Ideologies have specific structures. Teun van Dijk (1998, Chapter 5; 2011, 386, 395f) classifies the structure of ideologies the following way:

· Membership, identity: Who are we? Where are we from? What do we look like? Who can become a member of our group?
· Activities: What do we do? What is expected of us? Why are we here?
· Goals: Why do we do this? What do we want to realise?
· Values/norms: What are our main values? How do we evaluate ourselves and others? What should (not) be done?
· Position and group-relations: What is our social position? Who are our enemies, our opponents? Who are like us, and who are different?
· Resources: What are the essential social resources that our group has or needs to have?

This means that the production, reproduction and diffusion of an ideology is work that defines the membership, identity, activities, goals, values and norms, positions and resources of a dominant or exploitative group in relationship to a dominated or exploited group in such a way that the power of the first is with specific definition strategies that create particular meanings legitimatised, naturalised and presented as unproblematic. The structure of an ideology can be explained as a dialectical information process: it defines individual dimensions of a group, system or human being, the being-in-itself of the ideology:

identity, membership, activities, norms, values, goals, controlled resources. Then it relates this being-in-itself in a specific manner to a dominated group's being-in-itself (its identity, membership, activities, norms, values, goals, resources) and defines this relationship (being-for-another) in such a way that the dominant group's being-in-itself is justified and the dominated group's being-in-itself presented as inferior, but an inferiority that is necessary and justified. Ideology suggests that this relationship of two phenomena or groups should be resolved in a specific manner by taking specific measures that change reality in specific ways so that the asymmetric power relation between dominant group and the dominated group is maintained. This fusion and resolution is then an ideological being-in-and-for-itself. So ideology defines individual existences, relates them and suggests how this relationship should be shaped and changed. So a racist ideology describes a) a national group and a group of immigrants, b) a specific relationship between them by claiming e.g. that immigrants are criminals, do not work, speak different languages, have different customs etc and thereby negatively impact the lives of the national group, and suggests c) specific measures, such as the deportation of immigrants. Ideological work conducts the definition of ideological identities (ideological being-in-itself), relations (ideological being-for-another) and measures (ideological being-in-and-for-itself), the diffusion of these definitions into society, the crystallisation of these ideologies in groups, institutions, structures and orders and the maintenance and reproduction of ideology on all of these levels.

Ideological work employs different ways of how in the second step of the definition process the relation between the dominant group and the dominated group is described. Teun van Dijk (2011, 397f; 1998, 267) has logically formalised possible arguments in the Ideological Square Model. The model contains logical arguments of how ideologies justify dominative relationships. In reality, a concrete ideology often combines several of these logical possibilities that entail positive self-presentation and negative other-presentation. So ideology defines in-groups and out-groups and uses various ideological strategies:

· To express/emphasise information that is positive about Us,
· To express/emphasise information that is negative about Them,
· To suppress/de-emphasise information that is positive about Them,
· To suppress/de-emphasise information that is negative about Us.

Klaus Holzkamp (1985, 364, translation from German to English) stresses that ideology works by an "identification of general interests and partial interests" for the "perpetuation of the existing relations." Dominated and dominating individuals always have the possibility and therefore freedom to break through existing ideologies in order to think and act differently. This does however not automatically happen and in dominative relationships many "individuals by managing their everyday life in which they realise conditioned possibilities of action, relations and thought, reproduce 'with their own existence simultaneously bourgeois class relations' as unquestioned precondition" (Holzkamp 1985, 364, translation from German to English). In ideologies, "'possibilities for action and thought that are determined by heteronomous constraints' appear as the 'only 'thinkable' possibilities' for the creation of the conditions required to secure and unfold existence in 'freedom and equality'" (Holzkamp 1985, 365, translation from German to English). Holzkamp stresses that dominated groups' and individuals' reproduction of ideologies is grounded in existential fears and risks. Available ideologies, worldviews and power constellations condition individuals' specific worldviews and actions and the actuality of realising alternative thoughts and actions that are always possible. If one thinks through Holzkamp's argument then it becomes evident that the major fear that keeps people who are dominated from resisting or trying to organise resistance or joining resistance movement is the fear of death and related to it the fear of violence and torture and the experience of these negative realities not just for oneself, but for one's friends and family. Humans do not by nature subject themselves voluntarily to domination, rather their existential fears and needs for security, harmony, recognition, community is under conditions of domination often channelled into acceptance of one's own domination and exercise of domination against weaker groups and individuals (Holzkamp-Osterkamp 1983).

Many critical theories and analyses of discourse and ideologies in an idealistic manner focus on the level of texts and structures of ideologies and ignore the work or producing and reproducing ideologies. One needs to shed light on how ideologies operate and what their consequences are just like one needs to analyse who produces ideologies, under which circumstances, and with which motivations, goals and intentions. Ideology critique requires analysis of ideology structures and the work of ideology production just like the analysis of work requires an analysis of the structures and conditions of work, including the ideologies that shape workplaces and work cultures.

Table 2.2 gives an overview of various cultural workers in various dimensions of society. They all produce knowledge that is either ideological or critical. In heteronomous/class societies, ideological workers are almost found with certainty. They dominate specific fields and the resources within these fields. Critical workers produce critical knowledge that challenges ideologies.

TABLE 2.2   *Workers, ideologies and worldviews in various fields of society*

Realm of society	Ideological work	Critical work
Economy	Management gurus, consultants, managers: capitalist and liberal ideologies	Activists, unions, social movements, consumer protection groups, critical intellectuals: socialist worldviews critical of capitalism
Politics: government, parliament	Dominant or oppositional parties and politicians: political ideologies of inequality, domination and repression/violence	Critical parties, politicians, intellectuals: political worldviews of equality, participation and peace
Politics: civil society	Repressive social movements, NGOs and activists: political ideologies of inequality, domination and repression/violence	Emancipatory social movements, NGOs and activists: worldviews of equality, participation and peace
International relations	Nationalists: nationalist ideology	Anti-nationalists: global unity in diversity
News media	Uncritical journalists: one-dimensional, biased reports	Critical journalists: critical, engaging reports
Entertainment	Actors, entertainers, directors, artists: tabloidised, one-dimensional culture	Actors, entertainers, directors, artists: engaging, dialectical culture
Personal and gender relations	Hellbenders: hate, sexism	Altruists: love, care, solidarity
Belief systems, ethics, philosophy and religion	Demagogues: Conservatism	Public intellectuals: Progressivism
Science and education	Administrative scholars and teachers: administrative knowledge	Critical scholars and teachers: critical knowledge
Intercultural relations	Racists, divisionists: racism	Universalists: intercultural understanding

In heteronomous/class societies such work is always a potential, but not necessarily and not automatically an actuality because critique requires
resources that are not so easy to mobilise and often controlled by those ruling
the societal field(s).

The hegemony of ideologies and ideological workers can be challenged by
counter-hegemonic work. Gramsci (1988, 58) says in this context that making
a revolution needs "intense labour of criticism." In such cases, there is the
possibility for cultural class struggles, in which critical cultural workers oppose
and struggle against ideological workers. In such cases, critical workers – those
producing critiques as discursive knowledge in semiotic processes – create and
diffuse socialism, equality and participation, unity in diversity, dialectic, love,
care, Progressivism, critical knowledge, or understanding in order to challenge
the ideologies created, diffused and reproduced by ideological workers, such as
liberalism, inequality and domination, nationalism, one-dimensionality, hate,
sexism, conservatism, administrative knowledge and racism. Cultural struggles' emergence and outcomes are never determined, but highly uncertain.
Ideological work and critical work are highly fluid, dynamic and entangled.
Whereas one article in a newspaper may be ideological, another may be critical. But in general there is a tendency of institutional clustering so that ideologies and critique become crystallised in institutions that continuously create,
diffuse and reproduce certain ideologies or critiques. Such institutions have
internal contradictions (between dominant factions and their ideologies,
between dominant and subordinate groups and their discourses) and external
ones (between different institutions, institutions and other institutions,
systems and groups in society etc.).

Subordinated groups and individuals do not necessarily develop critical or
false consciousness. Ideology is a process with uncertain outcomes. Given the
power of dominant groups and the relative powerlessness of dominated
groups, the average likelihood of critical consciousness tends to be lower than
that of critical consciousness, unless dominated groups and individuals
empower themselves and learn to see through ideologies, to question them
and to struggle against them. Dominant classes and groups always try to
impose their ideologies on subordinated people. The dominated answer to this
ideological communication process in a positively (affirmation, hegemony),
negative (critique, counter-hegemony) or mixed way. As ideologists speak to
individuals through ideology, those addressed tend to react and to communicate back in specific ways that are not determined.

The existence of ideologies created and diffused by ideological workers on
behalf of a dominant group is independent of the question how people react
to ideologies. There are different possibilities, either that they are conscious

or unconscious that an ideology is an ideology or a mixed form, either that they follow, partly follow, question or resist ideologies. In the first edition of *Capital* (1867), Volume 1, Marx discussed the fetishism of commodities by saying that ideology is based on the logic 'they do not know it, but they do it'. Slavoj Žižek (1989, 25) suggests based on Peter Sloterdijk that today the cynical subject bases its action on the logic "they know very well what they are doing, but still, they are doing it." Žižek argues that humans partly know about the falseness of ideology, but follow it because they derive a surplus of enjoyment from it. Ideology is always false in that it contains dominant ideas aimed at justifying dominative reality. How human subjects react to ideology has to do with their subjectivity, i.e. their knowing and their doing in relation to ideology. Table 2.3 shows 16 logic combinations of how humans can react to ideology. The way Žižek describes ideology is just one of 16 possibilities of how humans can react to ideologies. They partly or entirely reproduce ideologies in their actions in the eight possibilities of the first two columns. They do not follow or struggle against ideologies in the eight possibilities displayed in the third and fourth column. The 16 logical possibilities have based on specific power structures different likelihoods. It is for example quite unlikely that

TABLE 2.3   *A typology of subjective reactions to ideology*

Action → Knowledge	Following an ideology	Following parts of an ideology	Not following an ideology	Resisting an ideology
Unconscious of an ideology	They do not know it, but they do it.	They do not know it, but they partly do it.	They do not know it and they do not do it.	They do not know it and they resist it.
Conscious of an ideology	They know it, but still, they are doing it.	They know it and they partly do it	They know it and they do not do it.	They know it and they resist it.
Partly conscious of an ideology	They partly know it, but still, they are doing it.	They partly know it and they partly do it.	They partly know it and they do not do it.	They partly know it and they resist it.
Critically conscious of an ideology	They oppose it and they do it.	They oppose it and they partly do (not) do it.	They oppose it and they do not do it.	They oppose it and they resist it.

people resist an ideology by accident, although they are unconscious of it, whereas it is much more likely that they are consciously aware and opposed to it when resisting it.

The production of ideologies and critiques requires workers who create the specific ideational content. But making ideologies and critiques that challenge them work is not just a knowledge production process, but requires multiple associated work processes within institutions and social systems. Take for example a school: there are teachers and pupils who engage in learning, which manifests, creates, reproduces and challenges critiques and ideologies to specific degrees. But work processes that are associated and necessary for enabling learning in schools are cleaners' maintenance of the school building; policy makers', consultants' and experts' design of the curriculum, food personnel's preparation of food in the cafeteria, etc. In order to understand the production of ideologies and critiques one therefore needs to consider the broader institutional foundations and contexts. This means that for analysing work that creates ideologies and critiques one should avoid cultural idealism and take, as suggested by Raymond Williams, a cultural materialist position that sees the embeddedness of culture, ideology and knowledge in different forms of work (information work, service work, physical work, etc).

Conclusion

I have argued that Marxist theory has too often treated the relationship of work on the one hand and culture, communication, language and ideology on the other hand in a dualistic manner. Based on Raymond Williams and Ferruccio Rossi-Landi's works, I have argued for a cultural-materialist approach that sees culture as work that produces symbols and meaning as specific use-values and communication as work process that circulates symbols and meanings in society. Ideology can based on these theoretical assumptions be considered as a form of labour conducted by ideological workers that aims at legitimating the interests of dominant groups and classes. Critical work in contrast challenges ideological work, but is at the same time in capitalism often confronted with an unequal distribution of resources that enable critical work.

A theory of culture, communication and ideology is a dialectical tool of theorising, understanding and helping to inspire struggles against capitalism. It stands in solidarity with those who work towards overcoming class societies along with all ideological labour that legitimate these structures.

References

Eagleton, Terry. 1991. *Ideology: An Introduction.* London: Verso.

Fairclough, Norman. 1995. *Media Discourse.* London: Hodder.

Fairclough, Norman. 2010. *Critical Discourse Analysis. The Critical Study of Language.* Harlow: Pearson.

Fuchs, Christian and Wolfgang Hofkirchner. 2005. Self-Organization, Knowledge, and Responsibility. *Kybernetes* 34 (1–2): 241–260.

Fuchs, Christian and Sebastian Sevignani. 2013. What is Digital Labour? What is Digital Work? What's their Difference? And Why do these Questions Matter for Understanding Social Media? *TripleC: Communication, Capitalism & Critique* 11 (2): 237–293.

Gramsci, Antonio. 1988. *The Antonio Gramsci Reader. Selected Writings 1916–1935,* ed. David Forgacs. London: Lawrence and Wishart.

Habermas, Jürgen. 1968. Arbeit und Interaktion. Bemerkungen zu Hegels Jensener "Philosophie des Geisters." In *Technik und Wissenschaft als "Ideologie,"* 9–47. Frankfurt am Main: Suhrkamp.

Habermas, Jürgen. 1976. *Zur Rekonstruktion des Historischen Materialismus.* Frankfurt am Main: Suhrkamp.

Habermas, Jürgen. 1984. *The Theory of Communicative Action, Volume 1.* Boston: Beacon.

Habermas, Jürgen. 1987. *The Theory of Communicative Action, Volume 2.* Boston: Beacon.

Hegel, Georg Wilhelm Friedrich. 1803/1804. *Jenaer Systementwürfe I.* Hamburg: Felix Meiner Verlag.

Hegel, Georg Wilhelm Friedrich. 1805/1806. *Jenaer Systementwürfe III.* Hamburg: Felix Meiner Verlag.

Hofkirchner, Wolfgang. 2013. *Emergent Information. A Unified Theory of Information Framework.* Singapore: World Scientific.

Holzkamp, Klaus. 1985. *Grundlegung der Psychologie.* Frankfurt am Main: Campus.

Holzkamp-Osterkamp, Ute. 1983. Ideologismus als Konsequenz des Ökonomismus. Zur Kritik am Projekt Ideologietheorie (PIT). *Forum Kritische Psychologie* 11: 7–23.

Hülsmann, Michael and Nicole Pfeffermann, eds. 2011. *Strategies and Communications for Innovations. An Integrative Management View for Companies and Networks.* Heidelberg: Springer.

Hund, Wulf D. 1976. *Ware Nachricht und Informationsfetisch. Zur Theorie der gesellschaftlichen Kommunikation.* Darmstadt: Luchterhand.

Hund, Wulf D. and Bärbel Kirchhoff-Hund. 1980. *Soziologie der Kommunikation. Arbeitsbuch zu Struktur und Funktion der Medien. Grundbegriffe und exemplarische Analysen.* Hamburg: Rowohlt.

Lukács, Georg. 1986. *Werke. Band 14: Zur Ontologie des gesellschaftlichen Seins. 2. Halbband.* Darmstadt: Luchterhand.

Marx, Karl. 1857/1858. *Grundrisse.* London: Penguin.

Marx, Karl. 1867. *Capital, Volume 1.* London: Penguin.

Marx, Karl and Friedrich Engels. 1845/1846. *The German Ideology.* Amherst: Prometheus Books.

Paul, Christopher. 2011. *Strategic Communication: Origins, Concepts, and Current Debates.* Santa Barbara, CA: Praeger.

Rossi-Landi, Ferruccio. 1977. *Linguistics and Economics.* The Hague: Mouton.

Rossi-Landi, Ferruccio. 1983. *Language as Work and Trade. A Semiotic Homology for Linguistics & Economics.* South Hadley: Bergin & Garvey.

Schiller, Dan. 1996. *Theorizing Communication. A History.* New York: Oxford University Press.

van Dijk, Teun. 1998. *Ideology: A Multidisciplinary Approach.* London: Sage.

van Dijk, Teun, ed. 2011. *Discourse Studies: A Multidisciplinary Introduction, Second edition.* London: Sage.

Williams, Raymond. 1962. *Communications.* Harmondsworth: Penguin.

Williams, Raymond. 1977. *Marxism and Literature.* Oxford: Oxford University Press.

Williams, Raymond. 1989. *What I Came to Say.* London: Hutchinson Radius.

Withalm, Gloria. 2006. Ferruccio Rossi-Landi. An Overview on His Ideas on Social Reproduction and Innovation. *Trans* 16. http://www.inst.at/trans/16Nr/01_2/ withalm16.htm (accessed February 28, 2014).

Žižek, Slavoj. 1989. *The Sublime Object of Ideology, Second edition.* London: Verso.

CHAPTER 3

Media Power and Class Power
Overplaying Ideology

David Miller

The media have a contradictory role in relation to class power. They do predominantly carry corporate and state friendly messages, but not exclusively. They do have a role in legitimating capitalist social relations, but the role of ideology in maintaining social order has been overplayed by some theorists. A variety of other mechanisms employed by the powerful to pursue their interests are arguably as important as the mass media in the maintenance of 'ruling ideas'. In attempting to rethink the relationship between media power and class power, this essay uses the work of Stuart Hall as the starting point for a critique of cultural and media studies. It argues that Critical Theorists such as Hall overemphasized the importance of ideology and the 'function' of the media in capitalist social order.

The primary interest of this kind of argument was in the alleged 'ideological effect' of the media on the public and how this might help to secure hegemony. A key assumption was that definitional power was 'always already' power in society. The argument advanced here is that definitional power is just power over definitions and has no necessary link with either popular ideology or societal power. The media do play a role in 'keeping America [and the rest of us] uninformed', as Donna Demac put it. (Demac 1984) They also mislead key sections of western populations about their own interests, and persuade some that happiness lies in the pursuit of goods. But this is not the only role of the media in relation to class power. The media play a direct role in the system of governance in which the public have very little say, or are really heard only *in extremis* (e.g. following successful campaigns or demonstrations—i.e. when opposition is effective). The public are in many circumstances mere spectators at what James Connolly in a different context described as the 'carnival of reaction'.

Furthermore, huge swathes of decision making and power-broking occur not just beyond the reach and influence of the public but also outside the purview of public and media debate. For example, the existence of the multimillion dollar/pound lobbying industry is a standing rebuke to those who argue that the media are overwhelmingly important. Ironically, then, a 'Marxist' analysis of the media assumes, along with liberal analyses, that the public have a fundamental legitimating role in liberal democracies, when in fact public consent is only needed to legitimize decision-making in certain circumstances. And even strong, consistent and popular protest can be ignored by the powerful under many circumstances. We need an alternative model of the relationship between media power and class power, on the lines outlined towards the end of this essay.

Media Power and Class Power

I have adapted the title of this essay from an essay written by Stuart Hall in the mid-1980s. It was a short and simplified piece for a book which attempted to make an intervention in media debates in the UK at the time. In it the media are said to be:

> *the machinery of representation* in modern societies. What they exercise is the power to represent the world in certain definite ways. And because there are many different and conflicting ways in which meaning about the world can be constructed, it matters profoundly what and who gets represented, *what* and *who* regularly and routinely gets left out; and *how* things, people, events, relationships are represented. What we know of society depends on how things are represented to us and that knowledge in turn informs what we do and what policies we are prepared to accept.
> HALL 1986:9

There are four points to be made here. First, what we know of society depends only in part on how things are represented to us, since we also experience the world directly. Second, the world is not only represented to us by the mass media. There is an elision here between representation in general and the mass media in particular. Third, this is a model which assumes fairly powerful media effects. Fourth, note the assumption that the argument stops at the level of the public. But what we are constantly being 'prepared to accept' is often not the same as what the public actually consents to.

Hall acknowledges the importance of ownership and control and of direct and indirect censorship and policing of the media in curtailing diversity. But he argues that these are not by themselves adequate explanations:

> there is also the way in which the hierarchy of *power* in the society is reproduced, in the media, as a structure of *access*. Or how the respect for, orientation towards and reproduction of power in the media surfaces as a set of limits and constrictions on knowledge. That is how, without a

single Ministerial or MI5 intervention, 'topics' come to be defined, agendas set and frameworks deployed which ultimately define the 'sayable and 'unsayable' in society. The area of what is considered as 'reasonable talk'about anything, as the appropriate and inappropriate registers, as the intangible boundaries which rule the inclusion or exclusion of certain things, certain points of view, is one of the most powerful of the ways the media's regimes of truth come to be established.

HALL 1986:12

This seems like a mysterious process. How is the structure of access determined? How exactly is it that topics come to be defined? What set of processes establish the boundaries of the sayable? Hall does acknowledge that 'we know far too little' of such processes. He asks: '[h]ow can we pinpoint, in the endless, diverse, flow of "talk" in the media, the precise ways in which the state stands as the "definer of the limits of political reality" for the media'. (Hall 1986:12)

The Ideological Effect?

Perhaps the mysteriousness of this process arises as a result of the simplified content of this particular article. But when we turn to Hall's earlier formulations, the process becomes if anything more mysterious. Here the media are the preeminent ideological institutions. They furthermore operate effectively to ensure the reproduction of capital:

[t]he 'definitions of reality', favourable to the dominant class fractions, and institutionalised in the spheres of civil life and the state, come to constitute the primary 'lived reality' as such for the subordinate classes. In this way ideology provides the 'cement' in a social formation.

HALL 1977:333

This assumes on the basis of theory (rather than evidence) that bourgeois ideology actually does indoctrinate the masses. But how does this happen? To understand this we need to look at the theoretical heritage on which Hall's work is based.

In particular we need to note the way in which two bodies of literature were drawn together in an attempt to renovate Marx. First there was contemporary work on language and semiotics. These approaches relied heavily on speculation about the meanings of texts. Drawing on semiotics, structural linguistics and anthropology via Levi-Strauss and Saussure, Hall attempted to posit a homology between Levi Strauss' proposition, that a speaker can use a language without any consciousness of its generative code, and Marx's famous statement that people make history but not in circumstances of their own choosing. The point of this was to show that language and discourse have their own determinate rules and can be seen to operate autonomously from the economic and political levels of society. On this basis Hall could argue for the 'relative autonomy' of the ideological and for an apparently autonomous 'class struggle in language', or for the 'specificity of the cultural'. (Schiller 1996)

Second and perhaps most importantly was the influence of Althusser. Althusser's work on ideology was an attempt to avoid the economism of certain strands of Marxism. Althusser conceived of society as being a complex totality of different 'levels' or 'instances'. (Althusser, 1969 & 1971) Of particular note was the instance of ideology, which had a 'relative autonomy' from the political and the economic. The economic level of society determined the ideological 'in the last instance'. (Kolakowski 1971) But if the last instance guarantees ideology for capital, relative autonomy is really not very autonomous at all and only narrowly, if at all, escapes the charge of economism. It certainly does not escape the charge of functionalism, as Hall notes, but his take on Althussser is also vulnerable to the same problem of assuming a function for the media even if it is only a 'systemic tendency'. (Hall 1977:346)

Hall's model blurs together, under the heading of ideology, the distinct moments of the propagation and promotion of particular ideologies by the dominant class, the work done on them to transform them into media products, the understanding and response to them of audiences and the impact of this in societal outcomes. (Miller 1997) It does this by conceiving of language and ideology as nearly indistinguishable and assuming that understanding language is tantamount to 'being spoken' by ideology. (Hall 1983:80)[1] Ideology, in other words, is an unconscious process. Hall discusses 'effective communication'(Hall 1977:344)[2] as the site of ideology. It is as if it were not

---

1   In a caveat Hall notes that language and ideology are not the same thing: '[a]n analytic distinction needed to be maintained'. But it is hard to see much of a gap between the concepts since he goes on to note the close relationship between understanding language and being spoken by ideology: 'one cannot learn a language without learning something of its current ideological inflections' (Hall, Stuart. 1983. 'The rediscovery of "ideology": return of the repressed in media studies', in M. Gurevitch et al., eds., Culture, Society and the Media, London: Methuen, p. 80). Once again this blurs together learning something, about which we might suspend judgement, with being 'spoken' by ideology.

2   see also Hall, Stuart. 1973. 'The "Structured Communication" of Events', Paper for Obstacles to Communication Symposium, UNESCO, University of Birmingham Centre for Contemporary Cultural Studies Stencilled Occasional Papers, Birmingham: CCCS; Hall, Stuart 1980a.

possible to step outside of ideology; language itself is ideological regardless of the intentions or views of the speaker.

To put it in its extreme form, a statement like, 'the strike of the Leyland tool-makers today further weakened Britain's economic position' was premised on a whole set of taken for granted propositions about how the economy worked... for it to win credibility, the whole logic of capitalist production had to be assumed to be true.

So far so good, but the key to this passage is the way that Hall goes on to assume that the statement wins credibility simply by virtue of having been understood:

> Much the same could be said about any item in a conventional news bul-letin, that, without a whole range of unstated premises or pieces of taken-for-granted knowledge about the world, each descriptive statement would be literally unintelligible. But this 'deep structure' of presuppositions, which made the statement ideologically 'grammatical' [was] rarely made explicit and [was] largely unconscious...to those who were required to make sense of it.
>
> HALL 1983:74

To win credibility for the proposition that strikes are a 'problem' for the nation (or whatever is the latest piece of capitalist ideology or state propaganda) certainly requires that it is repeated and elaborated on the 'unbiased' TV news as if it were simply a statement of fact; but it also requires that people believe it, which is not guaranteed simply by virtue of it being an intelligible statement. We may understand the message but not accept that it is true, valid or fair. This has been found extensively in critical audience research in recent years.[3] In formulations like Hall's the problem of the reproduction of capital is solved not by direct investigation of the relationship between the media, popular ideology and societal outcomes, but by theoretical fiat. (McDonnell & Robins 1980:160–161) In later formulations (in the early 1980s) Hall moved towards the Foucauldian notion of discursive practice, where ideology is said to speak through people without their knowledge:

'Encoding/decoding', in S. Hall, D. Hobson, A. Lowe and P. Willis, eds., *Culture, Media, Language*, London: Hutchinson.

3   See for example John Corner, 'Meaning, genre and context: the problem atics of public knowledge in the new audience studies', in J. Curran and M. Gurevitch, eds., *Mass Media and Society*, London: Edward Arnold, 1991; J. Kitzinger, 'A Sociology of Media Power: key issues in audience research', in G. Philo, ed., *Message Received*, London: Longman, 1999; David Miller, *Don't Mention the War: Northern Ireland, Propaganda and the Media*, London: Pluto, 1994.

when in phrasing a question, in the era of monetarism, a broadcasting interviewer simply takes it for granted that rising wage demands are the sole cause of inflation, he is both 'freely formulating a question' on behalf of the public and establishing a logic which is compatible with the dominant interests in society. And this would be the case regardless of whether or not the particular broadcaster was a lifelong supporter of some left-wing trotskyist sect...In the critical paradigm, ideology is a function of discourse and of the logic of social process, rather than an intention of the agent...The ideology has 'worked' in such a case because the discourse has spoken itself through him/her.

HALL 1983:88

It strains credulity to suggest that left journalists would not and do not notice their contributions to dominant ideologies. The MI5 vetting office in the BBC certainly does not take that view, nor did the management of Fox TV when they sacked two journalists in Tampa, Florida for their reporting of Monsanto.[4] But for Hall, what is important is the mysterious functioning of ideology, which we have imbibed so thoroughly that we no longer notice.

Hall, following Althusser, goes on to discuss ideology as an unconscious process:

important modifications to our way of conceiving dominance had to be effected before the idea was rescuable. That notion of dominance which meant the direct imposition of one framework, by overt force or ideological compulsion, on a subordinate class, was not sophisticated enough to match the real complexities of the case. One had also to see that dominance was accomplished at the unconscious as well as the conscious level: to see it as a property of the system of relations involved, rather than the overt and intentional biases of individuals; and to recognise its play in the very activity of regulation and exclusion which functioned through language discourse, before an adequate conception of dominance could be theoretically secured.[5]

HALL 1983:88

---

4 See http://www.foxgbhsuit.com.

5 This sits nicely with the appropriation of Lacanian psychoanalysis by Althusserians in the 1970s around the journal *Screen*, and later by Hall himself. The Lacanians saw the entry into consciousness as being the entry into ideology, via the mirror phase or the Oedipus complex. As late as 1996 Hall was hailing the importance of the 'suturing of the psychic and the discursive' (Hall, Stuart. 2001. 'Introduction: Who Needs "Identity"', in S. Hall, and P. du Gay, eds.,

If anything, however, the idea of the unconscious as the last guarantor of bourgeois ideology is less sophisticated than the model it seeks to replace, in the sense that it explains everything by a hidden principle. It does not match the complexities of actual societies in which people do continuously and consciously struggle for a better tomorrow. Elegant and sophisticated the theory and the delivery might be, but it does not conform to the available evidence on public belief and popular ideology. As McDonnell and Robins put it:

> ideology [is]...not a factor of the unconscious as Althusser maintains. This latter position would...make class consciousness impossible... Ideology does not permeate people's minds: the working class does not find it impossible to unmask the ideological mystifications of capitalist society. For ideology is far from watertight; it requires an incessant struggle by the capitalist class to maintain its precarious validity. A validity that is constantly called into question, not in a separate sphere of ideological struggle, but throughout the daily struggles in the workplace, the community etc.
>
> MCDONNELL & ROBINS 1980:160–161

This is a much more adequate position and lets us theorize the role of state and corporate information management, censorship and secrecy in the reproduction of inequality. It lets us see the importance not of the 'system of relations' but of concrete actions by concrete institutions and individuals in concrete historical circumstances not of their choosing. What else is the whole machinery of state and corporate public relations (together with confidentiality, intimidation, the use of the law etc.) but a massive daily attempt to 'nobble' the media and 'indoctrinate' the people? The capitalist class is perfectly aware of the need to brief, spin, dissemble and lie.

Gramsci to the Rescue?

Hall's greatest achievement, so far as many commentators are concerned, was his use of the concept of hegemony to avoid the disabling reductionism and functionalism of Althusserianism. Hegemony meant that consent was important and that the class struggle in language was or could be a two-sided affair. Hall noted that a problem with Althusser's work was that it was difficult to see

---

Questions of Cultural Identity, London: Sage, p. 16. For a critique of this position see Greg Philo and David Miller, *Market Killing*, London: Longman).

how anything but the dominant ideology could ever be reproduced.[6] Volosinov and particularly Gramsci were deployed to show that there can be a class struggle in language. This appeared to mean that intelligibility was not guaranteed and could be ruptured by oppositional codes or subordinate meaning systems. There was not always 'an achieved system of equivalence between language and reality'. (Hall 1983:78) This gave the possibility of a struggle for hegemony in language. This struggle was conceived as emanating from within the technical aspects of signs and language: there were 'mechanisms within signs and language which made the "struggle" possible'. (Hall 1983:78) These mechanisms included the multi-accentuality of a discourse, or the fact that some words can mean more than one thing or can be interpreted differently. Against this we can say that the struggle over language is made possible not by the alleged technical features of language, but by the material facts of conflicting power and interests. Instead of seeing challenges to hegemony as emerging from separate discourses, we need to see them as emanating from experience, material and ideal interests, and struggles in which ideology and language play a role that we can only sensibly grasp in terms of totality. The example Hall gives is the conflict over the term 'Black' as a term of abuse, or as a positive sign of beauty and empowerment. But it is the fact of racist discrimination and violence, on the one hand, and the struggle for self determination and self respect, on the other, which make this conflict possible, not the technical features of language. These conditions form the material circumstances in which people 'become conscious of conflict and fight it out', as Marx put it.

Hall discusses the level of the discursive as if it were a separate domain.

Gramsci's notion of the war of position is transposed from political and class struggles to the 'field of discourse'. As a result Hall holds that 'now we have to talk about texts that are never closed, about discursive systems that are not unified but the product of articulation and always contradictory; about the possibilities of transcoding and decoding the dominant definitions in play'. (Hall 1989:51) But we only have to talk in this way if we swallow all of this elegant theoretical edifice. Included in the bargain is the separation and elevation of discourse, as opposed to the importance of the reproduction of the means of survival. A materialist view holds rather that language is a product of human culture and is a part of the social relations of production of a 'whole way of life'.

---

6   In response to Thompson's *The Poverty of Theory*, Hall went furthest along the road of disavowing certain Althusserian positions, but this seems only to have had a limited effect on the extent to which the Althusserian 'problematic' continued to inform his thinking on ideology and media power. See Hall, Stuart. 1980b. 'In defence of theory', in Raphael Samuel, ed., *People's History and Socialist Theory*, London: Routledge and Kegan Paul.

It is a tool used by humans to communicate and negotiate, even if we do not understand the rules which generate it. To see the level of the discursive as a separate level is to privilege language over experience, consciousness, and material and biological reality. The problem is that this is not how 'discourse' functions. Discourses, or ideologies (as Hall seems increasingly unwilling to call them) arise out of the material and ideal interests of real people. There is no abstract struggle over language, only a struggle over power and resources of which ideological battles form part. There is no 'class struggle in language' which is separate and distinct from the class struggle over resources and the organization of society. Changing the word is not changing the world, as Sivanandan memorably put it. (Sivanandan 1990:49)

The notion that it was ideology that pre-eminently explained the reproduction of capital foundered on the rock of all sorts of evidence that people were able to understand the world (and the word). On the part of some formerly radical theorists, this led to some confusion about the possibilities of using concepts such as ideology and to a renewed pluralist emphasis on the indeterminacy of power. (Eagleton 1996; Philo & Miller 2001) The narrow focus on the media, or on the moment of decoding or interpretation, meant that the wider picture of the assault on social democracy seemed simply to vanish from the academic agenda of media studies.[7]

Back to Marx

As a potential way out of some of these problems I want to try and advance an alternative approach by going back to Marx and briefly re-examining his

---

7   Although it should be acknowledged that Hall and his colleagues had produced a pioneering account of such questions in *Policing the Crisis* (London: Macmillan, 1978). In addition Hall did produce a wide range of political writings on Thatcherism, collected in his books, edited with Martin Jacques, *The Politics of Thatcherism* (London: Lawrence and Wishart in association with *Marxism Today*, 1983) and *New Times*, (London: Lawrence and Wishart, 1989). Unlike *Policing the Crisis*, however, these writings were not based on original empirical research, and much of the political analysis derived from the theoretical agenda being described here. This work encouraged the left to abandon much of its radical platform and embrace a kind of left mirror image of Thatcherism in order to build a new counterhegemony. For critiques see David Harris, *From Class Struggle to the Politics of Pleasure*, London: Routledge, 1992; M. Rustin, 'The Politics of PostFordism and the Trouble with "New Times"', *New Left Review*, 175, 1989. This trajectory also fitted well with those tendencies which resulted in the virtual disappearance of the concept of class across academia. See Graham Murdock, 'Reconstructing the ruined tower: Contemporary Communications and Questions of Class', in M. Gurevitch and J. Curran, eds., *Mass Media and Society*, 3rd Ed. London: Edward Arnold, 2000.

classic formulations about the relations between economics, power and ideas. There are three main points I want to make here. The first relates to the misunderstanding of the notion of the social relations of production, the second to the base-superstructure metaphor, which has often been interpreted as indicating that the ownership of the means of production endows the capitalist class with fantastic powers of persuasion, and the third relates to the notion of ruling ideas.

1. In one of the most famous passages on the question of ideology Marx argued that:

> in the social production of their existence, men inevitably enter into definite relations, which are independent of their will, namely relations of production appropriate to a given stage in the development of their material forces of production. The totality of these relations of production constitutes the economic structure of society, the real foundation, on which arises a legal and political superstructure and to which correspond definite forms of social consciousness. The mode of production of material life conditions the general process of social, political and intellectual life. It is not the consciousness of men which determines their existence, but their social existence that determines their consciousness.
>
> MARX 1975:425

It is fairly clear from this passage that the 'social relations of production' are not simply a set of mechanistic 'economic' processes. They are a set of social processes which are determined by the need to reproduce the material basis of life and the forces of production. Such social processes act on the 'forces of production' and shape them in determinate, if historically contingent, ways. Social relations are profoundly ideological and are the real foundation on which capitalist self-interest—and opposition to it—are built. In other words, ideology is constitutive of the social relations of production. Further, ideology, and how people become conscious of their world, affects how those struggles are fought out and the resulting changes in both the forces of production and the social relations surrounding them. Ideology is not simply a reflection of the level of the economic, it is part of the means by which interests are welded to action and by which certain actions or states of affairs are justified and legitimated.

We should not reduce ideology to the system or structure of relations, but rather see the conscious (if ideological) actions of human beings as constitutive of the social totality and as causative agents in historical processes. This approach necessitates first and foremost empirical research to ascertain how human activities constitute history. It also means that we see the determinate actions of real human beings as being consequential for the reproduction of capital. Rather than seek power in some mysterious unobservable process of ideological interpellation or articulation, or simply in understanding language, we must seek it in the actions of real people in the (would-be) secret (but sometimes discoverable) low conspiracies which are a continuous and inevitable part of capitalist rule; in censorship, spin, lobbying, public relations, marketing and advertising; (Miller & Dinan 1995) in the institutions of 'disinformation and distraction' as Raymond Williams put it. (Williams 1985:268) These, in the context of economic power and resources, are some of the key means by which capitalism is reproduced, and we treat them as mere epiphenomena of the real, hidden nature of ideology at our peril.

2. The base/superstructure metaphor is rather unpopular these days. Critics have suggested that it reduces ideas and ideologies to the economic, whether in the first or last instance. And to be sure, in some hands it does. But following Terry Eagleton (Eagleton 1991:82), I would like to enter a few words for the defence.

Speaking crudely there were two interpretations of the base-superstructure metaphor. One was the vulgar Marxist interpretation which saw the media simply as an agency of class control and the population as brainwashed (or subject to 'ideological effects' in Hall's more sophisticated versions). The second was that associated with Raymond Williams, who suggested that we see the economic (the ownership of the means of mental production) as setting limits on what could appear in the media. (Williams 1980) This does seem to provide a reasonable description of much media behaviour. We could query it on the grounds that the imperative to make money sometimes pulls against the supposed imperative to support the system. Or we might query it on the issue of popular ideology, since it is arguably not that case that economic power determines popular ideology, at least not in a simple sense. But this again betrays a misunderstanding about the sources of power and experience in society. The position advanced here is that ideas come from and indeed are inseparable from interests. Accounts of the world and evaluations of it emerge from material experience as well as from the media and other symbolic systems. So there is every reason to suppose that there will always be sources of opposition to capitalism.

And who could deny that material factors have a determining role in moving culture in particular directions? To pick an example from California, which comes to hand as I write, it is apparent that the development of new forces of production in Silicon Valley has involved a set of changing social relations of production. Capital has been poured into the development of dot. com companies in the latter half of the 1990s (prior to the transformation from dot.com to dot.gone as the NASDAQ index plummeted). This made a small number of relatively young people very rich very fast. One consequence of this has been an alleged deleterious effect on social solidarity in some neighbourhoods in the Bay area. The *San Francisco Chronicle* reports:

> it was the new millionaires, made rich by cashing in their abundant stock options, that changed the playing field here. They thought nothing of bidding up houses several hundreds of thousands of dollars over the asking price or paying cash for $60,000 Mercedes-Benzes... For many, the irrationality of it all came at a price: skyrocketing housing costs, maddening traffic jams, shortages of skilled labor and perhaps most frustrating, a diminished sense of community. The nouveau riche were moving into old neighbourhoods, tearing down vintage homes, building bigger ones and erecting giant fences.
>
> WALSH & FINZ 2001

Now we might say that the 'culture' of the new rich and how they behave is not 'determined' in a mechanistic sense by the social relations of production. It was of course possible for the new rich to have given all their money away to anti-globalization protesters or for them to rip off the firms in which they work to fund the activities of revolutionary writers. The latter course was taken by Friedrich Engels at his family firm as a means of supporting Karl Marx. (Wheen 2000) But this has not happened -as far as we know- widely in the Bay area. Instead they put up fences and further dehumanized 'community'. Why must we say that this was simply a cultural matter with no deterministic link to the social relations of production? To say that the fences were built as part of a new cultural formation simply begs the question of what caused the culture to change. It seems more adequate to say that this was a 'determinate' outcome of the change in the social relations of production. Without wanting to reduce everything to such clear cut causation, it is clearly imperative to understand the social and material genesis of ideas and values and how these then ripple through the social fabric, provoking approval, desire, opprobrium or opposition. We cannot explain phenomena such as this without a model in which the social relations of production 'condition', 'determine' or 'influence' how people live in the world and relate to each other.

3. But the extent to which particular ideologies or ideas require to be believed (and by how many people) for the system to function is not a straightforward affair. The key question was how far does the ownership of capital allow the capitalist class to dominate the thinking of subordinated classes? According to Marx and Engels:

the ideas of the ruling class are in every epoch the ruling ideas, i.e. the class which is the ruling *material* force of society, is at the same time its ruling *intellectual* force. The class which has the means of material production at its disposal, has control at the same time over the means of mental production, so that thereby, generally speaking, the ideas of those who lack the means of mental production are subject to it... The individuals composing the ruling class possess among other things consciousness, and therefore think. Insofar, therefore, as they rule as a class and determine the extent and compass of an epoch, it is self evident that they do this in its whole range, hence among other things rule also as thinkers, as producers of ideas, and regulate the production and distribution of the ideas of their age: thus their ideas are the ruling ideas of the epoch.[8]

MARX & ENGELS 1947:39

The widespread interpretation of this is that those who own the means of production dominate the production of ideas, with the result that their ideas are adopted by the masses, thus assuring capitalist rule. This is the clear assumption in the work of Stuart Hall, quoted at the beginning of this essay.[9] But there is not much in the passage from Marx and Engels to encourage this interpretation. One way to pose this is to ask what a ruling intellectual force might be? Is it a set of ideas with which everyone agrees, or at least with which the mass of the (working class) population agrees? Or is it a set of ideas that rule because they are the most powerful in the society, or because they are the operating assumptions of the power structure, without necessarily commanding widespread consent?

If we assume that it is the first of these it is not very difficult to slip into a rather condescending view of the proletariat as being 'subject' to ideology. But suppose we take the second definition. It does not assume that a majority of the population agrees with or accepts every piece of bourgeois ideology. But then the question arises, if such ideas are not accepted how do they rule?

---

8   The example that Marx gives of the doctrine of the separation of powers as the dominant idea which is expressed as an 'eternal law' is also compatible with this interpretation. This is what is expressed in the 'dominant' ideology, but in order to rule it may not be necessary for it to be shared by the vast bulk of the population. This is particularly the case if we hold a weak model of hegemony where dominance need only be secured by the absence of effective opposition. See Miliband, Ralph. 1990 'Counter-hegemonic struggles', in *The Socialist Register 1990*, London: The Merlin Press.

9   To be fair it is not only 'Marxists' influenced by Althusser who have endorsed this interpretation.

To assume that capitalist societies are so transparently responsive to popular belief and opinion is to assume a rather pluralist version of the theory of democracy. (In fact Hall is explicit about this, observing that the advantage of pluralism is that it has a firm grasp of the place of consent in the social order. (Hall 1983:85)) But liberal capitalist democracies are founded on consent of an extremely limited and provisional sort.

Democracy

What does liberal democracy entail? Does it entail the government of the people, for the people and by the people? Or does it entail simply voting once every four or five years? Assuming for a moment that the will of the people in terms of votes cast is respected in Western countries,[10] we can probably agree that the practice of democracy is somewhere between these two poles. There are occasions, albeit rare, when popular pressure forces concessions— from the defeat of the Poll Tax in the UK to the anti-WTO protest in Seattle. But overall the exercise of power in society does not seem to bow easily to public opinion or the popular will—let alone to principles of justice and equality. While the media have a central role to play here, it also seems to be the case that much of the decisionmaking in society occurs elsewhere, out of sight of the population and sometimes of the media too. It is a task of social activism to illuminate such processes and bring them to wider atten-tion and sometimes that task is successfully accomplished. But we should be aware that class and corporate power occur 'behind our backs' in the sense that we do not know about them, rather than in the sense that we unconsciously consent to them via the mysterious mechanism of ideology. One neat way to sum this up is with Alex Carey's aphorism: 'the twentieth century has been characterised by three developments of great political importance: the growth of democracy, the growth of corporate power, and the growth of corporate propaganda as a means of protecting corporate power against democracy'. (Carey 1995:18)

Empirically this means widening the focus of media and cultural studies to examine the interaction of the symbolic and the material throughout society and to examine the communicative processes which accompany and make possible the operation of power. This means more than studying the media as texts or as institutions. It means studying their whole range of interactions

---

10   Which is somewhat adrift from practice, as the US election of George W. Bush in 2000 showed.

with the rest of the society. I would highlight two areas where this is especially important. The first of these is the role of corporations, states and activists in pursuing strategies for power and influence and the role that the media do (or do not) play in these. This means examining the intentions of actors and the planning and execution of strategies. Much of this will involve public relations and lobbying consultancies and these need to be a serious object of attention in media and cultural studies (and not just in terms of cultural industries). A second area is the question of the 'success' or failure of strategies. This is a much more complex area, which we might group under the heading of 'reproduction'. It involves questions about the role of the media in informing/influencing public opinion and the variety of questions associated with the notion of the 'active audience'. However, this notion has severe limitations, not least because it has not led on to questions intrinsic to the notion of reproduction, such as the question of outcomes. What happens as a consequence of popular belief or disbelief, or of 'negotiated' or 'oppositional' 'readings' of texts (to use the inadequate language derived via Hall from the pluralist Frank Parkin)? And what difference does this make to class power? We need to discuss these points under the specific heading of power in society, rather than in terms of media power alone.

Corporate Power and the Media

It is clear enough that corporations regularly get a good deal from the mainstream media in the UK (and even more so in the US). But, there are occasions on which essentially anti-corporate themes become major running news stories. In the UK, food safety issues such as Salmonella and BSE (Miller 1999; Miller & Reilly 1995), and the campaign against 'fat cats' in the mid-1990s, are good examples. (Bastion 1997; Vulliamy & Leigh 2000).

It is not that the coverage has always been progressive, although it sometimes has been, but that the stories' news values entail a concern for the 'public' as victims of state or corporate power, greed and arrogance. (It also helps that the corporations in question are not media corporations.) In such circumstances radical and liberal pressure groups can help to make the story run and can get some of their message across. Some recent writers describe this observation as a 'pluralist point', to which I would say the following: definitional power is not identical to political and economic power. It is important that we look beyond the front pages of the tabloids and the nightly news headlines to the issue of what happens as a result. In the examples of food safety, there can be little doubt, given the evidence of slump in the market for eggs, cheese and beef, that the radical view was widely shared by the public. Further evidence comes in the form of opinion poll and focus group research carried out by government and academic researchers (Macintyre, Reilly, etc. 1998), but the key question then is what happens as a result of this.

For a long time at the level of government, nothing beyond cosmetic changes occurred. Indeed after the 1988 salmonella scare in the UK public health interests were marginalized in policy-making, thus contributing to the appalling treatment of the issue of BSE. (Miller 1999)

Then under the Conservatives came an admission that BSE-infected meat was the 'most likely' cause of human deaths from CJD. Under New Labour this was followed by the BSE inquiry, and a Food Standards Agency -one of the key demands of the food activists from the late 1980s- was established. Both of these developments were 'nobbled' -the BSE inquiry by official spin, the Food Safety Agency by its limited powers and the fact that its head was a natural scientist unsympathetic to the critique of science and its increasingly close relationship with corporate power and money. There were no moves to reverse the deregulation which was at the root of the problems and very little 'political demand' (i.e. demand in policy circles as opposed to amongst the public) for change. So in terms of outcomes, even if we regard the media as having been on the side of the angels in this case- which would be a massive distortion- this does not lead us in a pluralist direction. The media may sometimes be the only ally that democrats and socialists have, given the foreshortened avenues for democratic change in current conditions, but they are not necessarily a powerful ally.

In what has been described as the information age, it is obvious that capitalism as a system, and corporations as institutions, require large amounts of information to function. Indeed the development of information technology has been an essential requirement for capital to increase its own mobility in the past couple of decades. (Babe 1994) Corporations need market data, data on their customers and potential customers, information on political movements and regulatory regimes. Some of this information comes from the media. But they also need to communicate to function. They need to debate internally and amongst their competitors in the same or differing industries. And they need to discuss issues with politicians and decision-makers. Much of this information and communication is private, confidential or secret. Some is public in a very limited sense and some is public and on view in the mainstream media, although it is often tucked away on the margins of the business pages. In the following section I outline four ways in which corporate and class power operate beyond the reach of the popular will.

Corporate and Class Power Beyond the Media

1   *Lobbying*

In recent years the power of the legislature has declined while lobbying and other covert means of influencing policy have massively expanded—from the hard money/soft money debate in the US to the 'cash for questions' and other lobbying scandals in the UK. (Drew 2000; Hollingsworth 1991; Lewis & the Center for Public Integrity 1998) Although there is some measure of transparency in terms of the regulation of lobbying in the US, lobbying itself is an almost completely covert business. It trades influence for cash and generally does not attempt to influence public opinion. In its day-to-day activities it is beyond the reach of public debate. It is an organized conspiracy against democracy in the sense that private interests try to influence legislation and decision-making directly, rather than democratically or by means of debate. The role of the media here is negligible, with one exception. That is when lobbying misdeeds are exposed in the media. This does not happen nearly regularly enough, but the role of the media is sometimes to undermine this or that piece of corporate selfinterest. Except in such cases, much decision-making in both the US and UK goes on in secret away from the prying eyes of the media and with precious little popular involvement. This is not an insignificant point given the very large sums of money and resources that the rich have managed to expropriate from the poor (especially in the US and UK) in the last couple of decades, through redistributive tax, cutting social spending and privatizing public assets.

Two examples might be worthwhile. The corporate campaign to open up China to global capital required that the US Congress pass the China Trade Bill. According to Public Citizen's Global Trade Watch at least $113.1 million was spent lobbying on this bill alone. (Woodall, Wallach, etc. 2000)

Yet this is not part of the agenda of mainstream news or of widespread public debate. In this example power is exercised away from the media rather than by the media. Secondly, let us take the example of the negotiations over the Free Trade Area of the Americas (FTAA), a major and audacious attempt to abolish the minimal democratic controls that still exist over the abuses of big money throughout North and South America. There is very little discussion of this in the mainstream media and the public are kept in almost total ignorance.[11]

To be sure, a lot more people may have heard of it after the protests against it in Quebec in April 2001, but one indication of where power resides is that the text of the agreement was kept secret by the state and corporate personnel negotiating it. 'Consumers' are almost completely ignorant of all such debates.

---

11   See http://www.ifg.org.

This does not suggest that they are dupes of the system or that they have been ideologically spoken—it is just that they don't know.

As the system of global 'governance' emerges the global public becomes more and more disenfranchised and powerless, denied basic information with which to make up its mind. The trend toward global 'governance' has been boosted by the progressive dilution of democratic controls on capital as corporations have increasingly sought to buy their way into the political process. There has been a flurry of books across the Anglophone world with very similar titles on this 'corporate takeover' and on the 'sleaze' and 'scandals' which go with it. (Derber, C. 1998; Lull & Hinerman 1997; Monbiot 2000; Tiffen 2000) These developments suggest a weakening of democratic controls. Do they also suggest that the role of the media as some form of check or balance within the system is becoming less important? On the contrary, media agendas are increasingly being set by corporate priorities to maximize profits. (McChesney 2000; Underwood 1995)

2   *Private Debates in Public*

There is also a sense in which much of what appears in even mainstream newspapers is not really for the bulk of the audience who consume the news. Private debates among the powerful can surface in the media as part of a struggle within the state apparatus or corporations, such as the struggle between the Special Branch of the Metropolitan police and the intelligence agency MI5 over antiterrorist operations in Britain (Miller 1993), or the 'dirty tricks' battle between British Airways and Virgin Atlantic (Gregory 1996), or a thousand other pieces of intrigue and power struggle. We can sometimes listen in if we are able to read between the lines, but there are few ways in which we can be part of the conversation.

3   *Withstanding Hostile Coverage*

The question is not 'is there definitional advantage?', but 'what difference does definitional disadvantage make?' When does it matter if the media are hostile? The issue of 'sleaze' in the UK did mean the end of ministerial careers and to some extent the unpopularity of the Tories and there was a field day on 'fat cats', as the bosses of the privatized utilities were dubbed. But this did not necessarily cause much angst in the business world—or at least it did not significantly materially alter board room pay rates which continued to rise, nor (beyond some populist rhetoric) did it result in any significant move by the Labour Government against boardroom pay rises or corporate power. Media coverage hostile to corporate interests often has little impact.

4   *Ignoring Public Opinion, Opposition and Protest*

There is a further stage beyond hostile coverage, which is the question of public opinion and action. Corporate and state decision-makers are able to ignore popular opinion and protest even when there is widespread support for or against a particular decision. Popular protest too can be resisted. In the UK the protests against the Poll Tax were ignored for a long time and it was only when the tax threatened to split the Conservative Party that it was removed. Throughout the counterinsurgency campaign in Northern Ireland virtually every opinion poll showed that the public was in favour of British military disengagement, yet no mainstream party ever attempted to carry through the will of the people on this issue (Miller 1994). In the UK and the US large sections of the population oppose corporate pollution and approve of public funding for everything from power and transport to health and education, yet governments in both states move further towards the market in their social and economic policy. The protests in Seattle 'shut down' the WTO talks, but they didn't stop the organization functioning and there is little sign of it fundamentally changing its course.

Conclusion

All this is only to say that change is hard to achieve. It has to be struggled for in language and in action. Changing the word is not changing the world. But this essay has also tried to draw attention to the fact that capitalism reproduces itself by means not just of ideology, but by a myriad of social processes in which ideology is ever-present, but only as part of a wider struggle for power and resources.

So what is the role of the media in the reproduction of class power? The media do have a role in promoting dominant ideologies and in spreading them variably amongst sections of the population. The media can on occasion help to convince elements of the public of states of affairs and evaluations of them which are thoroughly ideological, even where this is not in their own interests. But the media also have a direct role which is arguably as important for the reproduction of inequality as ideological power over the masses. Furthermore, there is a variety of mechanisms and practices in society, by which power is exercised and resources distributed, in which the media have a minimal role. Lobbying is an obvious example. Of course ideology and communication are ever attendant on such processes.

Consent is not simply an ideological process, but interacts with material and ideal interests, even though ideology can affect the perception of interests.

Consent, as in post-1945 Britain for instance, was gained not only by ideology but by real compromises such as the nationalization of key industries and the creation of the welfare state. Dependence on ideology as a privileged explanatory principle severs the connection between interests and ideas and neglects the importance of material interests in conditioning and creating ideas.

Secrecy, censorship and information management are all daily conspiracies against democracy. The way in which questions are ruled in and out are not mysterious processes but eminently researchable. Such research must not only examine media ownership, institutions and ideology, as much valuable work has, but also the real activities and strategies of corporations and states which are incessantly being planned and deployed. I am speaking of course of the promotional and information management activities of governments and corporations and of their secretive and covert lobbying and espionage activities. These are not distracting epiphenomena the state and capital could do without, but some of the key ways in which our system works.

Some people under some circumstances believe some things that are against their own interests and in the interests of the powerful. But the working classes do not believe every bit of bourgeois propaganda. Nor is it necessary for them to do so for capitalism to survive—or more accurately, if we take the current historical epoch, to go from strength to strength. There is no straightforward and automatic relationship between ideology and public consciousness. Ideology has been overplayed as an explanation of the reproduction of class and other divisions. 'Ruling ideas' rule by a variety of mechanisms. These include media propaganda and the systematic distortions of ideology which do successfully fool some of the people some of the time, but not all of us all of the time.

References

Arnold, Edward and J. Kitzinger. 1999. 'A Sociology of Media Power: key issues in audience research', in G. Philo, ed., *Message Received*, London: Longman.

Babe, R. ed., 1994. *Information and Communication in Economics*, Boston, Dordrecht, London: Kluwer Academic Publishers

Bastion, Lewis. 1997. *Sleaze: the State of Britain*, London: Channel Four Books.

Carey, Alex. 1995. *Taking the Risk out of Democracy: Corporate Propaganda versus Freedom and Liberty*, Sydney: University of New South Wales Press.

Corner, John. 1991. 'Meaning, genre and context: the problem atics of public knowledge in the new audience studies', in J. Curran and M. Gurevitch, eds., *Mass Media and Society*, London: Edward Arnold.

Demac, Donna. 1984. *Keeping America Uninformed: Government Secrecy in the 1980s*, New York: W.W. Norton.

Derber, C. 1998. *Corporation Nation: How corporations are taking over our lives and what we can do about it*, New York: St Martins Press.

Drew, Elizabeth. 2000. *The Corruption of American Politics: What went wrong and why*, Woodstock, NY: Overlook Press.

Eagleton, Terry. 1991. *Ideology: An Introduction*, London: Verso.

Eagleton, Terry. 1996. *The Illusions of postmodernism*, Oxford: Blackwell.

Gregory, Martin. 1996. *Dirty Tricks: British Airways' secret war against Virgin Atlantic*, rev. ed. London: Warner Books.

Hall, Stuart. 1973. 'The "Structured Communication" of Events', Paper for Obstacles to Communication Symposium, UNESCO, *University of Birmingham Centre for Contemporary Cultural Studies Stencilled Occasional Papers*, Birmingham: CCCS.

Hall, Stuart 1977. 'Culture, the media and the ideological effect', in J. Curran, M. Gurevitch and J. Woollacott, eds., *Mass Communication and Society*, London: Edward Arnold.

Hall, Stuart. 1980a. 'Encoding/decoding', in S. Hall, D. Hobson, A. Lowe and P. Willis, eds., *Culture, Media, Language*, London: Hutchinson.

Hall, Stuart. 1980b. 'In defence of theory', in Raphael Samuel, ed., *People's History and Socialist Theory*, London: Routledge and Kegan Paul.

Hall, Stuart. 1983. 'The rediscovery of "ideology": return of the repressed in media studies', in M. Gurevitch *et al.*, eds., *Culture, Society and the Media*, London: Methuen.

Hall, Stuart. 1986. 'Media power and class power', in J. Curran *et al.*, eds., *Bending Reality: The State of the Media*, London: Pluto, p. 9. Note the Foucauldian language which Hall had adopted by the mid-1980s.

Hall, Stuart. 1989. 'Ideology and Communication Theory', in B. Dervin, L. Grossberg, B. O'Keefe, and E. Wartella, eds., *Rethinking Communication: Vol I Paradigm Issues*, Thousand Oaks, CA: Sage.

Hall, Stuart. 2001. 'Introduction: Who Needs "Identity"', in S. Hall, and P. du Gay, eds., *Questions of Cultural Identity*, London: Sage, p. 16. For a critique of this position see Greg Philo and David Miller, *Market Killing*, London: Longman.

Harris, David. 1992. *From Class Struggle to the Politics of Pleasure*, London: Routledge.

Hollingsworth, Mark. 1991 *MPs for Hire: The secret world of political lobbying*, London: Bloomsbury.

Kolakowski, Leszek. 1971. 'Althusser's Marx', in R. Miliband, and J. Saville, eds., *The Socialist Register 1971*, London: The Merlin Press.

Lewis, Charles and the Center for Public Integrity. 1998. *The Buying of Congress: How special interests have stolen your right to life, liberty and the pursuit of happiness*, New York: Avon Books.

Althusser, Louis, *For Marx*, London: Allen Lane, 1969, and *Lenin and Philosophy and other essays*, London: New Left Books, 1971.

Lull, James and Stephen Hinerman eds. 1997. *Media Scandals*, London: Polity.

Macintyre, Sally., Jacquie Reilly, David Miller and John Eldridge. 1998. 'Food Choice, Food Scares and Health: The Role of the Media', in Murcott A., ed., *The Nation's Diet*, London: Addison Wesley Longman.

Marx, Karl and Friedrich Engels.1947. *The German Ideology*, New York: International Publishers.

Marx, Karl. 1975. 'A Contribution to the Critique of Political Economy', in *Early Writings*, Harmondsworth: Pelican.

McChesney, Robert. 2000. *Rich Media, Poor Democracy*, rev. ed., New York: The New Press.

McDonnell, Kevin and Kevin Robins. 1980. 'Marxist Cultural Theory: the Althusserian Smokescreen', in S. Clarke *et al.*, *One-Dimensional Marxism: Althusser and the Politics of Culture*, London: Allison and Busby.

Miller, David. 1993. *Official sources and 'primary definition': the case of Northern Ireland.* Media, Culture & Society, 15 (3), pp. 385–406.

Miller, David. 1994. *Don't Mention the War: Northern Ireland, Propaganda and the Media*, London: Pluto.

Miller, David. 1997. 'Dominant Ideologies and Media Power: The Case of Northern Ireland', in M. Kelly and B. O'Connor, eds., *Media Audiences in Ireland*, Dublin: University College Dublin Press, Miller.

Miller, David. 1999. 'Risk, Science and Policy: BSE, definitional struggles, information management and the media', *Social Science and Medicine* special edition 'Science speaks to policy', Vol. 49.

Miller, D. and W. Dinan. 1995. 'The rise of the PR industry in Britain 1979–1998', *European Journal of Communication*, 15(1), January 2000.

Miller, David and Jacquie Reilly. 1995. 'Making an Issue of Food Safety: The media, pressure groups and the public sphere', in Donna Maurer and Jeffrey Sobal, eds., *Eating Agendas: Food, Eating and Nutrition as Social Problems*, New York: Aldine De Gruyter.

Monbiot, George. 2000. *Captive State: The Corporate Takeover of Britain*, London: Macmillan.

Murdock, Graham. 2000. 'Reconstructing the ruined tower: Contemporary Communications and Questions of Class', in Gurevitch, M. and J. Curran, eds., *Mass Media and Society*, 3rd Ed. London: Edward Arnold.

Philo, Greg and David Miller. 2001. *Market Killing*, London: Longman.

Rustin, M. 1989. 'The Politics of PostFordism and the Trouble with "New Times"', *New Left Review*, 175.

Schiller, Dan. 1996. *Theorizing Communication: A History*, New York: Oxford University Press.

Sivanandan, Ambalavaner. 1990. *Communities of Resistance: Writings on Black Struggles for Socialism*, London: Verso.

Stauber, J. and S Rampton. 1995. *Toxic Sludge is Good for You: Lies, Damn Lies and the Public Relations Industry*, Monroe, Maine: Common Courage.

Tiffen, Rod. 2000. *Scandals: Media, Politics and Corruption in Contemporary Australia*, Sydney: University of New South Wales Press, 1999; John B. Thompson, *Political Scandals*, Cambridge: Polity.

Underwood, D. 1995. *When MBA's rule the newsroom*, New York: Columbia University Press.

Vulliamy, Ed and David Leigh. 2000, *Sleaze*, London: Fourth Estate.

Walsh, D. and S. Finz. 2001. 'Bay Area gloaters see upside in dot-com downturn', *San Francisco Chronicle*, Sunday 13 May 2001, pp. A1+A17.

Wheen, Francis. 2000. *Karl Marx: a life*, London and New York: W.W. Norton.

Williams, Raymond. 1980. *Problems in Materialism and Culture*, London: Verso.

Williams, Raymond. 1985. *Towards 2000*, London: Penguin.

Woodall, P., L. Wallach, J. Roach, and K. Burnham. 2000 *Purchasing Power: The Corporate-White House alliance to pass the China Trade Bill over the will of the American people*, Washington, DC: Public Citizen's Global Trade Watch.

CHAPTER 4

The Cultural Apparatus of Monopoly Capital
An Introduction

John Bellamy Foster and Robert W. McChesney

The past half-century has been dominated by the rise of media to a command-ing position in the social life of most people and nations, to the point where it is banal to regard this as the "information age." The once-dazzling ascension of television in the 1950s and '60s now looks like the horse-and-buggy era when one assesses the Internet, smartphones, and the digital revolution. For social theorists of all stripes communication has moved to center stage. And for those on the left, addressing the role of communication in achieving social change and then maintaining popular rule in the face of reactionary backlash is now a primary concern (McChesney 2013). The Arab Spring and the media battles of the elected left governments in Latin America are exhibits A1 and A2. Any serious left critique or political program must account for and embrace communication or risk being irrelevant and impotent.

To address these emerging concerns, over the past four decades the "political economy of communication" has emerged as a dynamic field of study, and one where considerable radical scholarship has taken place. The field addresses the growing importance of media, advertising, and communication in advanced capitalist societies, examining how the capitalist structure of communication industries shapes their output, as well as the role of media and culture in main-taining the social order. In particular, the field explores the way media "depo-liticizes" people, and thereby entrenches the privileges of those at the top. It highlights the importance of government policies in creating the communi-cation system, and the nature of the policymaking process in capitalist societ-ies. In North America the decisive founders of this area of research were Dallas Smythe and Herbert Schiller. In Europe a generation of scholars coming out of the 1960s launched the field, and there the work was more closely attached to a re-reading of Marx. Perhaps the most visible manifestation of the research in the United States has been the stellar critique of journalism produced over the years by Edward S. Herman and Noam Chomsky (McChesney 2007). Countless left activists are versed in the material today, a testament to the field's value and importance.

To no small extent, political economists of communication, including one of us, identified themselves as in the tradition of radical political economy, but with a sophisticated appreciation of media that had escaped their predecessors, locked in the past as they were. Paul Baran and Paul Sweezy were occasionally held up by political economists of communication as representing the sort of traditional Marxists who underappreciated the importance of media, communication, and culture.[1] Because of the preeminent role of their 1966 book, *Monopoly Capital*, Baran and Sweezy tended to receive more criticism than other radical economists who were likewise seen as negligent in this area. Smythe's seminal 1977 essay, "Communications: Blindspot of Western Marxism," while acknowledging *Monopoly Capital*'s strengths and importance, devoted more criticism to it than to any other work (Smythe 1977). The pattern has persisted in subsequent writings (Schiller 2006).

We were never especially impressed by this criticism (McChesney 2002). To us, *Monopoly Capital*, and the broader political economy of Baran and Sweezy, far from ignoring communication, provided key elements for a serious study of the subject. Its emphasis upon the importance of giant corporations operating in oligopolistic markets provided a very useful way to understand media markets. Specifically, Baran and Sweezy's take on the "sales effort" and the role of advertising in monopoly capitalism was and is the necessary starting point for any treatment of the subject (Baran and Sweezy 1966).[2] Few other economists came close to them in making advertising a central part of their political economy of capitalism. In doing so, they made the media and communication industries central components of modern capitalism.

Along these lines, one of our favorite pieces by Baran and Sweezy was their 1962 written testimony to the British Labour Party's Advertising Commission, headed by Lord John Reith, the iconic former director general of the BBC. The Advertising Commission was established as part of the Labour Party's reconsideration of the use of commercial advertising on British radio and television. Later published in *Science and Society* as "Theses on Advertising," and largely unknown to this day, Baran and Sweezy's testimony took the political-economic arguments concerning the role of advertising in contemporary capitalism, that were later developed in *Monopoly Capital*, and applied them foursquare to understanding media (Baran and Sweezy 1964). The analysis of

---

1   The critique tended to be more that *Monthly Review* underplayed the importance of media and communication than that it was wrong about these matters. On the rare occasions that *mr* covered the political economy of communication, it was sympathetic, and characterized the study as a necessary and logical part of monopoly capital. See the assessment of Herbert Schiller's work in Dowd 1974.

2   Many of the implications of Baran and Sweezy's analysis of the sales effort with respect to the development of modern marketing were developed in Michael Dawson, The Consumer Trap (Urbana: University of Illinois Press, 2005).

the deleterious effects of advertising on media operations and content, as well as society as a whole, is powerful and ages well. The piece also suggests that Baran and Sweezy, far from being determinists who thought any struggle for reform was a waste of time unless or until capitalism was overthrown, had a keen sense of the importance of media policy fights in the here and now. The Advertising Commission Report was finally published in 1966, and reflected the views of Baran and Sweezy with respect to the key roles played by oligopolistic markets, the decline of price competition, and the role of "the monopoly power of established firms" in the rise of modern mass media advertising (The Labour Party, 1966:33–40, 201, 204).[3]

In addition, Baran and Sweezy had sensitivity to the importance of technology and its capacity for changing the nature of capitalism and the nature of society that was mostly unrivalled among economists, left, right, and center. Their work placed emphasis on examining those "revolutionary" technologies, like the steam engine, electricity, and the automobile, which provided the basis for capitalist expansion for generations and turned the world upside down in the process. In 1957 Sweezy characterized the United States as being in the midst of a sweeping "scientific-industrial revolution," due to the confluence of the corporate expansion into directing research and the rise of permanent militarism in the 1940s. In a careful review of economic history, contemporary scientific and technological developments, and with a look toward the horizon, Sweezy put the invention of the computer and the emerging communication revolution at the center of a technological revolution that would be every bit as profound as that wrought by the steam engine. To those who found this hypothetical, if not preposterous, Sweezy responded: "Come back in another thirty years. The transformation of society implicit in the new technologies will then be in full swing and you will be able to see signs of it on every hand" (Sweezy 1957:7).[4]

---

3   Baran and Sweezy's testimony was solicited through the influence of Nicholas Kaldor, who was a member of the Advertising Commission but was forced to resign in 1964 when he was appointed special advisor to the Chancellor of the Exchequer. Kaldor's work on advertising, which was closely related to that of Baran and Sweezy's, was heavily quoted in the final report.

4   To support himself on top of his professional salary and to obtain funds for research, Paul Baran occasionally wrote reports for the Wall Street firm of Model, Roland and Stone. He was commissioned to do a report on technology but was pressed for time so he asked Sweezy to do it for him. The resulting report was issued by the firm with no author indicated, but Sweezy considered it one of his best pieces of writing. The original copy is in the Sweezy archives at Harvard University. Harry Braverman made use of Sweezy's argument on the scientific-industrial revolution in this pamphlet to construct much of his own argument on the scientific-technological revolution (see Braverman 1999:115).

Yet, to read *Monopoly Capital* one was left, somewhat paradoxically, with little sense that communication per se was of much interest to its authors.

This changed in 2011 when we discovered a missing chapter written for *Monopoly Capital* on culture, communications, and mental health, "The Quality of Monopoly Capitalist Society II" (Foster 2012). This chapter was originally drafted by Baran and was later edited and revised by Sweezy following the death of his coauthor. It had been intended as the penultimate chapter of *Monopoly Capital* (Baran and Sweezy 2012). Baran tragically died of a heart attack in March 1964 with a planned redrafting of this chapter undone. Sweezy was therefore left with the task of editing and completing the chapter, to which Baran had meant to add more material related to the mental health section, which was only loosely related to the culture section. Sweezy worked extensively on the chapter in November 1964 and perhaps later, editing the manuscript, cutting out considerable material from the original draft, and adding some new material related to communications. He gave this later version the title "The Quality of Monopoly Capitalist Society: Culture and Mental Health." In the end, however, he elected to leave it out of the book, recognizing that there were issues that the two of them had not sufficiently worked out together.[5]

But when we read this missing chapter, we immediately saw that the portion on culture was based on serious research and important theoretical insights. It also demonstrated a commitment to a "political economy of communication" before the field had even crystallized and far beyond what anyone, including ourselves, had imagined possible. It also provided a quite different perspective on Baran and Sweezy's goals for *Monopoly Capital*. Focusing on monopoly capital's creation of a mass society culture, it was in some respects

---

5 As Sweezy wrote in the preface to *Monopoly Capital*: "Whatever was drafted by one of us [for the book] was criticized at length by the other, and in most cases redrafted and recriticized more than once. Everything now in the book had been through this process before Baran's death. Apart from putting together the entire manuscript into finished form, the only thing I have done has been to leave out material that would have been two additional chapters. This material was in rough draft at the time of his death, but in each case one or the other of us had raised important questions which still remained to be discussed and resolved. Since neither chapter was essential to the theme of the essay as a whole, the best solution seemed to be to omit them altogether. I reached this conclusion the more easily since even without these chapters the book turned out to be longer than I had expected or we had originally intended." Paul M. Sweezy, "Preface," in Baran and Sweezy, *Monopoly Capital,* ix. From the first Sweezy had been concerned that the "cultural mess," given that it was left to the end of the manuscript, should not be given short shrift as a result (Paul M. Sweezy to Paul A. Baran, July 23, 1957, Baran Papers, Monthly Review Foundation). Baran had indicated that "if anything" he would "tend to accentuate its importance" (Paul A. Baran to Paul M. Sweezy, July 29, 1957, Baran Papers, Monthly Review Foundation).

intended to be the logical culmination of the book's argument. Its point was to provide an understanding of the political culture of monopoly capitalist society, and the implications for radical social change. Consequently, we have decided to publish the first two-thirds of this missing chapter for the first time in this issue, excluding the last third on mental health and re-entitling it "The Quality of Monopoly Capitalist Society: Culture and Communications."

Our motivation in publishing this piece is more than antiquarian. As we reviewed the work of Baran and Sweezy on culture and communication, as well as other pieces that appeared in *Monthly Review* in the late 1950s and '60s, it became clear that the missing culture chapter in *Monopoly Capital* was not an isolated occurrence nor an anomaly, but, rather, part of a broader emerging intellectual school. We discovered that some exceptional related work was done during this period by several major radical and Marxist intellectuals – people like C. Wright Mills, Herbert Marcuse, E.P. Thompson, Ralph Miliband, Eric Hobsbawm, and Raymond Williams, who were in regular communication with each other. All of these thinkers contributed to the critique of the cultural apparatus.

Mills, Miliband, and Williams, in particular, were all close to Sweezy and *Monthly Review* in this period. A key section of Mills's *The Sociological Imagination* (1959) was published first in *Monthly Review* (Mills 1958). Upon Mills's death, it was Miliband who wrote the memorial piece for *Monthly Review* (Newman 2002). As for Williams, he confided to Thompson in the 1960s that while he belonged to no faction or section, he "felt closest to the American Monthly Review" (Thompson 1988:310). Williams's (1960) article for *Monthly Review* was incorporated in his book *The Long Revolution (1961)*, while Miliband's early articles in *Monthly Review* undoubtedly influenced his *Parliamentary Socialism* (published in 1964 in the United States by Monthly Review Press).[6]

On the one hand, the work of this period demonstrates a creative and open-minded Marxism or radical social criticism that embraced the issue of communication and plunged into the problems it posed for social theory. It animated much of what would be most impressive about the New Left that was about to explode into prominence. On the other hand, the examination of communication gravitated from criticism of the deleterious effects of capitalist culture to being concerned with the politics of culture, and how control of communication systems was becoming a necessary political battlefield for the democratic left. As early as 1961, Thompson observed: "The task of creating an *alternative* means of communication has, from the start, been a major

---

6   Raymond Williams, The Long Revolution (New York: Columbia University Press, 1961), x; Ralph Miliband, Parliamentary Socialism (New York: Monthly Review Press, 1964b; original UK edition 1961). Raymond Williams' famous essay "Culture is Ordinary" appeared in Norman MacKenzie, ed., Conviction (New York: Monthly Review Press, 1958), 74–92.

preoccupation of the New Left" (Thompson 1980:8). In this sense these works anticipated many of the issues that concern the left today and the approach offers a clarity and insight that has considerable value for activists worldwide.

For that reason we decided it best not only to publish the missing chapter on culture from *Monopoly Capital*, but also to reprint a handful of related works on culture and communication from this period, by authors who were working along similar lines. In this introduction we will provide context for the times and the issues, as well as an explanation for the pieces we have elected to include. As we will suggest at the end of this introduction these works can be seen as providing some of the crucial foundations for a political economy of the media, helping us to construct the critical responses we need today in the age of the Internet, social media, and the ongoing attempts in Latin America and elsewhere to repossess the cultural apparatus of society.

Brecht, the Frankfurt School, and the Concept of Cultural Apparatus

In retrospect, the basis of Baran's, if not Sweezy's, concern for and awareness of culture and communication issues is obvious. Baran worked as a researcher under Friedrich Pollock, the associate director of the Institute for Social Research in Frankfurt, before fleeing Germany in 1933, following Hitler's accession to power. His experiences and associations in Frankfurt were to exert a strong influence on his writing; so much so that he is sometimes characterized as the foremost political economist associated with the Frankfurt School.[7] During the 1950s and early '60s, when he was a professor of economics at Stanford, Baran met with and corresponded with other figures whom he had known at the Institute for Social Research in Frankfurt in pre-Hitlerian Germany, such as his close friends Herbert Marcuse and Leo Lowenthal, and kept up with the writings of Erich Fromm, Max Horkheimer, and Theodor Adorno.[8]

Central to the Frankfurt School's concerns was the relationship of mass culture to politics and social change. Baran read widely and carefully in this area, and it

---

7 On Baran as the political economist of the Frankfurt School, see Howard and King (1992:114–115). Pollock himself, of course, was the main economist associated with the school, but Baran's work was to far eclipse him. Sweezy was less directly influenced by the Frankfurt School, but he had early on taken on many of the propositions on history and dialectics of Georg Lukács and Karl Korsch.

8 Peter Marcuse recalls: "I had only met Baran once, during the war, when my father was with the OSS [Office of Strategic Services].... I was maybe 12 at the time. Baran had come over to

was his passion for the subject that likely was the impetus for the prospective chapter in *Monopoly Capital*. He approached culture and communication as encompassing art, literature, entertainment, education, media, and the role of intellectuals.[9] His main concern was the undermining of affirmative culture, as a necessary form of human development, due to the relentless process of commodification promoted by monopoly capital. As he stated in 1950:

We have to understand the ideologically overpowering impact of bourgeois, fetishistic consciousness on the broad masses of the working population.... The heart-breaking emptiness and cynicism of the commercial, competitive, capitalist culture. The systematic cultivation of devastatingly neurotic reactions to most social phenomena (through the movies, the "funnies," etc.). The effective destruction in schools, churches, press, everywhere, of everything that smacks of *solidarity* in the consciousness of the man in the street. And finally, the utterly paralyzing feeling of solitude which must overcome any one who does not want to conform, the feeling that there is no movement, no camp, no group to which one can turn (Baran 1950).

In Baran's view, commodified culture comes to play a preeminent role under monopoly capitalism. The overarching critique is of the massive and growing gap between the actual quality of culture in the United States and what the society is capable of producing. This gap is both cause and effect of the absurdity of monopoly capitalism and evidence of its increasing destructiveness. It is a political-economic critique because it assesses the cause of the gap as being the capitalist nature of society and, more specifically, the capitalist nature of the "cultural apparatus." Baran and Sweezy took seriously the close examination of the structures of media and communication industries.

---

our house to talk to my father, and they stayed up a long time. I asked my father later why Baran had come, and he told me Baran wanted to talk about whether capitalism was ultimately bad for the capitalists as well as the workers, and I gather they agreed it was. My father was working on *Eros and Civilization* at the time (on the side, not at OSS!), and I assume that was the context. They really respected each other." Peter Marcuse to John Bellamy Foster, July 4, 2012. Baran referred to Adorno's work not only in the missing chapter on culture that he drafted for *Monthly Review*, but also in *The Political Economy of Growth*. His close attention to Adorno and Horkheimer's work was shown in his correspondence with Marcuse, e.g., Paul A. Baran to Herbert Marcuse, July 10, 1962 (Baran Papers, Monthly Review Foundation). Fromm is also discussed in Baran's letters.

9 In focusing on culture as a general way of viewing literary, artistic, and intellectual work Baran and Sweezy were, in Williams's terms, using the concept in "one of its predominant twentieth-century senses" and the one most related to questions of power. They differentiated this from more capacious anthropological uses of the term to refer to a definite way of life. See Williams (1989:199).

It was the concept of the cultural apparatus, derived from Bertolt Brecht, Fromm, Horkheimer, Marcuse, and Mills, that formed the central organizing principle in Baran's drafting of the discussion of culture and communications in *Monopoly Capital*. The earliest outlines for "The Quality of Monopoly Capitalist Society II" chapter had it covering the realms of the "mass media" and "mental health."[10] Baran was to transform this, however, into a treatment of specific media, particularly book publishing and broadcasting, as manifestations of what he and Sweezy called the development of "the cultural apparatus of monopoly capitalism." Indeed, their analysis in the missing chapter printed below begins and ends with the concept of the cultural apparatus.

To understand the significance of this it is important to know something of the history of this crucial Marxian concept. The notion of the cultural apparatus owed its centrality in Marxian theory primarily to the work of Brecht beginning in 1932 (see Eleanor Hakim's article in this issue).[11] Brecht saw what he referred to as the cultural "apparatus" or means of production and of technical control of cultural processes as applying to every realm of cultural production, such as the theatre, opera, radio, book publishing, and film. The crucial problem of the artist, who did not control the cultural apparatus in capitalist society, was then to find ways to gain control or to subvert the apparatus in order to promote critical, dialectical, and revolutionary ends. However, Brecht was under no illusions and in his view the dominant role of the cultural apparatus in bourgeois society was to reinforce existing power relations. As Rowitha Mueller has stated: "Thus the terminology itself points up the connection between culture and politics" (Mueller 1989:15–16). In Brecht's view, the cultural apparatus functions, among other things, to stabilize the existing social relations both politically and economically. He "saw this in terms of a selection process: 'Society absorbs via the (cultural) apparatus whatever it needs in order to reproduce itself'" (Brecht 1964:34).

In Brecht's view artists and intellectuals are not masters of the cultural apparatus, but rather their work is completely subordinated to it and capitalist objectives, and thus placed "out of their control." "The intellectuals...are completely dependent on the apparatus, both socially and economically; it is the only channel for the realization of their work. The output of writers, composers and critics comes more and more to resemble raw material. The finished article is produced by the apparatus." The capitalist order got in

---

10   Early outline of "Monopoly Capital," circa l957 (Baran Papers, Monthly Review Foundation).

11   The notion of the "apparatus" as representing the material conditions of art can already be seen in Hegel's philosophy of art where he refers to the "apparatus of its [art's] merely material nature" (Hegel 1886:72).

"the habit of judging works of art by their suitability for the apparatus without ever judging the apparatus by its suitability for the work." The result naturally was that "[cultural] work amounts to so much merchandise, and is governed by the normal laws of merchandise trade. Art is merchandise, only to be manu-factured by the means of production (apparati)" (Brecht 1964:34–35).

Brecht concretely explored various forms of the cultural apparatus – theatre, radio, film – with the idea of carrying out a kind of guerrilla war that would end up appropriating them for purposes of revolutionary change. He believed that ultimately "the socialization of these means of [cultural] production" was "vital for art." The goal then was to develop strategic approaches to asserting control over the various apparati, which were currently "wholly capitalist." This required empirical research and a deep understanding of the various ways in which the artist and intellectual could employ leverage. Brecht's drama was explicitly designed to subvert the apparatus of the theatre in this way. As he wrote: "When I read Marx's *Capital* I understood my plays" (Brecht 1964:23–48).

The artist and the intellectual in this perspective had a crucial role to play in the struggle over the cultural apparatus that was so vital to society. In Brecht's plays this took the form, to use a phrase of Baran's, of "the confrontation of reality with reason," through various dialectical devices. Brecht employed the concept of "inploitation" (a kind of reverse or internalized exploitation) to describe the complex, contradictory role of the consumer of the products of the cultural apparatus, who was simultaneously both a victim and a kind of complicit exploiter in the context of the struggle of the cultural producer or artist with the owners (Baran 1969:32, Mueller 1989:24; Oesmann 2005:107). The role of the artist and intellectual as revolutionary was to reestablish the relationship between the consumer and producer of cultural work by under-mining the estrangement from human needs and capacities enforced by the bourgeois society.

As Walter Benjamin, who was enormously influenced by Brecht, argued, the question of "the author as producer" was not so much a question of the "posi-tion [of the artist's work] vis à vis" the various forms of the cultural apparatus, as "what is its position *within* them?" The fundamental problem in cultural change then became "adapting the apparatus to the ends of the proletarian revolution" (Benjamin 1971:87, 102).

Brecht argued that the struggle over the cultural apparatus was not confined to those forms such as film and broadcasting that were new, but extended to the entirety of communication forms, all of which were being increasingly mechanized, commodified, and transformed. This included traditional forms such as printed books and the theatre. "The changes wrought by time leave nothing untouched, but always embrace the whole." A crucial aspect of this was "the mechanization of literary production," which could not "be thrown into reverse." The goal then has to be to refunctionalize or reconstruct the existing cultural apparatus to prevent these increasingly complex media from being removed further and further from the development of human needs and capacity and "the new possibilities of communication" (Benjamin 1971:47–52).

The concept of the cultural apparatus played a formative role in the work of the Frankfurt School. As early as 1932 it occupied a central place in Fromm's article, "The Method and Function of an Analytic Social Psychology" – published in the *Zeitschrift für Sozialforschung* and seen as the foundational work integrating historical materialism and psychoanalysis. As Axel Honneth explained the importance of this piece: "Within the intellectual circle of the Institute for Social Research, Fromm was entrusted with the task of working out a psychology that could be linked with economics without any fissure."

Fromm wrote that "the creation of the [governing] norms" in society was "not left to chance," but rather that "one whole basic part of the cultural apparatus serves to form the socially required attitude in a systematic and methodical way." The "cultural apparatus" was depicted as driving, in the language of psychoanalysis, the "libidinal structure of society" – or what Fromm later called "social character" – channeling it so that it was no longer a threat to the status quo. With respect to the working class, the cultural apparatus played a key role in forming what Fromm termed the social cement meant to counter the effects of alienation (Fromm 1970:158–160, Honneth 1991:23–26, Gebhardt 1978:387–388).[12]

Writing in a similar vein in 1936 in *Authority and the Family*, Horkheimer discussed how revolutionary periods remove some of these cultural controls depriving them of power, while in periods of restoration and reaction an "outmoded cultural apparatus as well the psychic makeup of men and the body of interconnected institutions acquire new power. Then there is a need to investigate the culture thoroughly." As a structure of power the cultural apparatus seeks to bond the population to the status quo by means of the promotion of particular ideas and ways of life, which are internalized within the psyche. In Horkheimer's words:

---

12   The concept of "cultural apparatus" was not specifically defined in Fromm's essay, but he was later to use the category mainly in the Brechtian sense. See Fromm (1955:163). It is noteworthy that Baran and Sweezy thought Fromm's early work (no doubt including his 1932 essay) was so important that they considered translating it for Monthly Review Press ("Notes on Planned Translations from the German," Monthly Review Press, no date, circa 1957, Baran Papers, Monthly Review Foundation).

One function of the entire cultural apparatus at any given period has been to internalize in men of subordinate position the idea of a necessary domination of some men over others, as determined by the course of history down to the present time. As a result and as a continually renewed condition of this cultural apparatus, the belief in authority is one of the driving forces, sometimes, productive, sometimes obstructive, of human history (Horkheimer 2002:59–60, 67–68).

But it was in Marcuse's "33 Theses" (written in 1947 and found in draft form in Horkheimer's archives, appearing only posthumously in Marcuse's *Collected Works*) that the issue of "the cultural apparatus of monopoly capitalism" was first raised. There Marcuse wrote, in thesis 15:

> The phenomenon of cultural identification demands that the problem of "cultural cement" (*Kitt*) be discussed upon a broader basis. One of the most important factors involved here is the leveling of the former avant-garde-oppositional forces with the cultural apparatus of monopoly capitalism (the transformation and application of psychoanalysis, modern art, sexuality, etc. in the work and entertainment process). First and foremost the effect of "*Kitt*" within the working class should be investigated: "scientific management," rationalization, the interest of the worker in increased productivity (and with it, in the intensification of exploitation), strengthening of nationalistic sentiments.
>
> MARCUSE 1998:221[13]

The concept of cultural cement, as articulated by Marcuse here, followed Fromm and Horkheimer. For Horkheimer it was this cement that was at all times the crucial object of analysis, since it "artificially held together the parts tending towards independence" (Honneth 1991:23–26). The intent of Marcuse's fifteenth thesis was to underscore the necessity of empirically researching how this cementing of workers to the dominant order was actually accomplished (in contradictory fashion) by the cultural apparatus of monopoly capitalist society.

---

13   On Marcuse's use of the concept of cultural apparatus, see also Marcuse (1955). Earlier in his 1941 article on "Some Social Implications of Modern Technology," Marcuse had presented what he called "the technical apparatus of industry, transportation, and communication" as the crucial, if partial, mediating factor, of modern mass alienation. He stated that, "the term 'apparatus' denotes the institutions, devices and organizations of industry in their prevailing social setting." There was, he said, "no personal escape from the apparatus." Yet, a social escape was perhaps conceivable, requiring a struggle over the cultural apparatus in particular. See Marcuse (1978:138, 143, 180).

This reflected the central problem governing the research program of the Frankfurt School. As Honneth has put it,

A major portion of the theoretical construction and social research of the Institute during the 1930s was an attempt to provide an empirical answer to the problem expressed in this tension [between exploitative socioeconomic conditions and cultural stability]. Its guiding motif is formed by the question "What psychic mechanisms have come about that enable the tension between the social classes to remain latent, even though it borders on conflict as a result of the economic situation?" The program of an interdisciplinary social science, outlined by Horkheimer at the beginning of the 1930s, is tailored to the investigation of this phenomenon (Honneth 1991:18).

Fromm was later to describe the "cultural apparatus" as a "filter" conditioning what entered society's "social unconscious" (Fromm 1992:56). As he wrote in *The Sane Society* in 1955 (a book that strongly impressed Baran): "Eventually, he [the alienated industrial worker] is under the influence of our whole cultural apparatus, the advertisements, the movies, television, newspapers, just as everybody else, and can hardly escape being driven into conformity, although perhaps more slowly than other sectors of the population" (Fromm 1955:163).[14]

Mills, Thompson, and Williams

Similar considerations led Mills, beginning in the late 1950s, to commence writing what was to be a major but never competed work, left unfinished at his untimely death – entitled *The Cultural Apparatus*. The historically specific context of Mill's entry into this sphere is powerfully described by Stanley Aronowitz:

Mills had come to the conclusion that it was not the economy or even self-interest in general that drove contemporary social agents to action or inaction. Mills concluded that in the epoch of what he termed "overdeveloped" capitalism, the masses were moved more broadly by "culture" than reason. He had become convinced that the cultural apparatus played a central role in reproducing the entire "set-up." But it is not the anthropological conception of culture – a whole way of life – that he believed determined politics or secured the domination by the leading institutional actors. Mill's invocation of the cultural apparatus...signaled that culture was no longer the spontaneous creation of the people but instead was an aspect of the organization and reproduction

---

14   Paul A. Baran to Paul M. Sweezy, November 28, 1956 (Baran Papers, Monthly Review Foundation.

of social and political domination. If social transformation was at all possible, its protagonists were obliged to understand the process of production and distribution of key cultural forms, especially the mass media. Clearly, the implication of his projected study was to argue for a new counterhegemonic strategy of the Left that matched the force of the culture industry (Aronowitz 2012:241–242).

Mills delivered three university lectures at the London School of Economics (LSE) in January 1959, utilizing a manuscript entitled *The Cultural Apparatus, or The American Intellectual.* These three lectures were later published as "Culture and Politics: The Fourth Epoch," "The Cultural Apparatus," and "The Decline of the Left." Together they constitute the main extant materials of his projected book on *The Cultural Apparatus* – left behind at the time of his death by heart attack at age forty-five in 1962.

Mills did not get very far in this unfinished work in defining what he actually meant by the cultural apparatus. His approach was broader and more obscure than the way the concept was being used in Marxist theory, where it was essentially equivalent to the cultural means of production including the technical means themselves. In contrast, Mills used the notion of cultural apparatus somewhat ambiguously in terms of "observation posts, interpretation centers, and presentation depots" and went on to say that it was "composed of all the organizations and milieu in which artistic, intellectual, and scientific work goes on." His emphasis was more on processes than on structures, allowing him to emphasize agency, namely the intellectual – to the point that he could say that "I have been studying, for several years now, the cultural apparatus, the intellectual – as a possible, immediate radical agency for change" (Mills 2008:204, 263). This tended to downplay the power dimension, reducing the question of the cultural apparatus itself to the question of the intellectual, of agency – rather than emphasizing the dialectical relation between cultural producer and the capitalist cultural apparatus as in Brecht and the Frankfurt School. Nevertheless, Mills went on to make the critical point that,

What intellectuals now confront is the expropriation of their cultural apparatus itself. We do not have access to the means of effective communication, but more than that, many of us are losing control of the very means of cultural production itself. The situation of the serious movie-maker – is not this the prototype of all cultural workmen? We are cut off from possible publics and such publics as remain are being turned into masses by those businessmen or commissars who do control and manage the effective means of communication. In their hands, these are often less means of communication than means of mass distraction.... What we ought now to do is repossess our cultural apparatus, and use it for our own purposes (Mills 2008:217–218, 221).

Mills's approach had a big impact on the New Left Marxists in Britain. Thompson attended the last of Mills's three LSE lectures on the cultural apparatus, and called it "absolutely splendid" (Mills 2008:213). But there was friendly criticism from a Marxist standpoint. In a long letter to Mills, Thompson wrote: "You argue that intellectual workers must repossess their cultural apparatus and use it for their own purposes. In what sense have they ever possessed it?" (Thompson quoted in Daniel Geary, 2009:196) For Thompson it was not a question of repossession of the cultural apparatus but of the construction of a left cultural apparatus. "The problem presents itself," he wrote in 1959, "as one of constructing (however painfully slow the process may seem – though steady progress is being made) an *alternative*'cultural apparatus' which bypasses the mass media and the party machinery, and which opens up direct channels between significant socialist groupings inside and outside the labour movement." Thompson was deeply involved in communications issues in the late 1950s and early '60s, and submitted a memorandum (as did Raymond Williams) to the 1960 Committee on Broadcasting (the Pilkington Committee); the Pilkington Report was presented to Parliament in 1962 (Thompson 1959).[15]

Williams shared with Mills and Thompson a concern to translate the critique of the cultural apparatus into a political strategy and program for the left. The starting point for his analysis was "the subordination of a general communications process to an increasingly powerful system of advertising and public relations" (Williams 1976:180–189). In 1961 Williams argued that,

Instead of the ritual indignation and despair at the cultural condition of "the masses" (now increasingly uttered even by their supposed friends) it is necessary to break through to the central fact that most of our cultural

---

15   Thompson's submission to the Pilkington Committee was listed in the report as connected to the publication *New University* and as having dealt with "Minority Interests and broadcasting," presumably referring to the issue of political minorities. Such issues were taken up in the Pilkington Report in sections on "Party Political Broadcasting" and "The News." Thompson's (1961) piece "The Segregation of Dissent," written for *New University* and addressing "minority causes" and "minority journals" fits this description. The New Left Review Ltd. also submitted a memorandum to the Pilkington Committee (published in *New Left Review* prior to the release of the Pilkington Report). Thompson apparently saw the New Left Review Ltd.'s submission as overly culturalist and reformist, focusing on issues of popular culture more than media control and making too many concessions with respect to the latter. United Kingdom, *Report of the Committee on Broadcasting, 1960* (London: HMSO, 1962), 92–101, 320, 327; "Which Frame of Mind? TV and Broadcasting: Evidence to the Pilkington Committee," *New Left Review* no. 7 (1961): 30–48; Thompson, *Writing by Candlelight*, 1–10; Michael Kenny, *The First New Left* (London: Lawrence and Wishart, 1995):103–108.

institutions are in the hands of speculators, interested not in the health and growth of society, but in the quick profits that can be made by exploiting inexperience. True, under attack, these speculators, or some of them, will concede limited policies of a different kind, which they significantly call "prestige" that is to say, enough to preserve a limited public respectability so that they will be allowed to continue to operate. But the real question is whether a society can afford to leave its cultural apparatus in such irresponsible hands.... We should be much clearer about these cultural questions if we saw them as a consequence of a basically capitalist organization, and I at least know no better reason for capitalism to be ended (Williams 1961:338–339).

Again it was Thompson who asked the hard question, observing in 1961 that Williams had failed to consider "the contrary problems of 'utopia'...and of an intellectual tradition associated with social groups opposed to established interests – which must make its way without the benefit of institutions or cultural apparatus of its own, and which is exposed to the dangers of sectarian aridity or of losing its best men in the institutions of the 'other side'" (Thompson 1961:34–39). Indeed, it was Thompson's lifetime struggle as a historian (in works such as *The Making of the English Working Class*) to show how the working class in England had sought to construct its own class consciousness and culture, despite its exclusion from the dominant cultural apparatus, i.e., the main means of intellectual production of the society (Thompson 1961).[16]

Toward a Wider Political Economy of Communication: The 1960s Critique

This was the state of the discussion in 1962 when Baran first set about drafting the analysis of culture and communications for *Monopoly Capital*. Baran and Sweezy's intention in this penultimate chapter of their book was to uncover the way in which the cultural apparatus of monopoly capitalist society was increasingly owned and controlled by the vested interests, undermining the critical and "intellectual side of civilization" and the possibilities for effective social change. Both the publishing and broadcasting industries, they wrote,

---

16 For Thompson the English working class of the nineteenth century developed a "resistance movement" to the acquisitive society that was not just backward looking but truly radical in its conception, and though it ultimately lost out in the struggle, partly through its inability to gain control of the means of production, including the means of intellectual production, and thus of the wellsprings of social and cultural existence, it nonetheless remained a "heroic culture" (Thompson, 1963:832).

demonstrated "the striking extent to which culture has become a commodity, its production subject to the same forces, interests, and motives as govern the production of all other commodities."[17]

Their analysis focused on "the cultural industries" as distinct forms of production, which as they "moved from handicraft to mass production" increasingly fell "under the sway of corporate business" geared to maximum profits and catering "to all the frailties and weaknesses of human nature." Under monopoly capitalism "cultural output...turned into its opposite," embodying a further fracturing of human reason and human action, and impeding rather than enhancing human development and historical change.[18]

Noting that book publishing had already lost out to newspapers and magazines as the "predominant form of reading," Baran and Sweezy nevertheless insisted on its "unique importance in society's cultural apparatus." From their experience, literacy, and access to literature and a broad range of political books were foundational to popular democratic politics. They were aware that progressive U.S. government policies and subsidies in the 1940s aimed at increasing literacy and expanding the publication and distribution of books had proven highly effective. They also were unsurprised that Senator Joseph McCarthy had singled these policies out as pro-Communist and anti-American.[19] Indeed, Leo Huberman, Sweezy's coeditor at *Monthly Review,* had been subpoenaed in 1953 by McCarthy's own Senate Committee due to the inclusion of several of his books in the State Department's overseas libraries. Huberman defiantly told the McCarthy committee: "A manifesto voted by the American Library Association on June 25, [1953] and concurred in by the American Book Publishers Council, opens with these words: 'The freedom to read is essential to our democracy. It is under attack'. Everyone knows that the main attacker is this committee of Congress and its chairman" (Huberman and Sweezy 1953:161).

Baran and Sweezy also saw firsthand that the changing nature of the book industry meant that the broad range of critical books that had proliferated in

---

17   Uncited quotations from Baran and Sweezy in this introduction are to "The Quality of Monopoly Capitalist Society: Culture and Communications" in this issue.

18   Baran and Sweezy's use of the term "cultural industry" in the introduction to their piece no doubt reflected the influence of Frankfurt School cultural theorist Theodor Adorno. See Adorno (1960:484). This essay by Adorno is cited in Baran and Sweezy's chapter. Baran, a close reader of Horkheimer and Adorno, as indicated in his correspondence with Marcuse, was also undoubtedly familiar with the chapter in *The Dialectic of Enlightenment* on "The Culture Industry: Enlightenment as Mass Deception." See Horkheimer and Adorno (1972:120–167).

19   We thank John J. Simon, who spent a career in book publishing and knew both Baran, Sweezy, and Huberman well in this period, for making this point to us.

the 1930s and '40s were becoming a thing of the past.[20] Without policies pushing in a different direction, the commercial book publishing industry was
undergoing enormous expansion, and although still "highly competitive,"
characterized by decreasing rather than increasing profit margins, was rapidly
becoming more and more concentrated, taking on the character of an "emerging oligopolistic...industry."

The mass-production and concentrated nature of the industry meant that
books were more and more standardized and sold in the same manner as cars or
cosmetics. This affected content, leading those who controlled the book-
publishing apparatus to emphasize: (1) conformist views (albeit a sophisticated
conformity that could include severe criticisms of the status quo as long as they
did not extend to the underlying structures or the possibility of radical actions);
(2) selectivity in issues discussed (problems of sex, individual psychology, and
even race were more admissible than the questioning of the economic and social
order); (3) a focus on celebrities; and (4) imitation of new successful fashions.

From there Baran and Sweezy went on to examine the character and content of the leading best-selling books, from religious books, to cookbooks, to
crime and detective novels, to general best-selling novels. They also included a
short discussion of comic books. The general conclusion pointed to the "steady
and methodical debasement of the book itself over the last few decades.
Transferring to the sale of books the methods used in marketing 'sex apparel'
and cosmetics, of liquor and cigarettes and nostrums of all kinds, undermines
all respect for literary work, and annihilates the book as a cultural medium."[21]

They paid close attention to the best-selling books of Mickey Spillane – six
of which belonged to the top fifteen best sellers of the twentieth century – and
his vigilante-murderer hero Mike Hammer. Spillane's anti-communism was
used frequently to justify his bloodlust and sadism, leading him to have
Hammer declare at one point: "But some day, maybe, some day I'd stand on the
steps of the Kremlin with a gun in my fist and I'd yell for them to come out and
if they wouldn't I'd go in and get them and when I had them lined up against
the wall I'd start shooting until all I had left was a row of corpses that bled on
the cold floors and in whose thick red blood would be the promise of a peace

---

20 On the active struggles over the cultural apparatus in the 1930s, including in the realm of
    publication, and how this faded in the 1950s and after, see Denning (1997).

21 Sweezy had suggested in his letter to Baran on December 5, 1962 the inclusion of a discus-
    sion of books for the elite and elite culture more generally in the chapter. Baran replied on
    December 7, 1962 that the point of the discussion of culture and communication was to
    focus on the cultural "state of the people," which is why books marketed to the elite were
    excluded in the draft. However, he indicated that he intended to add something on this
    (Baran papers, Monthly Review Foundation).

that would stick for more generations than I'd live to see" (Spillane 2001:132, see also Végső 2013:160–169, La Farge 1954:176–185, Saunders 1999, Palmer 2000:373–374). Spillane's best sellers were the perfect counterparts to the McCarthy era.

For Baran and Sweezy, Spillane was only an extreme example of the degradation of the mass distribution novel in which an artist's concern with "the representation of individual and social conflicts, of human passion, joy, and suffering," and had been replaced by books providing "a minute account of the hero's (frequently improbable) overt behavior without any attempt at the discovery, elucidation, and comprehension of the underlying causes and motivations. The purpose is merely to thrill."

Under monopoly capitalism, Baran and Sweezy argued, the cultural apparatus increasingly controlled the artist, "with the writer becoming more pronouncedly an employee of the publishing corporation and his independence increasingly turned into a sham." A few individual artists of course managed to struggle with this cultural apparatus and by various means transcend it. But the general tendency towards conformity and degradation within book publishing was not to be denied.

As Hobsbawm observed in a similar way in the *Times Literary Supplement* in 1964:

The economic facts are conclusive. The professional writer of books is in the position of the hand-loom weaver after the intervention of the power loom: two thirds or three quarters of his profession can earn less than a typist's income, and the number of writers who can live entirely by the sales of their books would fit into a single, not excessively large room....In certain branches of literature, such as utilitarian fiction, craft productions can persist, not only because the demand for it is smaller, more lasting and more intermittent, but also because the market can rely on large quantities of casual, part-time labour and the readiness of professional writers to turn themselves into hacks (Hobsbawm 2013:262–263).[22]

Television broadcasting, in contrast, though a far younger cultural apparatus, was not an emerging oligopoly, as in book publishing, but had already been established by government policies as a tight oligopoly. It was here that Sweezy in his work at *Monthly Review* had written two essays on American television with Huberman in 1958 and 1959. The first of these, published in April 1958, was a critique of the Federal Communications Commission (FCC), and its role in facilitating the concentration of broadcast media: both radio and television. The licensing of television stations, the facilitation of the dominance of

22   Baran and Hobsbawm, who were good friends, had coauthored a critique of Walt Rostow's *Stages of Economic Growth*. See Baran (1969, 52–67).

oligopoly, the deliberate squelching of competition, and the handing out of the airwaves for free to particular corporations (which Huberman and Sweezy compared to the handing out of western lands to the railroads in the nineteenth century) constituted an enormous "swindle" on the public, and the basis of monopoly capital in this area. The fact that this was often accompanied by outright corruption was not surprising. Profit margins from television they showed had been strong and increasing, reaching 22 percent by 1956. Sweezy and Huberman dug into the financial data of the television industry as few if any other scholars had ever done before, and systematically debunked the notion that regulation of private economic power in the public interest could ever be effective under monopoly capitalism; instead the only logical solution if one desired democratic media in the public interest was social ownership (Huberman and Sweezy 1958:401–411).

However, by the early 1960s it was already clear that the dominance of the three great networks had created a "tightly controlled oligopoly" in television.[23] Baran and Sweezy, who presented their "Theses on Advertising" to the Labour Party's Advertising Commission in 1962, the same year that Baran first drafted their treatment of culture and communication for*Monopoly Capital*, were under no illusion about what drove television broadcasting. They quoted 20th Century Fox Television President Peter Levathes's statement that "The sponsor buys a show to sell his product. That is the basic purpose of TV. To sell someone's product." The logic of this was clear. Monopoly capital (encompassing corporations as a whole and more specifically the TV networks and stations) was "interested in maximizing sales and profits by reaching the widest possible audience." This created the conditions for what FCC Chairman Newton Minow referred to in 1961 as "a vast wasteland" in the realm of television programming.

This "wasteland" was exposed for all to see in the 1959 quiz show scandal, which demonstrated the corrupt and mendacious way in which television broadcasting was organized with the aim of duping the public, and the moral and intellectual degradation of its content as a result. This was the basis for Huberman and Sweezy's second *Monthly Review* media piece on "The TV Scandals" in December 1959. The problem, they argued, lay not simply in moral decline, as so many commentators argued, but in a system that enforced such

---

23 Sweezy questioned the emphasis on the three great television networks as representing a "tight oligopoly" that controlled the industry in his early comments on the original draft of this chapter. As Sweezy wrote in a letter to Baran on December 5, 1962: "This whole paragraph stressing the great power of the networks seems out of focus in light of the statement on the next page that they are merely processors and agents. The latter is, in my view, a more accurate assessment of their role" (Baran papers, Monthly Review Foundation).

moral decline. "Can you imagine," they asked, "a morally responsible campaign to sell a remedy for 'tired blood?' A fantastic example perhaps? Not quite – it just happens to have been the product that Charles Van Doren was selling by his great intellectual feats on 'Twenty-One'" – the quiz show at the center of the "TV scandals." The whole point, they went on to argue, was put in a nutshell by Professor Seymour E. Harris, Chairman of the Harvard economics department, in an article entitled "Can We Prosper Without Arms?" which appeared in the *New York Times Magazine* of November 8th: "A high rate of investment would increase the nation's productive capacity.... But our private economy is faced with the tough problem of selling what it can produce. This is the reason for Madison Avenue." Quite so, and it is also the reason why neither Madison Avenue nor the [corporate] clients of Madison Avenue can afford the luxury of integrity or moral responsibility.

Adam Smith argued, with some degree of cogency for his day, that if everyone pursued "his" own private interests "he" would be led, "as if by an invisible hand," to serve the public interest. Nothing could be further from the truth today. When the giant corporation pursues its own private interests – as it must by the very law of its being – it is led by a not so invisible hand to degrade and corrupt the moral standards of a public which is completely dependent upon it not only for jobs and material goods but also for the "food of the mind." This is the plain lesson of the "TV scandals" (Huberman and Sweezy 1959:281).

Huberman and Sweezy went on to argue for: the creation of a nationwide, government-owned radio-television network under an authority representative of the best elements in the worlds of education, the arts, and entertainment. That this is no revolutionary proposal goes without saying. Both Britain and Canada have long had government-owned networks, and in both cases they were founded by conservative governments. Their performance has been infinitely superior to that of the private American networks. *The creation of an American counterpart should become one of the leading demands of everyone who recognizes the seriousness of the present situation* and understands the futility, or worse, of relying on the TV industry or its man Friday, the Federal Communications Commission, to initiate and carry through serious reforms (Huberman and Sweezy 1959:280) [our emphasis].

Huberman and Sweezy (together with Baran) thus followed Brecht, who contended that "the socialization of these means of [cultural] production is vital for art" and the development of communication (Brecht 1964:48–49).[24]

---

24   The influence of Brecht on Baran's thought was particularly evident as he was wont to quote him from memory. Paul A. Baran to Paul M. Sweezy, February 20, 1962

In their later analysis of the quiz show scandal in their chapter on culture, Baran and Sweezy referred to the sordid details exposed in the Congressional investigations, which showed that all elements of the television industry were caught up in the scandal. They responded not by calling for greater regulation, but by turning to the British government's 1962 *Report of the Committee on Broadcasting* (the Pilkington Report), which engaged in serious critique of the TV fare in the United States, and which characterized it – pointing to westerns – as containing "excessive violence and sadism." The Pilkington Report recommended an expansion of the BBC's role in television at the expense of further development of private programming – i.e., of the Independent Television Authority, with its channel Independent Television (ITV) set up in 1955 as a commercial competitor to the BBC.[25]

In Baran and Sweezy's view there was no effective form of regulation of the content of commercial broadcasting since:

It is not the particular form of swindle and deception that is important but the basic fact that it *is* swindle and deception that incessantly fill the air.

The dominance of the lie is not confined to explicit advertisements. The lie also permeates most of the television day. The world presented on TV is not the real world with its conflicting interests, its irrationalities, its destructive tensions, but also with its unending struggles and tremendous potentialities for betterment. It is an artifact which conjures up a tendentious, utterly misleading image of reality.

For Baran, who was a devoted reader of Kafka, the lesson to be drawn was clear. As Kafka wrote in *The Trial*: "'No', said the priest, 'it is not necessary to accept everything as true, one must only accept it as necessary'. 'A melancholy conclusion', said K. 'It turns lying into a universal principle'" (Kafka, Franz 1964:276).[26] Quoting Adorno, Baran and Sweezy referred to the dulling of the

---

(Baran Papers, Monthly Review Foundation). Nick Baran dimly recalls hearing Brecht's *Dreigroschen Oper* (*Threepenny Opera*) on his father's record player when he was a child. Nicholas Baran to John Bellamy Foster, April 24, 2013. It is not surprising then that the entire approach to the cultural apparatus in the Baran and Sweezy chapter on culture can be seen (particularly in the discussion of book publishing) as having a Brechtian emphasis, focusing on the relation of the artist to the apparatus and seeing the latter as an object of struggle.

25 United Kingdom, *Report of the Committee on Broadcasting* (Pilkington Report); see Milland (2009:95–107).

26 Mention of Kafka appears in Baran's correspondence. See, for example, the excerpt from Paul Baran to Paul M. Sweezy, July 4, 1963 in Sweezy and Huberman (1965:61). In 1938 Benjamin wrote on Brecht and Kafka: "The decisive thesis of all of these plays [by Brecht]

"capacity for life experience" promoted by most television broadcasting. In this respect "television and other mass media," they wrote, "contributes to a crippling of the individual's mental and emotional capabilities. By helping to instill in him a phantasmagoric image of existence it disarms him on the social and the individual plane." Worse still it gave rise to cynicism, and a sense that public life is a fraud, while undermining any sense that this is open to change.

Unfortunately, "the increasing awareness of the falsehood of what is conveyed by society's cultural apparatus," they noted, "does not result in a heightened search for truth, reason and knowledge, but rather in the spread of disillusionment and cynicism." Turning to Engels's description of ideology as "false consciousness," they interpreted this in a sophisticated fashion as including "a partial, biased view of reality, half truths, reflecting some important aspects of it without encompassing its totality." What was effectively foreclosed by this ideology was "the existing and expanding possibilities for a different more rational, more human existence." Indeed, they argued that "the cultural apparatus of monopoly capitalism," was aimed at the opposite end of making "people accept what is, to adjust to the tawdry reality and to abandon all hopes, all aspirations for a better society."

The political implications of the missing chapter are therefore decidedly despondent about the prospect of social change in the United States, or any other nation with a similar political and cultural apparatus. The reasons for this were readily apparent. Not only had the Progressive Party disappeared in the United States and with it much of the effective remnants of the New Deal Coalition, but also by the early 1960s the days of meaningful parliamentary socialism in Britain had essentially come to an end, as recounted at the time by Williams and Miliband in the pages of *Monthly Review*.[27] As Miliband commented on Mills's frequent despondency at the same time: "Often, particularly in his last years, the 'politics of truth' which he advocated sounded more like the politics of despair. Hopelessness is a weakness in a social scientist, almost as grave as mindless unconcern or the cultivation of the fixed grin" (Miliband 1964a:79).

Baran and Sweezy's position can be compared to that of Marcuse in his well-known work, *One Dimensional Man*, published in 1964. In the introduction, Marcuse stated that the main characteristics of the "one-dimensionality" of monopoly capitalist society were easily ascertainable if one were merely to

emerges clearly for the *reader*.... It can be summed up by a sentence from Kafka's prophetic novel *The Trial*: 'The lie is made into a universal system'." Benjamin (2002:332).

27   In "If Labour Wins," Miliband explained in *Monthly Review* 15, no. 6 (October 1963):328 that no "deep structural changes" would result.

subject oneself to "looking at television or listening to the AM radio for one consecutive hour for a couple of days, not shutting off the commercials, and now and then switching the station" (Marcuse 1964:xvii).

The dilemma was the Brechtian one. In Marcuse's words (paraphrasing Brecht): "The contemporary world can...be represented only if it is represented as subject to change." The current formally "rational universe" of monopoly capitalism was such that it "by the mere weight and capabilities of its [cultural] apparatus, blocks all escape." It invalidated "the cherished images of transcendence by incorporating them into its omnipresent daily reality." Marcuse ended his book by holding out the thin hope that "the spectre is there again, inside and outside the frontiers of the advanced societies.... The chance is that, in this period, the historical extremes may meet again: the most advanced consciousness of humanity, and its most exploited force" (Marcuse 1964:66–71, 257). Nevertheless, Marcuse's *One-Dimensional Man* was a deeply pessimistic book, centering on the containment and assimilation of the forces of social transformation as a result of the technical and cultural apparatus of late capitalist society.[28] "The legendary revolutionary," Marcuse wrote, "still exists who can defy even television and the press – his world is that of the 'underdeveloped' countries" (Marcuse 1964:71).[29]

Baran read Marcuse's book in manuscript in October 1963, in the midst of working on *Monopoly Capital*.[30] Marcuse's work had a profound effect on him. But Baran was also uncomfortable with the pessimistic conclusion that Marcuse's arguments reached. Baran thought the matter so important that rather than allowing this to affect the analysis of *Monopoly Capital* directly, he

---

28 These pessimistic conclusions were strongly criticized in Fromm's unpublished critique of Marcuse. See Fromm (1992:125–129).

29 Marcuse drew on Baran and Sweezy's analysis of monopoly capitalism in his later work. See, for example, Herbert Marcuse (1972:5).

30 A year before on October 7, 1962 Baran had written to Marcuse: "Oo, oh! Where did your manuscript get stuck? I am lusting after it like a thirsty man for water and I don't know how I can get hold of it. Send it to me, I beg you, even if it has not yet attained a condition of absolute perfection and even if you are still caught up in the process of 'purification'. It will be sent back to you as quickly as possible and I will be infinitely indebted to you in gratitude." This was followed by a discussion of new work by Horkheimer and Adorno. Baran to Marcuse, October 7, 1962 (Baran Papers, Monthly Review Foundation; original in German, translated by Joseph Fracchia). Marcuse replied a week later referring to "massive difficulties getting it published. At present there are three copies with different presses." Marcuse to Baran, October 27, 1962 (Baran Papers, Monthly Review Foundation, original in German, translated by Joseph Fracchia). We would like to thank Joseph Fracchia for his translations from the Baran–Marcuse correspondence.

proposed to Sweezy that they take up this challenge in their next book. In an extraordinary letter to Sweezy on October 10, 1963, Baran went directly at the existential challenge of Marcuse's analysis to Marxist theory and socialist politics:

> After having...shown how monopoly capital creates the muck that sur-rounds us on all fronts, we will have placed *this* part of the story "on the record" [in *Monopoly Capital*]. What is at the present time at issue and indeed most urgently so is the question whether the Marxian dialectic has broken down, i.e., whether it is possible for *Scheisse* [shit] to accumulate, to coagulate, to cover all of society (and a goodly part of the related world) *without producing the dialectical counter-force* which would break through it and blow it into the air. *Hic Rhodus, hic salta*! If the answer is affirmative then Marxism *in its tradi-tional form* has become superannuated. It has predicted the misery, it has explained full well the causes of its becoming as comprehensive as it is; it was in error, however, in its central thesis that the misery generates itself the forces of its abolition. I have just finished reading Marcuse's new book [*One-Dimensional Man*] (in MS) which in a laborious kind of a way advances this very position which is called the Great Refusal or the Absolute Negation. Everything is*Dreck* (filth): monopoly capital and the Soviet Union, capitalism and socialism as we know it; the negative part of the Marx story has come true – its positive part remained a figment of imagination. We are back at the state of the Utopians pure and simple; a better world there should be but there ain't no social force in sight to bring it about. Not only is Socialism no answer, but there isn't anyone to give that answer anyway. From the Great Refusal and the Absolute Negation to the Great Withdrawal and the Absolute Betrayal is only a very short step. I have a very strong feeling that this is at the moment in the center of the intellectuals' thought (and sentiment) – not only here but also in Latin America and elsewhere, and that it would be very much *our* commitment to deal with it.... What is required is a cool analysis of the entire situation, the restoration of a historical perspective, a reminder of the relevant time dimensions and much more. If we could do a good job on that – perhaps only a shortish booklet of less than 200 pages – we would make a major contri-bution and perform with regard to many a truly "liberating" act.[31]

Baran thus proposed to put into a restored historical context the apparent crisis of Marxism represented by the decoupling of social consciousness and agency from material contradictions and potentials. The perspective would have remained the critique of monopoly capital, but it would have required as

---

31   Paul A. Baran to Paul M. Sweezy, October 10, 1963. On Marcuse's view of Baran see Herbert
      Marcuse, "Tribute to Baran," in Sweezy and Huberman 1964:114–115.

an integral part of this critique a direct confrontation with the notion that the cultural apparatus was a permanent and irremovable roadblock to socialist politics, or even democracy. This was the direction that Mills and Williams were also going with their work. As Williams had put it in January 1960 in *Monthly Review*: "The central problem, as I see it, is cultural. The society of individual consumers which is now being propagandized by all the weight of mass advertising and mass publications, needs a new kind of socialist analysis and alternative" (Williams 1960:333).

Baran was moving in a definite direction of extending the cultural critique and merging it with political-economic analysis. However he was unable to work on this project, which he planned to pursue, with or without Sweezy, following the completion of *Monopoly Capital*. On March 26, 1964, while visiting Lowenthal and looking at a copy of Marcuse's just published *One-Dimensional Man* with a glass of brandy in his hand, he suffered his fatal heart attack (Sweezy and Huberman 1964:48).

With the decision by Sweezy to leave the chapter on culture out of the published version of *Monopoly Capital*, these struggles of Baran, together with Sweezy, to confront the cultural contradictions of capitalist society, and the existential as well as strategic questions for the political left, were unfinished.

Monopoly Capital avoided the pessimism implied in the unpublished culture chapter. Its conclusion, "The Irrational System," emphasized the tendency of the economic surplus to rise under monopoly capitalism and the necessity of the wasting of this economic surplus, even as human needs remained unfulfilled – pointing to the increasing irrationality of the entire economic and social order. Key to the whole development was the fact that "a tiny oligarchy resting on vast economic power" was "in full control of society's political and cultural apparatus." Under these conditions "improvements in the means of mass communication merely hasten the degeneration of popular culture." These were hardly conditions, they reasoned, that could prevail over the long run. Such a system was bound to find itself caught in ever more complex forms of irrationality and destruction. Hence, they concluded that it was only a matter of time until the contradictions of the social order generated forces of opposition that would overwhelm them: "We have reached a point where the only true rationality lies in action to overthrow what has become a hopelessly irrational system" (Baran and Sweezy 1966:339, 363).

There were "even indications," they wrote, "especially in the Negro freedom movement in the South, in the uprisings of the urban ghettos, and in the academic community's mounting protest against the war in Vietnam, that significant segments of the American people are ready to join an active struggle against what is being cumulatively revealed as an intolerable social order.

If this is so, who can set limits to the numbers who may join them in the future?"(Baran and Sweezy 1966:366) But it was the world revolt against capitalism based in the periphery that was the real agent of change, to which the United States, as the chief bastion of monopoly capital, was not in the end immune. Despite the enormous power of the system that controlled the means of production – and along with it the state and the cultural apparatus of society – social struggle was breaking out everywhere in the 1960s, creating the hope that monopoly capitalism would be both besieged and challenged from within.

The Critique of Culture and the Media in the 1960s

In deciding what to include (or exclude) in this issue directed at the 1960s political-economic critique of the cultural apparatus, we were guided by four main criteria: (1) whether the piece is original and holds value to people confronting politics in the twenty-first century; (2) the synergy with the political economy of the cultural apparatus of monopoly capitalism, as exemplified by Baran and Sweezy's missing chapter; (3) the extent to which the work was influential and part of current discussions; and (4) whether the work has received much (or any) attention since it was written. For example, William's pamphlet on *The Existing Alternatives in Communications* is practically unknown and is fully reprinted here. In contrast, Mills's work on *the cultural apparatus*, in the form of his three main articles on the subject, is fairly well known and has recently been reprinted, so while discussed in this introduction, it is not reprinted in this issue.

In addition to "On the Quality of Monopoly Capitalist Society: Culture and Communications" (the title given to it here), we are reprinting Baran and Sweezy's aforementioned "Theses on Advertising." Originally given as testimony to the Labour Party's Advertising Commission in 1962, this piece represents a classic exploration of the role of advertising under monopoly capital. Read together with their missing chapter on culture we are left with a coherent, and surprisingly wide-ranging, critique of culture and communication under monopoly capitalism.

During its first two decades *Monthly Review* was not known for its attention to culture and communication, which contributed to the notion that the editors did not care much about such matters. There were exceptions, though, that provide evidence of an important, critical approach. The two aforementioned critiques of commercial television by Huberman and Sweezy stand out as some of the most original work on media by *anyone* in the late 1950s. Other notable works, included F.O. Matthiessen's "Marxism and Literature" (March 1953), and Leo Marx's "Notes on the Culture of the New Capitalism" (July–August 1959).[32]

Monthly Review recognized the deficiency and launched a special supplement in 1965, *Review1*, which was to be a Marxist cultural review. Only a single edition was published. Although*Review1* gathered a lot of interest and was a success in that respect, it soon became clear that financial and editorial resources did not allow a continuation of the experiment. The third article in this summer issue, following Baran and Sweezy's contributions, draws from *Review1*and is by Eleanor Hakim, the managing editor of *Studies on the Left* (based at the University of Wisconsin) from 1960 to 1963. Hakim's article, "St. Brecht of the Theatrical Stock Exchange" has been excerpted and adapted for this issue from its original version in *Review1*. She discusses Brecht's use of the notion of "cultural apparatus," which he applied, as we noted above, to such varied forms as radio, theatre, and film – and that was to influence the way in which thinkers such as Fromm, Horkheimer, Benjamin, Marcuse, Mills, Williams, Thompson, and Baran and Sweezy would later use the term. As Hakim emphasized, Brecht asked: "Why shouldn't art try, by its *own* means of course, to further the great social task of mastering life?" (Brecht *1964:*96)

The fourth piece in this summer issue is a reprint of a section of Chapter 8 in Miliband's *The State in Capitalist Society* that addresses media. We find this a brilliant summary of the work on media being done in these circles, and what is striking is how Miliband seamlessly integrates a media critique into his analysis of politics under monopoly capitalism, expanding upon the Mills project. In particular, Miliband integrates a sophisticated critique of the media with a focus on the political constraints imposed by the media system. He concludes on a point implicit in all of the other work in this issue: the important ways that the capitalist media system encourages depoliticization in society. And if not always all-out depoliticization, this media system was shown to foster a "climate of conformity," helping to ensure that whatever occurs politically occurs within limits that are consistent with the preservation of the established order.

---

32   See Matthiessen (1953), Marx (1959:111–116); Huberman and Sweezy, "The TV Scandals." *Monthly Review* seemed particularly lacking in the critique of the news media. It is true that there were occasional forays into this area. In May 1964 the magazine published a piece entitled "Newspapers?" by former journalist Alexander Crosby. Crosby argued that "the press has been going down hill steadily" for decades as it became increasingly monopolistic and profit-obsessed. The result was a dull and reactionary news, all but worthless for a vibrant democratic society. Newspapers "have no heart and no energy." See Alexander L. Crosby, "Newspapers?" *Monthly Review* 16, no. 1 (May 1964):43–46.

The fifth and penultimate piece in the issue is a pamphlet by Williams that was published by the Fabian Society in 1962: *The Existing Alternatives in Communications*. This almost entirely unknown piece drew from his great work, *The Long Revolution* (1961), in which he addressed the question of the cultural apparatus, as well as the first, 1962 edition, of his book *Britain in the Sixties: Communications* (generally called *Communications*).[33] In 1962, Williams was another important figure, alongside Baran and Sweezy, to give testimony to the Labor Party's Advertising Commission, and their analysis clearly concurred on every point. (The Labour Party 1966:33–40, 201, 204; Williams 1967:155–156).[34]

That testimony influences the pamphlet as well. As noted above, Williams had submitted a detailed memorandum to the 1960 Committee on Broadcasting (The Pilkington Committee). His memorandum addressed the entire structure of the broadcasting industry, and may have influenced the 1962 Pilkington Report.

Like Baran and Sweezy, Williams was strongly impressed by the final Pilkington Report, released shortly after the first edition of *Communications*, and discussed it in the second (1966) edition of his book, where he referred to it as "the classical point of reference for all reform in this field" (Williams 1962:156).[35]

In *Communications*, Williams defined communications as "the institutions and forms in which ideas, information, and attitudes are transmitted and received," while communication (without an "s") referred to "the process of

---

33   See Williams (*1961:366*).

34   While Baran and Sweezy provided written testimony to the Labour Party's Advertising Commission, Williams was listed as a submitter of oral evidence.

35   The Pilkington Report indicated that Williams's memorandum to the Committee on Broadcasting had addressed the following topics: "BBC and ITA: Existing Services: License Fee: Third television programme: Regional broadcasting: Local sound broadcasting: ITA to collect advertising revenue direct: Broadcasting and Television Council: Educational Broadcasting: Consumer Research programs." *Report of the Committee on Broadcasting* (Pilkington Committee), 329. Since Williams' memorandum to the Pilkington Committee was completed at the same time that he was working on his "Existing Alternatives to Communications" (reprinted in this issue) and on his book*Communications,* his Pilkington Committee memorandum likely reflected similar concerns (as suggested by the Committee on Broadcasting's listing of its contents here). Williams also referred to the Labour Party's Advertising Commission Report (to which he and Baran and Sweezy had given testimony) in the second edition of his book; however, it was released while the book was in press, so he was only able to add a footnote indicating that "its majority recommendations amount to a useful short-term programme of action and ought, in my view, to be firmly supported" (Williams 1976:156).

transmission and reception." Williams argued that the spectacular growth of communications in modern times "have created social problems which seem to be of a new kind." Communication, he argued, joined economics and politics as "equally fundamental" to understanding society. "We have been wrong in taking communication as secondary," Williams wrote. "The struggle to learn, to describe, to understand, to educate, is a central and necessary part of our humanity. This struggle is not begun, at second hand, after reality has occurred. It is, in itself, a major way in which reality is continually formed and changed." This emphasis, he argued, "is exceptionally important in the long crisis of twentieth-century society" (Williams 1962:17–19).

Accordingly, Williams argued that control over communication was of paramount importance, and commercial control of media was a disaster for humanity, not to mention democracy. "The only alternative to a control by a few irresponsible men, who treat our cultural means as simple commodities, is a public system." Williams insisted there was an important place for consumer information and advice in a communication system, "but advertising is a very primitive way of supplying it." He recognized the "genuine difficulties" of establishing a public cultural system, but that did not alter his belief in its central and immediate importance as a political project. What was required was "no direct control by government" over content, but nonetheless a strong public role, along with public debate and deliberation over the "actual allocation of resources." He was emphatic that the Old Left model of state monopoly and censorship was no legitimate or attractive alternative. Indeed the bankruptcy of the Soviet-style system was demonstrated most decisively in its hideous communications structure and policies. Until socialists "can show a convincing alternative, which is free of these dangers," people would have no rational reason to change. "The idea of public service must be detached from the idea of public monopoly, yet remain public service in the true sense. The only way to achieve this is to create new kinds of institution" (Williams 1962:129–130, 166–173).

In "*The Existing Alternatives in Communications*" in this issue, Williams sums up these points and argues that the Labour Party needs to make reconstruction of the media and communication system a central part of its political program going forward. Implicit in his argument is that the very nature of a socialist regime can be gleaned by assessing its communication system, for that is where the rubber hits the road and the commitment to genuine democracy moves from words to practice. In Williams' view, what was essential was a well-funded public system with true independence and legitimate access for ordinary citizens, not just for socialism but also for democracy itself. The point was to create a system where the means of production in this area were held in trust by the public and leased out to individuals without control from the top, in ways that would create a dynamic, popular, decentralized, and democratic media system. Unless the Labour Party – and by extension, the left everywhere – made restructuring communications a high priority, it would increase their likeliness of irrelevance and ultimate failure.

The New Left and Communication: The 1960s and '70s and Today

The New Left, as Thompson had said, was in many ways defined from the beginning by its focus on culture and communication – seen primarily in a political-economic context. The fact that there was in the 1960s a historical moment for reform in broadcasting, after which change would become far more difficult (and British broadcasting would begin to move in the direction of the U.S. system with its commercialism and cultural degradation) was made clear in Williams's comments on the Pilkington Report in the second edition of *Communications*. "It is now more than ever certain," he wrote, "that we shall have to get rid of a commercial television structure, and especially of this one, with its close connexions in ownership with our already concentrated commercial press." Although the BBC had gotten a second channel as a result of the implementation of some of the Pilkington Report recommendations, it was already being forced to mimic the commercial system, competing for audiences "on the basis of profit rather than use" with the ITV channel of the Independent Television Authority. If another commercial channel were established, he predicted, "we shall have lost for a generation any chance of making a genuinely public system." The real goal, he insisted, ought to be "to start dismantling both the present commercial structure of ITV and the present centralization of BBC," replacing them with a system of public control over the technical and transmission apparatus, holding it in trust, coupled with "genuinely independent programme companies" which would lease the technical facilities and take responsibility for policy and content (Williams 1962:156–158).[36]

Williams in many respects captured the core arguments of all the other writers from this period. He took elements of the critique initiated by Baran and Sweezy, the Frankfurt School, and Mills about the growing importance of the cultural apparatus under monopoly capitalism and developed it into a broader and more coherent intellectual vision. More important, he used this as

---

36 The long-run response to the Pilkington Report and the decline of the BBC-centered system are described in Garnham (1990:128–132).

a gateway not to despair over the duping of the masses, but, to the contrary, as a new crucial political battleground where the political left could rejuvenate itself and create a truly democratic socialism. It was no small accomplishment. At the same time as this work was being done, Jürgen Habermas had just completed his dissertation in Germany. When one reads what became *The Structural Transformation of the Public Sphere* today – it was not available in English until 1989 – one is struck by the manner in which the analysis and arguments are complementary with those of Baran, Sweezy, Miliband, and especially Williams and Mills. Indeed, Habermas closes the book by invoking Mills approvingly (Habermas 1989:249–250).

By the early 1970s, accompanying the global upsurge in political activism, there was considerable attention given to communication issues on the left. In the global South, the newly liberated nations organized for a New World Information and Communication Order in conjunction with a New International Economic Order to redress the global imbalances in control over communication networks and media resulting from centuries of imperialism. It was the first time in global politics that communication was put on the same level as the economy, or better yet, seen as being integral to the political economy.

In Britain, Nicholas Garnham, who would go on to be a central figure in the political economy of communication, wrote a manifesto for media activism in 1972 that drew directly from Marcuse and Williams. "The media of mass communication clearly play a vital role and the control of those media is a matter of central political concern," he wrote. "The media are not neutral in the struggle for democracy. In the Long Revolution the pen may indeed turn out to be mightier than the sword. The outcome of that battle will therefore depend upon which side gains control of the pen." In Garnham's view, a problem with much of the "counterculture" media activism of the times was the belief that "alternative cultures, life styles and the institutional forms to go with them could be constructed within the existing social formation and alongside the more traditional social forms" (Garnham 1980:14). Williams shared this concern, noting in 1975 that the commercial system had succeeded in "incorporating large areas" of alternative popular culture into its own domain (Williams 1976:184).

In his 1975 retrospective look at the preceding fifteen years in British (and, to a certain extent, western) communication, Williams found some hope that the counterculture that had developed in that period might have lasting progressive value. But he was also skeptical. The idea of an alternative culture is radical but limited. It can very easily become a marginal culture; even, at worst, a tolerated play area. It is certainly always insufficient unless it is linked with effective opposition to the dominant system, under which the majority of people are living.

Williams was especially heartened by the emergence of cooperatives to generate communication and culture, but here, too, direct political confrontation with the powers-that-be was unavoidable: "One of the key developments, that of the workers' or producers' or contributors' cooperative, depends, in the high-capital areas, on active support by a reforming government, and that takes us back to one of the central areas of conflict" (Williams 1976:186–187).

In the United States, there was an explosion in developing such "alternative" media in the form of community theater and, especially, alternative newspapers and periodicals. But policy activism also emerged. In the early 1970s, African-American groups and other community and civil rights organizations participated in hundreds of license challenges to existing commercial radio and TV broadcasters before the FCC in a failed effort to claim their channels for community use. By the mid–1970s this activism contributed to the creation of scores of new community FM radio stations and public-access TV. The activism was a testament to the vision Williams and the others laid out a decade earlier.

By the end of the 1970s and thereafter the political projects associated with the writers in this volume disappeared with the collapse of the left and the rise of neoliberalism. As Garnham acknowledged in 1978, the "need" for radical media reform was growing "more acute" at the same time that the prospects for such reform were much further away (Garnham 1980:9). The new fields of the political economy of communication and cultural studies downsized their immediate political ambitions and crystallized as academic undertakings, finding a toehold in a handful of universities where they provided a muscular critique while maintaining a tenuous institutional existence thereafter. Williams regarded the emergence of academic media studies as "significant," though he added that it was "ironic that this work should have developed in the same period in which the general situation was so sharply deteriorating" (Williams 1976:183). Much of critical communication research subsequently turned away from the structural issues that were central to the work of the 1960s as institutional reform, not to mention socialism, appeared impossible. At its most extreme this devolution ended up in the varieties of post-structuralist, postmodernist, and postcolonial schools. In such an environment it was easy for this 1960s political-economic and structural-reform tradition to be forgotten, even by some of the people associated with it.

In the past decade, with the emergence of global corporate media empires and the Internet, radical media reform has returned as a major political issue in countless nations. At times the reform efforts can be marginal, especially when they are not associated with popular movements and an organized political left that can provide vision and courage. But what is more important – since it represents a precondition of any forward movement – is how the left has now come to embrace the central importance of structural media reform and communication issues as never before, much as the writers in this issue desired. Nowhere is this more apparent than when one looks at Latin America today, where many of the great struggles concern how progressive forces can get elected-left governments to create truly independent media systems free of the traditional domination of a few capitalist clans in every nation, as well as the state. The capitalist forces are determined to use their media power to maintain their class privileges. The fate of these governments and socialist politics writ large may well ride on the outcome. Recently, notions about the creation of a public media system that would be "accountable to the public rather than the state" – or the market – perhaps similar to the general approach adopted by Williams have been informally broached by some individuals in the current period of experimentation and debate in Cuba (Burbach 2013).

It has been said that Beethoven's late string quartets were so far ahead of their time that we have not yet caught up to them. So it is with this work by Williams and the other contributors to the struggle over the cultural apparatus under concentrated capitalism that have been all but lost to history until now. Activists today still have much to learn from this visionary work about how to think about communication. All of these contributors, for example, were aware of the radical changes that new communication technologies were going to create in the decades to come, but none of them thought these technologies would magically solve fundamental political problems on their own. If anything the left has been too timid with regard to communication politics; it is time to be realistic, as the 1960s saying goes, and demand the impossible.

The reason that these issues are returning to the fore today is that capitalism is in crisis and facing political challenges in a manner not seen for decades. Evidence suggests that these political-economic contradictions will deepen in what we have termed an "endless crisis" (Foster and McChesney 2012). Moreover, the larger planetary threat posed by capitalism is coming to the fore as never before. As Baran wrote in the 1960s (with the nuclear threat in mind): "the issue now is not even capitalism or socialism...the issue now is world survival or world catastrophe" (Baran 1969:436).

The final piece in this summer issue therefore returns to political economy. The basis of all the pieces in this issue is coming to grips with the nature of monopoly capitalist society. Here Baran and Sweezy's economic analysis was in many respects the lodestar for all the contributors. But how does their understanding of monopoly capital hold up five decades later?

We conclude therefore with John Bellamy Foster's new introduction to the second edition of his *The Theory of Monopoly Capitalism*, which was first published in 1986. This piece takes the core elements of *Monopoly Capital*'s political economy and addresses how the theory has developed over the past three decades. It provides a context for appreciating how the political-economic basis of the work in the 1960s can be adapted to the present times. The moral of the story: with regard to the political economy of communication, the present is history.

References

Adorno, T.W. 1960. "Television and the Patterns of Mass Culture," in Bernard Rosenberg and David Manning White, eds., Mass Culture, Glencoe, IL: The Free Press.

Aronowitz, Stanley. 2012. Taking It Big: C. Wright Mills and the Making of Political Intellectuals, New York: Columbia University Press.

Baran, Paul A. (writing under the pseudonym Historicus) 1950. "Better Smaller But Better," Monthly Review 2, no. 3 (July 1950): 85–86.

Baran, Paul A. 1969. The Longer View (New York: Monthly Review Press.

Baran, Paul A. and Paul M. Sweezy. 1964. "Theses on Advertising," Science and Society 28, no. 1 (Winter 1964): 20–30. Reprinted in this issue.

Baran, Paul A. and Paul M. Sweezy. 1966. Monopoly Capital, New York: Monthly Review Press.

Baran, Paul A. and Paul M. Sweezy. 2012. "Some Theoretical Implications," Monthly Review 64, no. 3 (July–August 2012): 24–59.

Benjamin, Walter. 2002. Selected Writings, Cambridge, MA: Harvard University Press.

Braverman, Harry. 1999. Labor and Monopoly Capital, New York: Monthly Review Press.

Brecht, Bertolt. 1964. Brecht on Theatre, New York: Hill and Wang.

Burbach, Roger. 2013. "A Cuban Spring?" Counterpunch, April 13, 2013, http://counterpunch.org.

Dawson, Michael. 2005. The Consumer Trap, Urbana: University of Illinois Press.

Denning, Michael. 1997. The Cultural Front: The Laboring of American Culture in the Twentieth Century, London: Verso.

Dowd, Douglas. 1974. "Monopoly Capitalism and Mind Management," Monthly Review 26, no. 11 (November 1974): 32–36.

Foster, John Bellamy and Robert W. McChesney. 2012. The Endless Crisis: How Monopoly-Finance Capital Produces Stagnation and Upheaval from the USA to China, New York: Monthly Review Press.

Foster, John Bellamy. 2012. "A Missing Chapter of Monopoly Capital: Introduction to Baran and Sweezy's 'Some Theoretical Complications'," Monthly Review 64, no. 3 (July–August 2012): 3–17.

Fromm, Erich. 1955. The Sane Society (New York: Rinehart and Co.

Fromm, Erich. 1970. The Crisis of Psychoanalysis, Greenwich, CT: Fawcett Publications.

Fromm, Erich. 1992. The Revision of Psychoanalysis, Boulder: Westview Press.

Garnham, Nicholas. 1980. Structures of Television, revised edition, London: British Film Institute (First published in 1973).

Garnham, Nicholas. 1990. Capitalism and Communication, London: Sage.

Geary, Daniel. 2009. Radical Ambition: C. Wright Mills, the Left, and American Social Thought, Berkeley: University of California Press.

Gebhardt, Eike. 1978. "Introduction to a Critique of Methodology," in Andrew Arato and Eike Gebhardt, eds.,The Essential Frankfurt School Reader, New York: Urizen Books.

Habermas, Jürgen. 1989. The Structural Transformation of the Public Sphere, Cambridge, MA: MIT Press.

Hegel, G.W.F. 1886. Introduction to Hegel's Philosophy of Fine Art, London: Kegan Paul, Trench, and Co.

Hobsbawm, Eric. 2013. Fractured Times: Culture and Society in the Twentieth Century, London: Little, Brown.

Honneth, Axel. 1991. The Critique of Power, Cambridge, MA: MIT Press.

Horkheimer, Max. 2002. "Authority and the Family," in Horkheimer, Critical Theory: Selected Essays, New York: Continuum.

Horkheimer, Max and Theodor Adorno. 1972. The Dialectic of Enlightenment, New York: Continuum.

Howard, M.C. and J.E. King. 1992. A History of Marxian Economics, vol. II, Princeton: Princeton University Press, 114–15.

Huberman, Leo and Paul M. Sweezy. 1953 "A Challenge to the Book Burners," Monthly Review 4, no. 4,August 1953.

Huberman, Leo and Paul M. Sweezy. 1958. "Behind the FCC Scandal," Monthly Review 9, no. 12, April 1958.

Huberman, Leo and Paul M. Sweezy. 1959. "The TV Scandals," Monthly Review 11, no. 8, December 1959.

Kafka, Franz. 1964. The Trial. New York: Modern Library.

La Farge, Christopher. 1954. "Mickey Spillane and His Bloody Hammer," in Rosenberg and White, eds., Mass Culture (Originally published in The Saturday Review, 6 November 1954).

Marcuse, Herbert. 1955. Eros and Civilization (New York: Vintage Books.

Marcuse, Herbert. 1964. One-Dimensional Man, Boston: Beacon Press.

Marcuse, Herbert. 1972. Counter-Revolution and Revolt, Boston: Beacon Press.

Marcuse, Herbert. 1978. "Some Social Implications of Modern Technology," in Arato and Gebhardt, eds., The Essential Frankfurt School Reader New York: Urizen Books.

Marcuse, Herbert. 1998. "33 Theses," in Marcuse, Collected Papers, vol. 1, London: Routledge.

Marx, Leo. 1959. "Notes on the Culture of the New Capitalism," Monthly Review 11, no. 3 (July–August 1959): 111–116.

Matthiessen, F.O. 1953. "Marxism and Literature," Monthly Review 4, no. 11 (March 1953) 398–400.

McChesney, Robert W. 2002. "What Ever Happened to Cultural Studies?" in Catherine A. Warren and Mary Douglas Vavrus, eds., American Cultural Studies, Urbana: University of Illinois Press, 76–92.

McChesney, Robert W. 2007. Communication Revolution: Critical Junctures and the Future of Media, New York: New Press.

McChesney, Robert W. 2013. Digital Disconnect: How Capitalism is Turning the Internet Against Democracy, New York: New Press.

Miliband, Ralph. 1964a. "Review of C. Wright Mills, Power, People and Politics," British Journal of Sociology 15, no. 1.

Miliband, Ralph. 1964b. Parliamentary Socialism (New York: Monthly Review Press (original UK edition 1961).

Milland, Jeffrey. 2009. "The Pilkington Report: The Triumph of Paternalism?" in Michael Bailey, ed., Narrating Media History, London: Routledge.

Mills, C. Wright. 1958. "Psychology and Social Science," Monthly Review 10, no. 6 (October 1958): 204–249.

Mills, C. Wright. 2008. The Politics of Truth, Oxford: Oxford University Press.

Mueller, Rowitha. 1989. Bertolt Brecht and the Theory of the Media, Lincoln: University of Nebraska Press.

Newman, Michael. 2002. Ralph Miliband and the Politics of the New Left, New York: Monthly Review Press, 2002), 65–68.

Oesmann, Astrid. 2005. Staging History: Brecht's Social Concepts of Ideology, Albany: State University of New York Press.

Palmer, Bryan. 2000. Cultures of Darkness, New York: Monthly Review Press.

Saunders, Frances Stoner. 1999. The Cultural Cold War, New York: New Press.

Schiller, Dan. 2006. How to Think About Information, Urbana: University of Illinois Press, chapter 1.

Smythe, Dallas. 1977. "Communications: Blindspot of Western Marxism," Canadian Journal of Political and Social Theory 1, no. 3 (Fall 1977): 1–27.

Spillane, Mickey. 2001. The Mike Hammer Collection, vol. 2, New York: New American Library.

Sweezy Paul M. (writing anonymously, no author listed) 1957. The Scientific-Industrial Revolution, New York: Model, Roland, and Stone.

Sweezy Paul M. and Leo Huberman, eds. 1964. Paul A. Baran (1910–1964): A Collective Portrait, New York: Monthly Review Press.

Sweezy, Paul M. and Leo Huberman, eds., 1965 Paul Alexander Baran (1910–1964): A Collective Portrait, New York: Monthly Review Press.

The Labour Party. 1966. Report of a Commission of Enquiry into Advertising, London: Labour Party.

Thompson E.P. 1959. "The New Left," The New Reasoner, no. 9 (Summer 1959), 1–17, http://marxists.org.

Thompson, E.P. 1961. "The Long Revolution—II," New Left Review, I/10, July–August 1961, 34–39.

Thompson, E.P. 1963. The Making of the English Working Class, New York: Vintage.

Thompson, E.P. 1980. "The Segregation of Dissent," in Thompson, Writing by Candlelight, London: Merlin Press.

Thompson, E.P. 1988. "Last Dispatches from the Border Country: Raymond Williams, 1921–1988,"The Nation, March 5.

Végső, Roland. 2013. The Naked Communist: Cold War Modernism and the Politics of Popular Culture, New York: Fordham University Press.

Williams, Raymond. 1958 "Culture is Ordinary" in MacKenzie, Norman ed. 1958. Conviction, New York: Monthly Review Press, 74–92.

Williams, Raymond. 1960. "Class and Voting in Britain," Monthly Review 11, no. 9 (January 1960).

Williams, Raymond. 1989. What I Came to Say, London: Hutchinson Radius.

Williams, Raymond. 1961. The Long Revolution, New York: Columbia University Press.

Williams, Raymond. 1962. Britain in the Sixties: Communications, Harmondsworth: Penguin.

Williams, Raymond. 1967. Communications, New York: Barnes and Noble.

Williams, Raymond. 1976. Communications, third edition, London: Penguin.

CHAPTER 5

The War against Democracy in the UK

Nick Stevenson

The ideal of a deeper democracy than that offered by either authoritarian state societies or overtly capitalist societies remains central to any attempt to think critically. Here we perhaps need to remember that the Left in the European setting has a less than spotless record when it comes to questions of democracy. However the roots of a more emancipatory project in a period of human rights abuse, growing inequality, privatisation and authoritarian states remains the development of more genuinely democratic forms of the communication. If the wider media system continues to enforce a horizontal flow of information from centre to periphery then more critical social movements need to be able to offer visions and practices that challenge this logic. Intellectuals and social movements need to be able to offer visions of a more inclusive world where questions of voice, freedom and the right to communicate are meaningful. Such a world can-not be fostered by a mostly capitalist run media, a top down public service model or indeed a new communications media focused upon the spectacle. The possibility of a more authentic democracy depends upon a critical spirit sceptical of capital, the state and more 'official' forms of journalism. As George Orwell (1968a, 407) argued it is the responsibility of critical intellectuals to 'keep the spirit of liberalism alive'. While Orwell is sometimes remembered as an ideologue of the cold war this is at best a form of displacement. Orwell warned against the arrival of a world where state's and accepted political positions closed down different political positions thereby silencing criticism and independent thinking. In this quest criticism needs to move beyond simplistic ideas of good and bad and value different dissenting positions. Orwell adopted a democratic politics that sought to press for the reform of common institutions like the media and education system so that they can become places where citizens experimented with different ideas. Orwell is best understood as being part of a liberal generation of socialists who sought to construct a genuinely democratic state that would seek to manage the economy, reduce inequality and provide an alternative to the indignity of a life of poverty and servitude. In this respect, Orwell was not a utopian, but fearing the ideological rigidity of both Left and Right he was committed to a struggle for a more humane and less cruel society.

Orwell's (1999) novel Nineteen Eighty-Four describes a world where political and intellectual pluralism had disappeared. This was a society where

technology and state oppression manufactured conformity and blind obedience through fear and intimidation. The totalitarian features of Communism
and Fascism had sought to eliminate all forms of dissent and ideological opposition. These were ideologies that could not admit to any idea of the social
good beyond collective conformity.

While Orwell (1968b) was explicit that his dystopian novel was meant to act
as a satirical warning against a society that 'could' arrive, his passionate plea
to think beyond the ideological rigidities of the time remain with us today.
If Orwell warned against the conformism required by state dominated societies it is likely he would have been just as alive to the conformity required by the
liberal capitalism of today. If during Orwell's time it was the state that governed society then today it is the capitalist market. Orwell's nightmare remains
our own the extent to which he offered a dystopian world that manages the
consciousness of the many. If by liberal society we mean a world where citizens are generally free to become the people they wish to be and where freedom is as much of an everyday practice as it is a matter of law then current
British society falls a long way short of these ideas. Despite the fact that England
has a long heritage of sceptical liberalism including Orwell, but also other
thinkers like Bertrand Russell, John Stuart Mill and Leonard Hobhouse this tradition currently seems to be in decline. The Labour Left is mainly caught up
with a discussion of communitarianism that values civic renewal through
work, family, faith and flag with its more liberal dissenting wing in decline. The
conservativism of the Left is however not surprising given the increasingly
marginal position it occupies within English society more generally. In this
respect, the project of third way socialism that brought modest forms of redistribution while remaining relaxed about the neoliberal domination of culture
and the broader society has now come to an end. New Labour's support for the
war on terror, the development of academy schools and failure to democratise
public institutions has signalled the end of social liberalism.

If the period of social liberalism that built the welfare state, the NHS, comprehensive schools and the BBC lasted until about 1979 its mark on the culture
is now being forgotten. In the wake of totalitarian Europe social liberalism
sought to reconcile ideas of liberty with more collective values. Social liberalism (or democracy) sought to articulate three different kinds of freedom.
Firstly there was the idea that if culture was completely ruled by the market it
could end up squeezing out important artistic works that would not necessarily appeal to a majority. The paradox about freedom was that it required a balance between the market and the state or between individualism and
collectivism. Secondly social liberalism recognised that freedom required
security from market failure. That unless citizens had a sense of security should

their actions end in failure they would be unlikely to live autonomous and adventurous lives. Finally social liberalism sought to reduce inequality and promote a sense of equal opportunity so that citizens could live with some degree of autonomy. It was the aim of the workers movement to ensure working people had some of the experiences and choices usually confined to elites.

All of these features are now in decline in the new neoliberal orthodoxy. The arrival of the global 24 hour economy has served to progressively remove the social protections of pervious eras and impress a new kind of ideological conformity. Neoliberalism, as is well known, operates as a form of class power that attacks the social aspects of liberalism and replaces them with the market. If Orwell feared the authoritarian state in his own time in ours he would have been concerned as the state becomes progressively reduced to its core security features and freedom is reduced to a market ideology. Freedom is now a lifestyle built upon hyper-consumption, aspiration, positive thinking and upward mobility. To be free means to never be depressed, encounter moral complexity or to wonder whether one is leading a good life. The ideology of freedom as such is hostile to all forms of state involvement (which needs to be reduced to a minimum) and prizes a life of market success. Here it is at least arguable that market freedom is coming to resemble a totalitarian ideology. The poor become the waste products of the system, social limits to market ideology are readily dismissed and inequalities are becoming increasingly pronounced. As Tzvetan Todorov (2011) argues the attempts to balance ideas of the good against one another are abandoned through the assumption that freedom equals market freedom. Neoliberalism presses a one-eyed view of the world reducing ideas of political pluralism to the idea of gaining freedom through the market. Here democracy, welfare and the environment are increasingly subject to the logic of the balance sheet. Further this logic increasingly impresses itself into the inner life of citizens as everyone is encouraged to take 'personal' responsibility for their own affairs and subject their actions to cost benefit forms of analysis.

If Orwell warned that the conformity of state domination would produce power worship and fearful conformity the age of the market is where we learn to be remorselessly positive while subjecting our decisions to the calculator. The Orwellian world of mind control has not disappeared. The development of neoliberalism, new technologies of communication and more cognitive therapies focused on positive thinking are all part of the same matrix of control. If neoliberalism advocates thin citizenship and a life of consumption, new technologies are mainly driven by advertising and the market while positive forms of thinking seek to banish darker thoughts and ideas of unrest. The world of restless faced paced journalism, mobile phones and the commodification of the self fails to deliver what it promises. Mostly these features leave unquestioned the rule of capital, the down grading of democracy and the col-lapse of the environment. As Jodie Dean (2009) argues the claim that the development of a world of computers, mobile phones and the rapid expansion of television screens has had a radical democratising effect needs to be care-fully criticised. By communicative capitalism Deane means the emergence of a society built upon the spectacle of consumption where what matters are that messages are passed on rather than interpreted and understood. This is a world where the flow of digital meanings has increasingly come to resemble the flow of commodities. The fantasy here is that by writing a blog or responding to a text message we are actually engaging in democracy. Indeed Deane is harshly critical of the American Left who rather than criticising the development of a hyper-capitalist society engage in a form of cyber-radicalism. Here the assump-tion is that the arrival of the new technological society has potentially offered everyone a voice and a platform. The over enthusiastic adoption of communi-cations technology has meant that the vastly unequal communicative power of the rich and powerful escapes criticism. The ideology of 'anyone can start a blog' displaces concern about a world where the most powerful communica-tions media continue to be run by corporate interests. As Robert McChesney (2008) argues that in terms of communications media the main paradox of our time is that there has been on the one hand a massive increase in communica-tions media and evidence of enhanced forms of civic withdrawal. Much of the new media content has not been driven by a renewal of civic activism but by the downgrading of journalism and the development of hyper-consumerism. This of course does not mean that if the digital economy collapsed tomorrow that there would be a sudden upsurge of democracy, but such features should at least begin the process of developing a more critical attitude towards tech-nology. Douglas Kellner (2003) has argued that visual media has become one of the central organising features of the economy. What Debord (1998) had origi-nally termed the society of the spectacle back in the 1960s is enhanced by the arrival of a new generation of mobile phones, I Pads, flat screen televisions, home cinemas and a host of other 'must have' technological gadgets all of which serves to impress the logic of capital into everyday life under the guise of 'harmless fun' and 'entertainment'. As the spectacle gains a grip on our soci-ety increasingly the way you look, style and the presentation of the self becomes the most important features. Further the love of money, celebrity and greed more generally are more powerful than other values such as social responsibility, justice and of course democracy. It is then market driven ideas and consumerism that have become society's dominant values.

Here those seeking to press for a more substantive democracy can-not of course be seen to become anti-technological. Such a position would indeed prove to be self-defeating. However it is the job of an anti-authoritarian Left to point to some of the democratic limitations of the technologically driven society. As Hirshkop (1998) argues the cyber-enthusiasts who argue that new technology would lead to a wave of newly engaged citizens have under-estimated the extent to which the dominant capitalist society is instrumental in the creation and construction of new knowledge and popular realities. That is it is the needs of the economic system rather than citizens that is dominant in the construction of the media system. If capitalism requires a weak democracy and generally passive citizens then the attempt to open up spaces of dissent, passionate exchange and a more questioning attitude will require more contested forms of culture than exist in the context of the present. Similar to the comments made by Dean (2009) a new wave of democratic thinking, resistance and critical questioning will not be simply handed to us by technology but will require a much broader based citizen movement for change. If this were to emerge as Hirschkop (1998) suggests then cyber-technologies would inevitably have a role to play, but without such a movement much computer technology much of the time is likely to serve the interests of capitalism. As Castoriadis (1997, 394) argues if we seek to answer the question as to why we prefer the democratic life to one fostered by hyper-consumption then we can-not point to a 'foundation' in human nature, but we can argue that such a project is as socially and historically constructed as hyper-capitalism. Here the struggle for the democratic and good society always has to take place under less than perfect conditions. However, while recognising the inevitability of constraints, Castoriadis (1997 415) continues, we also need to recognise that the progressive privatization and commodification of public (and virtual) space has handed over power to powerful elites and vested interests. As Castoriadis argues, the economic system,

> seems to have succeeded in fabricating the type of individual that 'corresponds' to it: perpetually distracted, zapping from one pleasure [jouissance] to another, without memory or project, ready to respond to every solicitation of an economic machine that is increasingly destroying the planet's biosphere in order to produce illusions called commodities.
>
> IBID., 415

In other words, capitalism is already pushing up against its bio-physical limits with the long term sustainability of a society built upon consumerism increasing the need for a more democratic alternative. Thinking over the long term a society continually being 'enchanted' through new technological gadgets cannot last in the longer term. The demand for a more self-critical life requires new forms of public space that are not dominated by the spectacle where these questions can be asked and different alternatives imagined. As David Orr (2009) suggests such features not only ask that we reimagine ourselves in terms of a wider web of life, but also ask that we seek to develop a new way of life where we seek to take responsibility for generations yet to come. This is a crucial question, and yet what is not clear is how this can be turned into an urgent issue. Here Orr points attempts to use less, construct community gardens, develop low carbon lifestyles and other features, but the question remains how to give the future a voice. Here we will need a new generation of film makers, media activists, artists and cultural commentators seeking to imagine the life available for generations to come in a world dominated by the spectacle. These new forms of culture would need to find cultural narratives beyond the usual shock and awe tactics of advertising that leave the consumer shaken but not enlightened. If the new digital citizen is restless and on the move then more critical and ecologically orientated citizens will need to become more future orientated and learn to think over longer time frames than is common at present. This will only be possible if there is a substantial renewal of democratic thinking that aims to ask tough questions of capitalist modernity and encourages citizens to live in ways that recognise our shared vulnerability.

Such features will not be delivered by a new wave of shiny eye catching gadgets. However if the media relentlessly focuses our attention on what is happening right now it also has a nostalgic orientation. If 24 hour news and continual updates focuses the attention of citizens on the immediate then the post-modern re-running of television programmes from a previous era gives the media a nostalgic aura. This is also evident in the new Conservative-Liberal coalition government in the UK. There is an attempt by the government to return Britain to the 'security' of a pervious era when elites ruled for the good of everyone and the state was shrunken down to the levels before so called new Labour excess. What we are nostalgic for seemingly is a world where the lower orders knew their place and there was a proper deference to those in authority. This can be seen in the overt elitism of some of the cuts to the arts and libraries budgets as the presumption seems to be that only the well-heeled middle-classes use such services. The arts budget is being cut by 30% and the BBCs by 16% in the so called age of austerity (Edgar 2012, Toynbee 2012). The programme of government austerity has generally attacked the provision of the public sector and yet the power of large conglomerations remains unchecked. Recently the Leveson committee investigated the so called 'free' press in the wake of a widely reported phone hacking scandal. Despite public out-cry and revulsion at malpractice there is little chance of the inquiry focusing on the ownership and control of a mostly Right wing and capitalist run press. Instead the 'media storm' created around the phone hacking scandal is busy searching for individuals to blame. While the printed word is in long term decline it is highly unlikely that the current neoliberal government will call for the break-up of the corporate press. While the scandal did prevent the government handing overall control of Sky television to Rupert Murdoch the long term trajectory of the media industry remains away from public control to corporate ownership. The current down-sizing of the BBC (public broadcasting network) and public arts organisations ultimately presses a model of commercial culture for the masses and artistic culture for elites. This trajectory is especially evident in terms of the cuts to higher education spending and the reform of the education system more generally which will inevitably push working-class students in a vocational direction while maintaining 'choice' for the most privileged. Further the development of academy and so called 'free' schools where educational institutions are largely removed from public and democratic and accountable forms of control with increase power given to school heads (and the government) to control the labour of teachers.

The austerity government using the 'fig leaf' of economic necessity (so far escaping the need to increase the tax burden of the wealthy, close tax loop holes, cancel expensive weapons systems and scale back imperial ambitions) has actually seen a concerted attempt on the part of ruling elites to roll-back the existing democratic settlement and re-inscribe the rule of elites. The lack of power of the working-class movements and the re-emergence of deference has seen renewed attacks on the ability of ordinary citizens to gain a decent and comprehensive education, attacks on the welfare state and cuts in the public sector more generally. It is in this context perhaps that cyber-optimism and the celebration of the democratizing effect of new technology looks increasingly misplaced.

These more hierarchical and overtly class ridden times perhaps find their best expression in popular television. There has been increasing amount of concern demonstrated by cultural critics for the ways in which popular drama and so-called reality television focuses on the 'shameless' lifestyles of working-class people. The popular use of the derogative term 'chav' has rightly been criticised for the evident class racism that lies behind the representation of lower class people who are presumed to have neither taste nor a sense of common morality (Jones 2011). Poor working-class people are the Other of the new consumer democracy where it is presumed that we can all find an equal voice on the internet. More nostalgically the popularity of television series such as 'Downton Abbey' and 'Upstairs Downstairs' continue to speak of an English obsessions with the cultural codes of class where the lower orders are fixed into place and status distinctions are more definite than they are today. This also links into the new wave of popularity being experienced by the British Royal Family (evident in last year's Royal Wedding and the coming Jubilee celebrations) which continues to be the state organised spectacle that celebrates the continuation of class hierarchy. Class hierarchy and deference then have made a come-back in the age of increasingly powerful elites and the diminishing case being made for democratic forms of accountability.

However in terms of the communications and public sphere there are a number of political and cultural developments that offer hope for a more emancipated future. The first is in the revival of critical documentary film making. Work by Michael Moore and Morgan Spurlock and others has been very suggestive in terms of the ways in which documentary can become the site of democratic practice. Through the use of humour, montage and the displacement of more 'objectivist' accounts documentary film in some of its guises offers the possibility of genuinely democratic forms of criticism. In the British context, recent films by Ken Loach (Spirit of 45) and Fanny Armstrong (The Age of Stupid) have sought to open up questions concerning the power of corporations, democratic criticism and responsibility for the environment in the context of global climate change. This work is often used by educators and social movements seeking to develop more critical ideas and sustain debate outside the dominance of the mainstream media. Further there have been other possibilities for critical protest opened up by the revival of anarchism. Anarchist arguments concerning the violence of the state, the undesirability of hierarchy and control from above has led to the explicit development of more autonomous social movements engaging in direct forms of action. The global development of Occupy and other groups like UK Uncut have all explicitly rejected the idea that political opposition requires leaders. The idea of direct action and decentralised decision making has a long history of being critical of the kinds of intellectual hierarchy that often inspire more Marxist or trade union led opposition (Ward 1973). Further the anarchist tradition has long criticised the ways in which deference to established forms of authority not only blind people to their own creative potential but equally strangles dissent within authoritarian contexts of control. The possibility (if not the probability) of creating a new society is prefigured by more everyday encounters that mostly depend upon co-operation and mutuality than control from above or competitive individualism.

Many of the groups inspired by these ideas have used new technological forms like facebook and twitter to organise themselves in less hierarchical ways. As Joss Hands (2011) argues the more horizontal possibilities suggested by new media have been effectively utilised by many different movements and networks seeking to develop less top down forms of mobilisation. Further new media networks have helped to develop a shared cultural commons on the internet that is often more democratic in orientation than more centrally controlled publications. However as Joss Hands (2011) also points out new media can still be used in more centralised ways and is no guarantee of more democratised forms of practice. However we need to recognise along with David Graeber (2002:61) that much of the 'creative energy for radical politics' is coming from autonomous movements using humour, theatre and other cultural forms to suggest more grass roots versions of democratic practice and argument. Like the documentary film makers I described above much of the protest is creative, explicitly criticises different kinds of violence and aims through its practise to demonstrate what a more politically and democratically engaged society might look like. Rather than deferring to elites or bureaucratic agreements the new cultures of protest capture what a more emancipated and non-violent society in the process of becoming. Here there is a sense of hope that more direct forms of action on the part of citizens can begin to carve out both real and virtual spaces whereby the rule of capital and an increasingly repressive state can be questioned and confronted. If indeed new forms of class hierarchy are being imposed by neoliberalism from above they are most effectively challenged by arguments and critical practices from below that seek to develop associations and networks that have broken with pyramid like structures. These arguments suggest a utopia yet to come far beyond the reaffirmation of the rule of capital and a security driven state. As James C. Scott (2012) argues it is unreasonable to expect citizens who live in a class dominated society increasingly based upon hierarchical forms of control from above to suddenly become critical citizens in the public sphere. If the dominant model of citizenship depends upon voting for a particular political party every four years and then becoming passive it is not surprising that many people are uninterested in politics. In increasingly economically insecure and impoverished times many people use what reserves they have simply trying to survive. Further the dominance of experts and elected politicians on television news often hiding behind ideas of 'neutrality' serves to disempower many citizens. As Scott (2012:127) argues there exists within most Western democracies a huge 'antipolitics machine' this effectively takes debate out of the hands of ordinary citizens suggesting it is only a matter for the elite decision. More democratic and participatory forms of engagement however can act as an alternative form of education suggesting that citizens are capable of making decisions and formulating arguments for themselves. However this becomes a difficult (if not impossible achievement) where many people are prevented from using their own discretion and creativity by the kinds of control that exist within most large organisations across the public and private sector.

As I have sought to argue cyber-optimism continues to mask the continuation and entrenchment of class hierarchies within media and education. Capitalist consumerism continues to empower the voices and perspectives of elites, turn the poor into an Other while laying waste to the environment. If the Left are to begin the process of talking about democratic alternatives to the current crisis it would need to build a more substantive oppositional movement developing shared spaces of dissent and criticism. Such features will require a new democratic cultural imaginary that is both critical of the way of life offered by neoliberalism and a new sensibility that speaks as much about justice as it does about sustainability. Of course in this process citizens would need to discover new uses for communications technology and most pressing of all a new passion for democratic forms of engagement. This is why in the final analysis it is less a case of being against technology than the way it is currently shaped by capitalism. However lest we become too pessimistic in our analysis there is much to learn from the re-emergence of Anarchist ideas that might yet led to more inventive forms of protest and civic involvement in the future. The historian Peter Linebaugh (2014) has reminded us of the similarity between our time and that of the eighteenth century dominated by forced acts of enclosure when peasants were thrown off common land. The violent acts of enclosure which began the rule of capital are being replicated today as increasing areas of social life are being turned into a factory where capital rules and workers are controlled from above. In these times of austerity, deference and authoritarian rule from above it has become increasingly urgent that citizens learn new tactics of dissent. Undoubtedly technology will have a role to play in this process, but so will the necessity of courage, defiance and intelligent criticism. Rebecca Solnit (2004) argues that even when faced with the darkness that hope remains a permanent possibility, but it does require action. There have been times in the past when the ruling elite have seemed even more powerful than they are today. If the official media landscape is increasingly under the control of corporations and political elites then we should also remember that the Arab Spring, Occupy and other grass roots movements remind us that we are not without hope. As a peace activist in the early 1980s people often told me that the Cold War would go on for ever. That I was wasting my time marching against nuclear weapons and there was nothing I could do against the might of the great super powers. It is of course always easier to give into those voices than it is to risk action based upon human rather than technological hope.

References

Castoriadis, Cornelius. 1997. Done to be Done. In The Castoriadis Reader, ed. David A. Curtis, 361–417. Oxford: Blackwell.

Dean, Jodi. 2009. Democracy and Other Neoliberal Fantasies: Communicative Capitalism and Left Politics. Durham and London: Duke University Press.

Debord, Guy. 1998. Comments on the Society of the Spectacle. London: Verso.

Edgar, David. 2012. Why Should We Fund the Arts? The Guardian, January 5 http://www.theguardian.com/culture/2012/jan/05/david-edgar-why-fund-the-arts (accessed January 5, 2012).

Graeber, David. 2002. The New Anarchists. New Left Review 13, Jan Feb, 61–73.

Hands, Joss. 2011 @ Is for Activism, London, Pluto Press.

Hirschkop, Ken. 1998. Democracy and New Technologies. In Capitalism and the Information Age: The Political Economy of the Global Communication Revolution, eds. Robert W. McChesney, Ellen Meiksins Wood, and John Bellamy Foster, 207–217. New York: Monthly Review Press.

Jones, Own. 2011. Chavs: The Demonisation of the Working Class. London: Verso.

Kellner, Douglas. 2003. Media Spectacle. London: Routledge.

Linebaugh, Peter. 2014. Stop Thief! The Commons, Enclosures and Resistance, Oakland, Spectre.

McChesney, Robert. 2008. The Political Economy of Media. New York: Monthly Review Press.

Orr, David. 2009. Down the Wire. Oxford: Oxford University Press.

Orwell, George. 1968a. Writers and Leviation. In The Collected Essays, Journalism and Letters of George Orwell, Volume IV, eds. Sonia Orwell and Ian Angus, 407–414. London: Secker and Warberg.

Orwell, George. 1968b. Letter to Frances A. Henson. In The Collected Essays, Journalism and Letters of George Orwell, Volume IV, eds. Sonia Orwell and Ian Angus, 62. London: Secker and Warberg.

Orwell, George. 1999. Nineteen Eighty-Four. London: Secker and Warberg.

Scott, James. C. 2012. Two Cheers for Anarchism, New Jersey, Princeton University Press.

Solnit, Rebecca.2004. Hope in the Dark, New York, Cannongate.

Todorov, Tzvetan. 2011. The Totalitarian Experience. London: Seagull.

Toynbee, Polly. 2012. How the Badly Maimed BBC Can Stand Up to Parasitic Sky. The Guardian, January 2. http://www.theguardian.com/commentisfree/2012/jan/02/maimed-bbc-parasitic-sky (accessed January 5, 2012).

Ward, Colin. 1973. Anarchy in Action, London, Freedom Press.

CHAPTER 6

Infamy and Indoctrination in American Media and Politics

Arthur Asa Berger

Practice

As I sit at my computer, writing this article, on January 9, 2012, Republican presidential candidates in New Hampshire are insulting one-another at town-meetings in New Hampshire, having bickered with one another in a dozen so-called 'debates' between the candidates held in various sites in the United States.

The Republican Debates

The first primary of the American presidential election will be held tomorrow and Mitt Romney, a multi-millionaire entrepreneur who was governor of Massachusetts for one term, is expected to win by a large margin. He won the caucuses in Iowa by only eight votes, which was a victory in one sense and a loss in another. After the primary in New Hampshire, the action moves to South Carolina, where the next primary will take place.

And what have American's learned from watching these debates? Mostly that none of the Republicans running for the presidency trust Romney and they don't like one another. They believe he is really a moderate and the Republicans want (or think they want) a 'true' conservative, whatever that is. During the campaign, when the 'anyone but Romney' feeling was strong, a variety of candidates momentarily led the field, only to flame out and be replaced by another candidate. Herman Cain, a former pizza executive who boasted that he had no political experience at all, led for a while and entranced Republicans with his 9-9-9 plan. It soaked the poor and middle classes but was great from the wealthy – like all Republican plans. But when a number of women who claim they had had affairs with Cain attracted media attention, Cain 'suspended' his campaign. When Rick Perry, the governor of Texas, entered the contest, he immediately became the front runner, but that only lasted until he participated in the debates and stumbled terribly, showing that he was not ready for 'prime time', and for the presidency. He had a famous 'oops' moment on television when he could only name two of the three governmental departments he would eliminate when he became president. He still has a lot of money to spend on advertising from his billionaire backers but now seems to be irrelevant.

Next came Newt Gingrich. He has been divorced twice and worked as a lobbyist (it was discovered) but conservatives were willing to forgive him because they though he could stand up to Obama in debates and because he actually had some ideas about the economy and other topics. Gingrich comes across on television as smug, nasty and hostile. His claim to fame was shutting down the United States government when he was Speaker of the House. While Romney spent his time attacking President Obama, a Super PAC (Political Action Committee) full of former staffers and others sympathetic to Romney spent three million dollars attacking Gingrich, which more or less destroyed his lead and his candidacy. Super PACS can spend money however they want but they cannot coordinate with the candidates. This left Rick Santorum, who spent the better part of a year in Iowa, as the only candidate standing, more or less, and he almost defeated Romney in Iowa. Santorum was defeated soundly when he ran for his seat in the Senate a number of years ago but that seemed to be of no concern to him or his backers.

The last two Republican debates in New Hampshire were notable because of the poor questioning by the moderators in the first one and the expressions of loathing by Gingrich towards Romney and the attacks by all the other Republican candidates on Romney in the second. Assuming Romney wins News Hampshire and South Carolina, he will have more or less assured himself of getting the nomination. He has offered an economic plan that, when analyzed, also was very beneficial to the 'rich, well-born and able', and which, like so many other Republican plans, took money from poor people and the middle classes and transferred it to the wealthy.

Gingrich argues that Romney, despite his claims, actually is a 'career politician' (which Republicans think isn't something to be proud of) and has been running for president for a dozen years. Gingrich pointed out that Romney spent 200 days out of the state of Massachusetts when he was governor running for president, and that his performance in the business world as head of Bain Capital wasn't anything to boast about. The other candidates attacked Romney on every front, arguing that he was really a moderate claiming to be a conservative and that he 'flip-flopped' on everything – that is, he didn't stand for anything except running for president, but he brushed off the attacks, saying he's used to being attacked and has 'broad shoulders'. It looks like conservative Republicans will have to grit their teeth and vote for him unless there is a third party conservative candidate. The debates were characterized by self-promoting comments by each of the candidates on their achievements, and by attacks on each other when not attacking Romney.

The Press and the Debates

Meanwhile, journalists, politicians and other so-called experts, have spent endless hours and written numerous columns and articles speculating about any and every aspect of the debates and the participants in them. The subtext of my report is that the election of the American president is now a multi-year media event. Because the United States is so large, the fight for the presidency is now, in large measure, waged on television, with attack advertisements and commercials by Democratic and Republican Super PACS and 'positive' or 'vision' advertising by the candidates. Obama is expected to have close to a billion dollars for his campaign and Romney (or whoever the Republican nominee is) and the Republicans will also have enormous amounts of money. Generally speaking, because Republicans own many newspapers and television stations, Republican candidates for office have had a considerable advantage over Democrats in elections at every level of government.

January 11, 2012

It is January 11. Mitt Romney won 'big' in New Hampshire, getting 38% of the votes in the Republican primary. He gave a victory speech attacking Obama as a 'failed' president who wants to bring a European-style welfare state to America. Ron Paul, a libertarian who is far outside of mainstream Republicanism, finished second with 22% of the votes and Jon Huntsman, who had staked his campaign on New Hampshire, finished third, with 17% of the votes. A billionaire casino-owner and long time friend of Gingrich sent a check for $5 million dollars to 'Winning Our Future', a Super PAC full of Gingrich supporters, which led the *New York Times* to write (Jan. 10, 2012, page 1) "The last-minute injection underscores how last year's Supreme Court ruling [that allowed Super PACS] has made it possible for a wealthy individual to influence an election." (Confessore and Lipton 2007). Gingrich's Super PAC is spending the money to buy $3.4 million dollars worth of time on South Carolina's television stations to attack Romney and his record at Bain Capital. The money is also being spent producing a 30 minute anti-Romney film.

The action now moves to South Carolina, a state that is much more conservative than New Hampshire, where Romney faces a more difficult task. Polls suggest he has a big lead there but we cannot know what impact that attacks from Gingrich and other Republicans running for the nomination will have on Romney's fortunes in South Carolina. Most pundits suggest that if Romney wins in South Carolina, he will get the nomination. He has taken pains to present himself as the inevitable Republican candidate and barring a big surprise in South Carolina, it looks like he was right in doing so.

January 12, 2012

The Republican candidates are now in South Carolina, a more religious and conservative state than New Hampshire. Gingrich is running ads saying that Romney was in favor of abortion and showed he was when he was governor of Massachusetts, and other Republican candidates are attaching Romney as a 'vulture' capitalist, who looted companies and destroyed countless jobs. Romney claims he created 100,000 jobs, but there is no way of determining how accurate this claim is. Romney has $19 million in his campaign chest and many Super PACs that support him have millions to use to attack the other Republicans in the race and President Obama.

If Rick Perry or Newt Gingrich don't do extremely well in South Carolina, and that seems to be the likely outcome, it is fair to say that they have no chance of securing the nomination. Ron Paul, who is running as an agitator and championing his Libertarian cause, will probably continue to participate in the primaries. He has no hope of winning the nomination but he wants to be able to help influence the Republican party's policies and agenda.

I will finish this section of this article after the results from South Carolina and Florida come in. By then, if Romney wins, the remaining candidates (aside from Ron Paul) will be in a hopeless position. Many Americans consider the lineup of Republicans running for the nomination to be second rate. Some have suggested that the 'best' Republican candidates didn't run because they were afraid the Republican party has become so ultra-conservative (right-wing) that they would be forced by the members of the Tea Party and others to adopt positions they don't like. The Republican party is now full of socially conservative and not highly educated blue-collar workers and a relatively small number of upper-class people who don't like to pay taxes. The image many Americans had of their country as a classless, all-middle class country (with minor exceptions at the top and bottom) has been revealed to be an illusion as information about the economic inequality in the United States became more widespread.

January 19, 2012

Rick Perry, the 'oops' candidate, suspended his participation in the race and threw his support to Newt Gingrich. Perry was a 'dead man walking', and it was only a matter of time before he realized he was in a hopeless situation. He was leading the Republican candidates until he opened his mouth. Yesterday, Mitt Romney revealed he pays taxes at the 15% level, which is about half of what most middle class Americans pay. He pays at this level because most of his income is from investments and is taxed at that level. The other Republicans who are running are putting pressure on Romney to release his tax reports so people can see how wealthy he is and where he gets most of his income. Romney is reportedly worth around $250 million. There is also news of a recount in Iowa that would give Santorum the win – by some 38 votes. But things are a mess in Iowa as far as the recounting of votes is concerned and nobody knows whether Santorum or Romney came in first.

A recent poll showed Romney ahead of Gingrich by ten percent but Perry's decision to 'suspend' his candidacy and his decision to support Gingrich may allow Gingrich to come very close to Romney. Sarah Palin also indicated, indirectly, that she liked Gingrich and he said that if he became president, he'd find an important place for her in his administration. But Palin doesn't like to work; she loves making money as a media celebrity and issuing comments about politics, from time to time.

I will end my comments on the Republican candidates when the results from South Carolina and Florida come in. Most Americans consider the field of candidates the Republicans put forth as extremely weak, except, perhaps, for Huntsman (who suspended his candidacy a number of days ago, saying he found the experience of running for the presidency 'toxic' and supporting fellow Mormon, Romney) and Romney. Huntsman didn't contest in Iowa and the good people of Vermont put him third, even though Huntsman had spent months in New Hampshire and participated in something like 140 events. Huntsman's father is a billionaire and helped his son a bit. Romney has a problem of seeming to have no core beliefs, other than a talent for and love of making money and an idée fixe – an all-powerful, all-consuming desire to be president. His candidacy raises the question – why shouldn't a multi-millionaire who has been on both sides of most major political issues – become

president? Should we hold his wealth against him? He keeps arguing that he's
a success and American should reward success, not look down on it.

January 23, 2012

A funny thing happened to Mitt Romney on the way to his coronation. He lost
South Carolina by 12 percentage points (Gingrich gained 40 percent of the vote
and Romney 28 percent) and all of a sudden, Romney looks like he is in big
trouble. Even people who though the most important issue was being able to
defeat Barack Obama voted for Gingrich, and he beat Romney with just about
every other socio-cultural group in the state. Romney led by double digits in
polls conducted a few days before the election. But Gingrich performed well in
the debates just before the election – attacking the media for asking him about
his adultery and Romney for not posting his tax returns – and Romney didn't
do well at all, and so now it looks like Romney's house of cards may come tum-
bling down. His national lead has collapsed and, as I write this, Gingrich has
momentum and could possibly win in Florida. Romney was fortunate in that
100,000 Floridians already voted by mail – when Romney's aura of invincibility
hadn't been shattered. Now, he may lose in Florida, even though he has a great
deal of money and a large staff in the state. If Romney wins in Florida, Gingrich
will have a much more difficult time getting the nomination.

If Romney loses, the battle to win the nomination between Romney and
Gingrich could last for many months. It is even conceivable that the Republican
establishment, which is terrified of Gingrich winning the nomination (since he
would alienate many independents, who will ultimately determine who wins
the presidency) may induce someone else to come in – though that would be
extremely difficult. Gingrich's Super PAC also got another $5 million from the
wife of the billionaire who gave it $5 million earlier, and Gingrich got another
$1 million from people who support him. The airwaves in Florida are now full
of dueling radio ads and television commercials in which Gingrich and Romney
attack one another, and there are countless robotic-telephone calls being made
and millions of letters full of campaign literature being sent out on behalf of
the two leading candidates. Santorum, who has been described as a 'choir boy',
is no longer a significant factor in the race – or so it seems.

January 31, 2012

Romney spent five times as much money (sixteen million dollars) in Florida
as Gingrich did and defeated him soundly. And so, it looks like the loss in

South Carolina was just a bump in the road for Romney, who also had a very strong organization in Florida as well as help from the Republican establishment. He can now resume the narrative he was carefully generating as the "inevitable" Republican candidate. Newt Gingrich vowed to fight on all the way to the Republican convention. The question we must consider now is whether the Republican candidates have damaged themselves so much that they are going to be defeated by Obama with relative ease. Rick Santorum describe the battle between the Republicans as a 'mud wrestling' match, but he is essentially irrelevant, though he vows to continue to campaign. The turnout in Florida was a bit low this year, which suggests a lack of enthusiasm for the Republican candidates and twenty percent of the Republican voters indicated that they would have preferred to have other candidates to consider.

Now it is time to move from practice to theory and the relation of the mass media to politics.

Theory

The problem Democrats face (generally speaking) is exacerbated by the amount of consolidation in the media, which is owned, as a rule, by conservative Republicans (see Table 6.1).

TABLE 6.1   *Top 10 media conglomerates, 2010*

Conglomerate	Revenues in billions of dollars
Comcast/NBC Universal	41.33
Walt Disney	28.71
Murdoch News Company	24.73
Viacom/CBS	20.54
Time Warner	20.28
Sony	16.09
Bertelsmann	15.79
Vivendi	12.45
Cox	11.01
Thomson Reuters	9.86[1]

Problems Caused by Media Consolidation

Because of the consolidation of media properties, we now have relatively small number of media conglomerates that control enormous numbers of book publishers, newspapers, radio stations, and television stations. They promote Republicans who pass legislation that is favorable to the conglomerates. Fox News can be considered a branch of the Republican Party because it is so partisan in its coverage of events. It is owned by Rupert Murdoch, who also owns the *Wall Street Journal.*

Ben Bagdikian, formerly dean of the School of Journalism at the University of California in Berkeley, called our attention to this matter a number of years ago. He writes:

> In 1982, when I completed research for my book, 50 corporations controlled half or more of the media business. By December 1986, when I finished a revision for a second edition, the 50 had shrunk to 29. The last time I counted, it was down to 26. [When the latest edition of *The Media Monopoly* was published in 1993, the number was down to 20.] A number of serious Wall Street media analysts are predicting that by the 1990s, a half-dozen giant firms will control most of our media. Of the 1,700 daily papers, 98 percent are local monopolies and fewer than 15 corporations control most of the country's daily circulation. A handful of firms have most of the magazine business, with alone accounting for about 40 percent of that industry's revenues (1987).

This consolidation also has taken place in other areas connected to the media. For example, there are now just four or five giant global advertising corporations that own most of the important advertising agencies. Companies that want to hire advertising agencies now demand, in many cases, that they be part of these global conglomerates so the advertisers can have a global reach.

This control of the media is counteracted, to some degree, by the development of social media sites such as Facebook and Twitter. During the debates, there were many running blogs and Twitter accounts of the debates and political and other events are now widely read and debated in the blogosphere and social media. What impact, short term and long range, Tweets and comments on Facebook will have on political life in America remains to be seen.

The Question of Media Effects

There is a dilemma we face when thinking about the media: we cannot "prove" that they have significant and long term effects, but you only have to look at elections to recognize that the media play an all-important role now in the political process in America. This problem of media effects was dealt with by Denis McQuail:

> The entire study of mass communication is based on the premise that the media have significant effects, yet there is little agreement on the nature and extent of these assumed effects. This uncertainty is the more surprising since everyday experience provides countless, if minor, examples of influence. We dress for the weather as forecast, buy something because of an advertisement, go to a film mentioned in a newspaper, react in countless ways to media news, to films, to music on the radio, and so on. There are many reported cases of negative media publicity concerning, for instance, food contamination or adulteration, leading to significant changes in food consumption behaviour. Our minds are full of media-derived information and impressions. We live in a world saturated by media sounds and images, where politics, government and business operate on the assumption that we know what is going on in the wider world. Few of us cannot think of some personal instance of gaining significant information or of forming an opinion because of the media (1994, 327).

Right now, *The New York Times* and many other newspapers are full of analyses of the Republican debates and speculations about what will happen in the primaries in other states and what the Romney candidacy means, assuming he wins the nomination, for the Republican party. In the past, the Republicans have been able to get many blue-collar and white-collar voters to vote against the economic interests in social issues such as abortion or gun rights.

Whether these social issues will work now, when the American economy is in bad shape and when reports on the distribution of income in the United States show that a small percentage of the public owns most of the country, remains to be seen. Newspapers have carried reports recently on the fact that social mobility in the United States lags behind social mobility in a number of other countries. The so-called 'American Dream' no longer is operative and the notion people had that they could succeed if they had enough 'luck, pluck, and virtue' has been shown to be just that – a dream. The 'Occupy Wall Street' movement brought the unequal distribution of wealth to the attention of the American public.

The Problems of Privatism and Hegemonial Ideological Domination

Some media theorists have argued that one reason the Republicans win is that large percentage of Republicans, who tend to be white and well to do, vote and smaller percentages of Democrats, who tend to be people of color and poor, vote. It is only when people of color and poor people vote in large numbers that the Democrats win. This happened last in 2008 when Obama was elected president. One reason that many people don't vote is that they don't recognize the impact that elections have on their lives. Another reason in what I describe as 'privatism'.

Privatism argues that viewers of television and other media focus their attention on their own lives and personal concerns, especially as they participate in consumer culture, and neglect social matters and the public realm. The media help generate materialism. Thus, for example, many people know little about our history, but know everything about pop culture celebrities and have incredible 'product knowledge' (learned from advertising). This privatism or lack of interest in politics on the part of the general public means that small groups that are politically motivated and organized, like the Tea Party, exercise inordinate power over our political agenda. Many people do not vote in elections because they are all wrapped up in themselves, so the argument goes, and can't be bothered with anything else, even though decisions made by elected officials affect their lives in important ways.

Another reason is that we are "victims," so to speak, of hegemonial domination. The British media theorist Raymond Williams, in his book Marxism and literature, the used the term "hegemony" to describe the process by which the ruling classes shaped the consciousness of the masses. Williams distinguished between rule, which is political, and hegemony. As he explained:

> Hegemony is then not only the articulate upper level of 'ideology', nor are its forms of control only those ordinarily seen as 'manipulation' or 'indoctrination'. It is a whole body of practices and expectations, over the whole of our living: our senses, our assignments of energy, our shaping perceptions of ourselves and our world. It is a lived system of meaning and values – constitutive and constituting – which as they are experienced as

practices appear as reciprocally confirming. It thus constitutes a sense of reality for most people in the society, a sense of the absolute because experienced reality beyond which it is very difficult for most members of the society to move, in most areas of their lives (1978, 110).

We can characterize 'hegemonial ideological domination' as that 'which goes without saying'. We are dominated but cannot recognize that this is the case because it is ubiquitous and seems to be nothing more than common sense. This domination has the function of helping maintain the status quo and solidifying the role of the ruling classes in society.

Another Perspective: Grid-Group Theory

Let me offer another theory that will help explain the relations between media and politics in the United States – Grid-Group theory. Let me explain what Grid-Group theory is by quoting from a book, *Cultural Theory*, written by Michael Thompson, Richard Ellis and Aaron Wildavsky:

> Our theory has a specific point of departure: the Grid-Group typology proposed by Mary Douglas. She argues that the variability of an individual's involvement with social life can be adequately captured by two dimensions of sociality: group and grid. *Group* refers to the extent to which an individual is incorporated in bounded units. The greater the incorporation, the more the individual is subject to group determination. *Grid* denotes to the degree to which an individual's life is circumscribed by externally imposed prescriptions. The more binding and extensive the scope of the prescriptions, the less of life that is open to individual negotiation (1990, 5).

What Grid-Group Theory argues, then, is that our behavior is shaped by two different forces: one is the 'strength of the groups' to which we belong (and the amount of control they have over us) and the other is the 'number of rules and prescriptions' to which we are subject. The group boundaries can be very strong or relatively weak and the number of rules and prescriptions can be few in number or numerous. This theory derives from the work of social anthropologist Mary Douglas.

Thus, Catholic priests have strong group boundaries and many rules, while Reform rabbis have weaker group boundaries and fewer rules. Soldiers in the United States Army and other military branches have strong boundaries and many rules. Armies are hierarchical with a very strong and elaborated chain of command. People who belong to sports clubs have weak group boundaries and few rules. It isn't difficult to join them and they don't have many rules.

Douglas & Wildavsky (1982) explained why we form political cultures or, outside of politics,

what Mary Douglas describes as 'lifestyles:

> What matters to people is how they should live with other people. The great questions of social life are "Who am I?" (To what kind of a group do I belong?) and What should I do? (Are there many or few prescriptions I am expected to obey?). Groups are strong or weak according to whether they have boundaries separating them from others. Decisions are taken either for the group as a whole (strong boundaries) or for individuals or families (weak boundaries). Prescriptions are few or many indicating the individual internalizes a large or a small number of behavioral norms to which he or she is bound. By combining boundaries with prescriptions... the most general answers to the questions of social life can be combined to form four different political cultures (7).

In Table 6.2 below, I take these two dimensions, Grid and Group, and show how they lead to four different lifestyles depending on the strength or weakness of the group boundaries and number of rules and prescriptions.

Different theorists have given these lifestyles different names, but the names all suggest what it is that generates the lifestyle. The names for the lifestyles I've used were used by Aaron Wildavsky in his work on political cultures; Mary Douglas had different names for Egalitarians and Fatalists: Enclavists and Isolates.

TABLE 6.2   *Lifestyes, group boundaries and rules and prescriptions*

Lifestyle/Political cultures	Group boundaries	Numbers and kinds of prescriptions
Hierarchical elitists	Strong	Numerous and varied
Egalitarians (Enclavists)	Strong	Few
Competitive individualists	Weak	Few
Fatalist (Isolates)	Weak	Numerous and varied

Wildavsky explained how these groups are formed. He writes:

> Strong groups with numerous prescriptions that vary with social roles combine to form hierarchical collectivism. Strong groups whose members follow few prescriptions form an egalitarian culture, a shared life of voluntary consent, without coercion or inequality. Competitive individualism joins few prescriptions with weak boundaries, thereby encouraging ever new combinations. When groups are weak and prescriptions strong, so that decisions are made for them by people on the outside, the controlled culture is fatalistic
>
> WILDAVSKY 1989, 6.

Douglas used the term 'isolates' for Wildavsky's 'fatalists' and 'enclavists' for his 'egalitarians', and Wildavsky changed the terms he used at times. The important thing is that each of these groups can be located in the figure relative to their relationship to group boundaries and number of rules to which they are subject.

We must recognize that people are not aware of the fact that they are in one of Douglas' 'lifestyles' or Wildavsky's 'political cultures'. The important point for Grid-Group theorists is that our everyday lives and the decisions we make about all kinds of different things are shaped, to a considerable extent, by our Grid-Group affiliations or lifestyles. In her seminal article In Defence of Shopping, Douglas (Table 6.3) offers some insights into the nature of each lifestyle and points out that an acceptance of one lifestyle involves a rejection of the three other lifestyles.

Douglas argues that there are four and only four lifestyles and each is in competition with the three others, and they all need each other in order to function. There is movement possible between lifestyles, though the fatalists/

TABLE 6.3   *Nature of lifestyles*

Individualist	Hierarchical elitist	Egalitarian	Isolates
High Tech	Formal	Simplicity	Withdrawn
Sporty	Traditions	Not formal	Unpredictable
Arty	Established institutions	Anti-authoritarian	Few Friends
Competitive	Family network basic	Intimate friendships	Alienated
Open Network		Spiritual values	

isolates are generally at the bottom rung of the economic ladder and rely on luck to get them out of their lifestyle.

What grid-group theory claims is that many of our decisions about who to vote for, who to marry, what to buy when we go shopping, where to travel on vacations, what shows to watch on television, what movies to go to, ad infinitum, are shaped by unconscious imperatives found in our group memberships – that is, the lifestyles to which we adhere – that shape our behavior.

We must assume that people do not realize the source of much of their behavior. Aaron Wildavsky, who was a friend of mine, once said to me, 'Arthur... if people really understood why they did the things they do we would not have any need for psychologists, political scientists, economists, sociologists or any other kinds of social scientists'. People may think they know why they do things but their ideas about these matters are mistaken. This notion, that people don't really understand why they do things, explains why we have social scientists of all kinds as well as psychoanalysts and other kinds of therapists. Grid-Group theorists make the same argument, except that it is our social arrangements, the lifestyle groups to which we belong, and not our unconscious, that tends to shape our behavior.

Let me summarize the points I've made. First, Grid-Group theory suggests that individuals face two problems in establishing an identity: 'who am I?' and 'what should I do?' Second, they arrive at their identities by becoming members of groups – Douglas calls them 'lifestyles' and Wildavsky deals with 'political cultures' – with either very strong boundaries that contain them tightly or with weak boundaries that allow them to pass in and out of the group with ease. Third, they answer the second question by becoming members of groups that have either few rules or numerous and varied rules and prescriptions.

Douglas offers an important insight about these four cultural types in her article on shopping:

> None of these four lifestyles (individualist, hierarchical, enclavist, isolated) is new to students of consumer behaviour. What may be new and unacceptable is the point that these are the only four distinctive lifestyles to be taken into account, and the other point, that each is set up in competition with the others. Mutual hostility is the force that accounts for their stability (1997, 19)

These groups are important, Douglas suggests, because they shape our consumer choices.

It is our cultural alignments, she explains, that are the strongest predictors of our consumer preferences. When we are wandering around shopping

centers or doing any shopping we are, without being aware of the full significance of what we are doing, actualizing the lifestyle to which we are attached
and rejecting the kinds of choices made by members of other lifestyles. She
writes:

> We have to make a radical shift away from thinking about consumption
> as a manifestation of individual choices. Culture itself is the result of a
> myriad of individual choices, not primarily between commodities but
> between kinds of relationships. The basic choice a rational individual has
> to make is the choice about what kind of society to live in. According to
> that choice, the rest follows. Artefacts are selected to demonstrate that
> choice. Food is eaten, clothes are worn, cinema, books, music, holidays,
> all the rest are choices that conform with the initial choice for a form or
> society.
>
> IBID., 17

When she writes the word 'society' she is referring to lifestyles. Her thesis flies
in the face of those who argue that it is individual taste and preferences that
shape our decision making and consumer behavior. What seems to be individual taste, her argument suggests, is based on unconscious imperatives
located in the lifestyle to which people belong. What it more interesting,
according to her theory, cultural bias shapes our behavior. "Shopping," she
writes, "is agonistic – a struggle not to define what one is, but what one is not"
which means that shopping is, since we are rejecting other lifestyles, ultimately
an act of cultural defiance (Douglas 1997, 30). The kind of 'shopping' we are
interested in here involves 'buying into' one or another political candidates
and political parties.

Once we have selected a political culture, and we are not always aware that
we are doing so, everything else is shaped by the decision and our choices of
politicians follow almost mechanically. Since people can change their lifestyles, it is not possible to argue that they do not have freedom and all their
choices are "determined," but if Wildavsky is correct, most of our political decision making is shaped by our political cultures and our antipathy toward other
political cultures. What we must recognize is that, to a considerable extent, our
"choice" of a political culture, is shaped by our exposure to the mass media.

Wildavsky describes what kind of leadership we get from each of the four
political cultures:

> Under fatalistic regimes, leadership is *despotic* – continuous and total;
> under sectarian [egalitarian] regimes, leadership is ipso facto *inegalitarian*

and therefore illegitimate or it is *charismatic* – a legitimate ring of new law unlimited in scope. Hierarchic regimes have autocratic leaders; within their spheres they are supreme, but their scope is limited. Market regimes [individualist] are led by *meteoric* leaders who flame bright and burn out quickly – the right person in the right place at the right time for the right purpose!...The nature of the cultural theory I am expounding may become clearer if it is understood that power relations among participants constitute the political aspect (which I call regime) of its organizational structure (1989, 31).

So our decision-making in political campaigns is the result of many different factors, involving the media we consume which often determines the political cultures to which we belong. Where Mitt Romney and Barack Obama fit in the schema involving political cultures is somewhat ambiguous, but it would be fair to suggest that Obama and Democrats might be described as egalitarian and that Romney and Republicans would reflect some kind of combination of hierarchical elitist (he was born with, as we put it, "a silver spoon in his mouth") and individualist.

> Successful presidents tend to be emotionally secure. The have none of the social resentments and desperate needs that plagued men like Richard Nixon. Instead they were raised, often in an aristocratic family, with a sense that they were natural leaders of the nation. They were infused, often at an elite prep school, with a sense of obligation and responsibility to perform public service.
> BROOKS 2012

The growth in the number of independents in America (not Democrat, not Republican) can be explained as a kind of political culture identity confusion, as members of these political cultures find themselves torn between Individualists and Elitists, on the one hand, and Egalitarians, on the other.

These two political cultures tend to be the "establishment" in the United States with egalitarian Democrats functioning as loyal opposition. The election of 2012 will determine what kind of president we get and what kind of government we will have in the United States. The media, especially advertising, will play a major role in the campaign, with close to two billion dollars (estimated) being spent on the campaigns, most of it on political advertising. The day after the winner is determined for the 2012 presidential election, the battle for the 2016 presidential election will begin, which means that in the United States, someone is always running for president. Presidential campaigns should be seen as epic dramas that never end, which means that Americans are always in a state of anxiety (who will win?) over the presidency and the political order.

References

Bagdikian, Ben. 1987. The 50, 26, 20...Corporations That Own Our Media. *Fairness & Accuracy in Reporting*, June 1. http://fair.org/extra-online-articles/the-50-26-20 -corporations-that-own-our-media/ (accessed 11 October 2011).

Brooks, David. 2012. The C.E.O. of Politics. *New York Times*, January 13. http:// www.nytimes.com/2012/01/13/opinion/brooks-the-ceo-in-politics.html (accessed January 13, 2012).

Confessore, Nicholas and Eric Lipton. 2007. A Big Check, and Gingrich Gets a Big Lift. *New York Times*, January 9. http://www.nytimes.com/2012/01/10/us/politics/shel don-adelson-a-billionairegives-gingrich-a-big-lift.html?pagewanted=all&_r=0 (accessed January 9, 2007).

Douglas, Mary. 1997. In Defence of Shopping. In *The Shopping Experience*, eds. Pasi Falk and Colin Campbell, 15–30. London: Sage.

Douglas, Mary and Aaron Wildavsky. 1982. *Risk and Culture*. Berkeley: University of California Press.

McQuail, Denis. 1994. *Mass Communication Theory: An Introduction*. London: Sage.

Thompson, Michael, Richard Ellis and Aaron Wildavsky. 1990. *Cultural Theory*. New York: Westview Press.

Wildavsky, Aaron. 1989. Political Leaders Are Part of Political Systems: A Cultural Theory of Leadership. In *Political Leadership from Political Science Perspectives*, ed. Byron D. Jones, 253–282, Lawrence: University Press of Kansas.

Williams, Raymond Williams. 1978. *Marxism and Literature*. New York: Oxford University Press. http://fair.org/extra-online-articles/the-50-26-20-corporations -that-own-our-media/.

CHAPTER 7

U.S. Media and the World

Gerald Sussman

Media and Popular Culture: The U.S. Transnational Power Context

The post-Second World War era has been marked by epochal political, economic, social, and technological transformations, particularly those centered on the extension of U.S corporate hegemony at home and overseas, the principal focus here. The dialectics of global power struggles turned in part on the wave of Third World revolutionary and independence movements and on the challenge of the postwar Soviet state and its allies. As the main material beneficiary of the war, the U.S. emerged as an industrial and technological superpower, initially overwhelming the world economy with its industrial output, its military reach, its network of Cold War propaganda, and its popular cultural and international "soft diplomacy" penetrations. Seizing on the collapse of the Soviet Union and its socialist bloc, the U.S. organized a more extensive global market integration under the guiding ideology of neoliberalism, leading to greater wealth polarizations and a decline of worldwide movements for social democracy. And on the ashes of Soviet socialist internationalism, the United States exploited the weakened opportunities for revolutionary resistance by perfecting the instruments of mass persuasion and propaganda on a domestic and global scale.

In the early decades of the post-war period, the world's popular media were, and to a considerable extent remain, U.S.-dominated. This can be measured, *inter alia*, by its exports of recorded music (just three U.S.-based companies have 60% of the world market) and DVDs, book publications, blockbuster movie and TV programs, and the worldwide recognition of its celebrity icons, from Michael Jackson to Bill Gates. Almost all of the world's top-grossing films (i.e., over $200 million in earnings) were produced in whole or in part by Hollywood studios. By one estimate, over 80% of children's shows and TV movies and 75% of TV dramas sold in world markets are products of U.S. companies. The spread of the mobile phone, the internet, and digital media, all originating in the U.S., has not lessened cultural hegemony, indeed only added to it, and the dominant language of transmission and server content, English, perpetuates the privileges of the English-speaking countries. Even the illegal trade in pirated DVDs and CDs, despite the protests of Hollywood and music industry moguls, only increases the long-term market share of the American

cultural industries. This is not to say that non-U.S. media simply take on specific American cultural values but rather that the private commercial and
monopolistic tendencies of the U.S. media, including their emphasis on entertainment and profit-seeking, continue to influence the media elsewhere,
including the fledgling private media in Central and Eastern Europe, where
media 'independence' is largely associated with denationalization and privatization, and "freedom" with corporate freedom.

Decades of Third World and allied resistance to U.S. cultural hegemony,
including the 1970s' and early 1980s' demands for a New World Information
and Communication Order, have not altered this cultural power imbalance,
even if countries such as India, China, and Brazil have since developed their
own impressive international movie and TV markets. India, by far the largest
producer of commercial films, has protected its own movie production and
resisted film imports, and a number of countries, such as Cuba, Ghana, and
South Korea, have strong domestic music industries. But even in France, with
committed cultural protectionist policies, only a third of films exhibited are
French-produced (and in the U.K. in terms of revenue only about 5%). Under
the false rubric of 'free trade', global information and culture flows remain
heavily one-sided. The E.U. imports more than ten times the value of cultural
products it exports to the U.S. London's 2012 Olympic Games, which cost
British taxpayers $17 billion, were festooned with advertising from such com-
panies as Coca Cola (the Game's official soft drink), McDonald's (the exclusive
supplier of french fries), Visa, and the greenwashing propaganda of environmental polluters British Petroleum (BP) and Dow Chemical, the latter of which,
after taking over Union Carbide, ignored its responsibility for the Bhopal
disaster.

The usual rhetoric of 'globalization' is quite misleading, as it implies a shared
set of values and practices, when it is in fact a euphemism for economic imperialism. For this reason, the term transnationalization, meaning the imposition
of one state's production system upon the division of labor of other countries,
makes more sense. Although migration patterns have altered the ethnic
makeup of many Western countries and might suggest a form of globalization,
there is little evidence that power elites in the more privileged states encourage policies of cultural diversity. There is in fact a vicious backlash against
immigration in the United States, Australia, and most of Europe, and Japan has
never tolerated cultural diversity or assimilation. A people-centered globalization would mean that global governance on various important issues (world
peace, environmental justice, health and safety conditions, education, poverty,
women's emancipation, racial, gender, and ethnic equality, secure and quality
employment, and related issues, including cultural development) would have

broad international and social representation. Instead, what we see is intensified intervention of u.s. and other international oligarchs (the World Bank,
IMF, WTO, NATO, the u.s. military, the transnational corporations, and their
various intellectual, political, and economic subalterns), constituting a global
ruling class, imposing threats of destabilization, exclusion, or invasion against
non-compliance.

The transnational capitalist class structure has transcended but not eliminated the nation state. And although there is considerable variation among the
capitalist states in the degree of social democracy, everywhere it is under
assault. Indeed, the transnational ruling class has no desire to crush the state,
which remains an irreplaceable instrument for mass mobilization, economic
expansion, coercion, and legitimation: for military adventures, infrastructure,
international commerce and capital accumulation, research and development, legal preservation of property rights, policing and political repression,
cultural hegemony. The mainstream media (MSM) play a crucial role in fostering the circulation of capital and regularly renewing the legitimacy of the class
structure and the ruling order while pacifying the public. Under modern capitalism, as Althusser (1994) argued, it was principally the education system that
reproduced the ideological norms; in the Middle Ages it had been the Church.
These days the MSM exercise even greater hegemony over the minds of working people than formal, now more corporatist, educational institutions.

American Media and Internal Colonization

In the United States, the most radical and least reformist (or humane) of state
capitalisms, risk-averse MSM follow standardized program rules in order to
maximize profits and please their advertisers on whom their revenues almost
completely depend. A few national consulting companies ever conscious of
the advertising dollar suggest to local TV stations a format focusing on crimes
and disasters, weather reporting, inserts from the parent station or network
(called plugola), and usually a cooling-off feature at the end of the news, such
as a penguin born that day at the local zoo. Many stations use pre-packaged
video news releases from the government or from corporations that are made
to look like locally-produced news stories. Typically stations do not advise
their audiences of the actual source.

Extensive use of product placement further commodifies media culture,
creating a slippery convergence of advertising and programming. So-called
'reality shows' are marketing vehicles that often use branded products as part
of their story lines. According to a study of John Foster and Robert McChesney

(2003), an NBC reality show, 'The Restaurant', which ran for two seasons, was produced by a giant among international ad agencies, Interpublic. Other programs ('American Idol' and 'The Apprentice') are packed with product placements, which render them infomercials. The former AOL Time Warner retroactively digitally inserted products in TV reruns, such as in the popular show, 'Law & Order', a practice they called 'virtual advertising'. 'Guerrilla marketing' is used in erstwhile public places where people least expect them (to catch their unaware attention and stir up a viral sales response through social networking). Children's programming is a particularly favored specialty for American advertisers, and ad industry managers openly discuss the 'nagging' strategy they employ in getting kids to pester their parents to purchase the items advertised on their favorite TV programs. Coke and Pepsi battle on high school and university campuses for 'pouring rights'. Western Europe on the other hand has much stricter regulations on advertising directed at minors.

For years, ExxonMobil has run ads and editorials on the New York Times op-ed page to try to influence readers about the positive character of the company. It has also been one of the major 'underwriters' (a euphemism for advertisers) of the Public Broadcasting Service, along with other corporate behemoths, such as Pfizer, a sponsor of 'Sesame Street', Chevron, Archer Daniels Midland, Dow Chemical, Pacific Life Insurance, and the far-right political campaign financier, David Koch. PBS has rejected union funding for programs on its network out of concern for partisanship, though it does not reject corporate funding for pro-business programming, such as Franklin Templeton Investments' underwriting of PBS's 'Nightly Business Report' or until its end in 2005 the sponsorship of the network's 'Wall Street Week' by such companies as Lockheed, Martin Marietta, Enron, and a range of Fortune 500 investment firms. In the current U.S. political economy and political culture of the two corporatist political parties, one can only expect a greater degeneration of mainstream media into ever more conspicuous apparatuses of commercial and state ideology and propaganda.

The Future of Capitalist Media

In blocking the formation of common carriers in the broadcast media, the Federal Communications Commission effectively turned over speech rights to licensed companies. The few 'public service' standards that existed in broadcasting were largely abolished beginning with the Reagan administration and FCC's elimination of the Fairness Doctrine, first introduced in 1949, which was intended to assure diverse voices on controversial public issues. This led to the creation of the extremely partisan and blaring right-wing Fox TV News, owned by Rupert Murdoch, the u.s.-based tycoon put under investigation in the u.k. and u.s. for his companies' involvement in bribery, corruption, and illegally hacking the phones of celebrities, royalty, and ordinary citizens. With its tabloid and reactionary style of 'public affairs' programming, Fox ranks as the number one source of TV news in the United States, cnn a distant and declining third. The triumph of private monopolization was sealed with the Clinton era Telecommunications Act of 1996, which extended the term of TV licenses, reduced competitive restrictions on the number of TV stations that could be owned by one corporation (and eliminated entirely that restriction on radio station ownership), permitted cross-media ownership (TV-radio combinations in top-50 markets and broadcast-cable cross-ownership), enlarged the limits of national audience share by a single corporation, and eliminated restrictions on conglomerate-scale mergers and acquisitions and vertical integration. The Act enabled a reduction of major media players in the u.s. from 50 in 1983 to 6 in 2005.

Late capitalism has mapped out public consciousness as its final frontier. After restructuring their economies toward services and severely reducing manufacturing employment, the u.s., u.k., France, and other leading capitalist states now have to 'sell' industrial commodities that are produced elsewhere. This has brought about a rapid rise of the promotional industries – advertising, marketing, PR, branding, sales management, political consulting, and related occupations – which is reflected in explosive productivity growth in the service and informational sectors. The staggering proliferation of business and personal communication devices has converted much of everyday economic and social interaction into promotional practices, leading to 'systemic propaganda' (the infrastructural collectivity of promotional behaviors) and the growing importance of ideology (commercial and state) and ideological state apparatuses (Althusser 1994) in maintaining a stable social order to the benefit of corporate elites. Propaganda is no longer simply about state persuasion; it now is employed as a legitimate exercise in a broad range of social institutions and interactions. This is obvious in the expanding uses of marketing in politics, in the intrusive, ubiquitous, and unregulated manipulative forms of commodity advertising, in the professional branding of public places (even cities and whole countries) and in the self-branding (e.g., Mac people) of consumers, from internet and Facebook pages to the logos on clothing that construct their identities. The new propaganda society transmits an infomercialization of news and a spectacularization of mass media displays, awash with subliminal advertising and subterranean prejudices, the commercialization of public space and public events, the encouragement of self-promotion and self-commodification, and inducements toward an informalization of labor in which people voluntarily source their identities and ideas as value-producing free labor to production and marketing industries.

Why do American audiences appear to be pacified by degenerated mass media, especially news programming? In fact, they do not, or at least the evidence is contradictory. On the one hand, broadcasting, continually infantilizing media programming, remains the most influential form of culture and information in the U.S. But according to polling data by Gallup and regular studies by the Pew Research Center for People and the Press, a growing majority of Americans do not trust MSM news (Mendes 2013; Project for Excellence in Journalism 2013). The Nielsen ratings company reports that the number of TV households in the U.S. has been declining (Nielsen 2011). And even with the MSM's best efforts to divert the public gaze away from where the power actually resides, namely the corporate boardrooms, numerous polls suggest that a large majority of Americans, even in the midst of a media truth embargo imposed upon them, see corporations in general as wielding far too much power in society and especially in the political sphere. The public is answering back with various forms of resistance: Occupy Wall Street, piracy of online films and music, hacking of corporate billboards, anti-corporate and anti-state graffiti, independent websites, videos, and databanks, support for Wikileaks, successful opposition to SOPA (Stop Online Piracy Act), seeking alternate sources of information based inside and outside the country, and a range of other expressions of rebellion, organized or otherwise, against the corporate state – which are likely to intensify in the years ahead.

Beyond America, the main threat to cultural sovereignty does not turn most essentially on whether the U.S. is or is not the leading media exporter. The real threat to cultural independence is the commercialization of media, regardless of the main source of international media flow – the reduction of culture to commodity status. When commercial media, backed by a neoliberal state, take over public and personal space, the meaning of citizenship and identity is converted to consumerism and spectatorship. What is missing in the magic of the market fable is that modern communications exists only because vast amounts of public expenditure was and is appropriated by the state and put into research and development of electronic circuitry, communication satellites and launch vehicles, computer programs, and other information and communication technologies, at the same time that corporate rights to public space are legislatively codified.

Under the plutocratic system, the democratic potential of communications will never be realized. Only a governance structure that converts state subsidies for the exclusive purpose of non-commercial media offers the promise of a communications system in the service of the public interest. The escalation of deception needed to sustain the capitalist propaganda society may be close to if not already beyond the tipping point. As social and political movements in the Middle East and elsewhere have shown, once the state loses its legitimacy, to politically interpolate a popular nursery rhyme, all the king's horses and all the king's men can no longer put it together again. It is incumbent upon public intellectuals to break the legitimacy of the ruling order and make the argument for a socialist and citizen-based ideological alternative to capitalism, consumerism, and possessive individualism as a social, political, cultural, and thought construct and as a way of life.

References

Althusser, Louis. 1994. Ideology and Ideological State Apparatuses (Notes Toward an Investigation). In *IdeologyMapping*, ed. Slovoj Žižek, 100–140. London: Verso.

Foster, John Bellamy and Robert W. McChesney. 2003. The Commercial Tidal Wave. *Monthly Review* 54 (10). http://monthlyreview.org/2003/03/01/the-commercial-tidal-wave (accessed March 17, 2014).

Mendes, Elizabeth. 2013. Americans' Confidence in Newspapers Continues to Erode. *Gallup Politics*, June 17. http://www.gallup.com/poll/163097/americans-confidence-newspapers-continues-erode.aspx (accessed March 17, 2014).

Nielsen Company. 2011. Nielsen Estimates Number of U.S. Television Homes to be 114.7 Million. *Newswire*, May 3. http://www.nielsen.com/us/en/newswire/2011/nielsen-estimates-number-of-u-s-television-homes-to-be-114-7-million.html (accessed March 17, 2014).

Project for Excellence in Journalism. 2013. State of the Media 2013. http://stateofthemedia.org/2013/local-tv-audience-declines-as-revenue-bounces-back/ (accessed March 6, 2014).

CHAPTER 8

The Evolving Business Models of Network News?

Oliver Boyd-Barrett

Introduction

This paper critically appraises the shifting business models and practices of US television news 1940–2010, with particular reference to the terrestrial and cable news networks and the relationship of television news to centers of power. I review the networks' origins, history and principal content characteristics. I examine major trends of the 2000s and ponder their significance in terms of a long-term transition from 'network' to a 'post-network' supply of news. I investigate one area of coverage as spectacularly revealing of networks' relation to major centers of US power, namely war and the military industrial complex, which I call a relationship of complicity.

Some scholars have pondered the approaching "death" of television (Katz and Scannell 2009), taking their cue from the rise and fall of US terrestrial television network audiences – from a peak of 50 million homes in 1980, falling to 22 million in 2009. Yet this audience considerably exceeded the total reached by any one cable television channel. Pronouncements of the 'death' of television are perhaps a way of marking the decided transition from the exclusive networks of old to a 'post-network' society of abundant television, anywhere and at any time. Factors contributing to this transition have included: (1) proliferating competition of supply across platforms (including terrestrial, cable, satellite, wireless delivery to computer, phone and other mobile devices); within a framework (2) of industry concentration, corporatization and conglomeration; (3) combination of technological advance and diminishing human resources; (4) apparent abandonment of public service criteria in favor of market orientation and infotainment.

Numbers of Television Journalists

According to US Census and the Bureau of Labor Statistics, quoted in Weaver et al. (2007), the full-time editorial workforce in U.S. news media in 2002 was 116,148 with the largest concentration (58,769 or 50.6%) in newspapers, followed by weekly newspapers (21,908 or 18.9%), television (20,288 or 17.5%), radio

(13,393 or 11.5%), news magazines (1,152 or 1%) and news services (638 or 0.5%). Television news staffs were spread across approximately 1,300 stations nation-wide. In the period 1971–2002, the total size of the full-time editorial workforce in the traditional mainstream U.S. news had grown 67%. In absolute numbers there had been growth in all but two categories: news magazines shrank slightly, from 1,900 to 1,152 and news agency services had shrunk dramatically from 3,300 to 638. Numbers of television journalists had increased the most dramatically of all, by 190% for the period as a whole, but slipping in the 2000s.

News networks each employed 1000–1400 staff in 2010. The 2004 Pew report on the State of the News Media noted general declines in investment. Numbers of free-to-air (ABC, CBS, NBC) network news correspondents were down by a third from the 1980s, the number of foreign news bureaus had fallen by half, while correspondent workload was up by 30%. In local television, almost 60% of news directors reported either budget or staff/cuts. Cutbacks were noted again in the 2006 report, with older journalists being replaced by younger. Broadcast network news had experienced a total 10% reduction of expenditure in the period 2002–2006. In cable, Fox expenditure was up 11%, CNN up by 5% while MSNBC was still cutting. Staff in local television news experienced an average size increase of 36% in this period, although journalists were expected to do more: hours of news on local television stood at a record high (3.8 hours a day). ABC News reduced its worldwide news staff from 1500 to 1100 in 2010. CBS reduced by 70. Only one of the free-to-air networks, NBC, was robustly profitable ($400 m annually), the only one of the three linked to a cable news channel, MSNBC, with which it shared costs and from which it benefited from advertising and subscription revenues (Stelter and Carter, 2010)

Network History

Origins
Over several decades three principal US networks delivered audiovisual news to US citizens: they were ABC, CBS and NBC. A contender, the DuMont net-work, ceased broadcasting in 1956, lacking the safety-net afforded its rivals from radio network revenues. DuMont assets contributed to the assembly of Metropolitan Broadcasting Corporation, a small network renamed Metromedia in 1961, then sold to News Corporation and Twentieth Century Fox Film Corporation in 1985, forming the Fox Broadcasting Company in 1986. This grew to become, in effect, the nation's fourth network.

Together the three majors reached almost the entire television population, constructing a 'national' portfolio of news that was considerably attractive to advertisers, who provided almost all the revenue. Then, in reaction to a series of 1970s FCC deregulatory measures that favored cable, an increasing number of households converted to receiving the traditional networks within their basic-tier cable or satellite portfolios, where the networks constituted an important but tiny cluster within 100–500 + channel universes. One-time 'free-to-air' services were now increasingly bundled into cable or satellite packages that by the 2000s cost subscribers in the range of $30–$80 monthly. In this way, cable operators easily recouped the payments they made for the right to distribute network services. For audiences, the trade-off bought higher quality signals and more channels. In the early 2000s, less than one in five households continued to receive networks by roof-top antennae as opposed to coaxial cable or satellite dish delivery. The federally mandated switch from analogue to digital transmission in 2009 obliged those audiences to purchase (discounted) set-top converter boxes (sometimes requiring new antennae) if they wished to receive the digital versions of the old "free to air" services. Many elected to switch to cable or satellite providers.

ABC

The three 'terrestrial' channels emerged under the umbrella of parent radio organizations in the 1940s, transmitting first in black-and-white and, by the mid-1960s, in color. In 1940, the FCC broke up the radio duopoly headed by CBS and RCA's NBC, obliging RCA to abandon one of its chains. RCA's 'Blue Network', acquired by retail magnate Edward Noble in 1945, was renamed the American Broadcasting Company. Its first evening news anchors were H.R. Baukhage and Jim Gibbons (1948–1951). The ABC Television Network, broadcasting from 1948, was acquired in 1953 by United Paramount Theatres to form American Broadcasting – Paramount Theatres Inc (shortened to American Broadcasting Companies Inc. in 1968). The new company fostered strong relations with Hollywood studios, notably Disney, and in the 1970s set up a theatrical division, ABC Pictures, producing both for cinema and television. ABC introduced 'Good Morning America' in 1975. ABC was acquired in 1985 by Capital Cities Communications to form Capital Cities/ABC. In 1996, Capital Cities was taken over by Disney, which renamed its broadcasting group ABC, Inc. In 2004, it started a 24/7 channel, ABC News Now for online and mobile phone consumers. Principal news shows in 2009 included 'America This Morning', 'Good Morning America', 'Good Morning America Weekend Edition', 'This Week with George Stephanopoulos', 'ABC World News with Charles Gibson', 'ABC World News Saturday & Sunday', '20/20', 'Nightline', 'ABC World News Now', 'ABC News Brief', 'Primetime' (Auletta 1992; Barkin 2003; Barnouw 1968; Epstein 2000; Goldenson and Wolf 1991).

CBS

CBS Broadcasting Inc, previously known as the Columbia Broadcasting System, a radio network, was established in 1928. It had only one television station in 1950 but grew steadily during the following decade. 'CBS TV News' was introduced in 1948, extending from 15 to 30 minutes in 1963 (a move soon imitated by NBC and ABC). First evening news anchor was Douglas Edwards (1948–1962). Walter Cronkite began as anchor in 1952, and was succeeded by Dan Rather in 1981. Edward Murrow, with producer Fred Friendly, converted CBS' 'Hear it Now to See it Now' from 1951. CBS launched '60 Minutes' in 1968. The company was acquired by Westinghouse Electric Corporation in 1995, later coming under the control of Viacom in 2000. Viacom had started as a spin-off of CBS in 1971. In the late 2000s, Viacom's principal owner Sumner Redstone split the company into two: CBS Corporation, with the CBS television network at its core, and the new Viacom. But both companies continued to be controlled by Sumner Redstone through National Amusements. News shows in 2009 included 'CBS Morning News', 'The Early Show', 'The Saturday Early Show', 'CBS News Sunday Morning', 'Face the Nation with Bob Schieffer', 'CBS Evening News with Katie Couric', 'CBS Evening News with Jeff Glor' (Saturday edition), 'CBS Evening News with Russ Mitchell' (Sunday edition), '60 Minutes', '48 Hours Mystery', 'Up to the Minute', 'CBS NewsBreak' (twice-daily 90 second daytime broadcast), and 'CBS News'. (Auletta 1992; Barkin 2003; Barnouw 1968; Epstein 2000; Paper 1987).

NBC

The National Broadcasting Company (NBC) was formed in 1926 by Radio Corporation of America (RCA), which owned 50%, and its partners General Electric (30%) and Westinghouse (20%). The first NBC network television broadcasts began in 1939. First evening news anchor was John Cameron Swayze (1948–1956), succeeded by Chet Huntley and David Brinkley (1956–1970). 'NBC Today' the first television morning news magazine show, began in 1952. Ownership of NBC passed to General Electric in 1986, when General Electric purchased RCA. GE sold off the NBC Radio Network. By the late 2000s, amidst a gathering crisis in the news industry, there was evidence of growing disenchantment with NBC within GE, and negotiations commenced with the nation's largest cable company, Comcast, to purchase a major part of GE's shares in NBC. Principal news programs in 2009 were 'Dateline NBC', 'Early Today', 'Meet the Press', 'NBC Nightly News', and 'Today'. (Auletta 1992; Barnouw 1968; Barkin 2003; Epstein 2000).

The major terrestrial networks (and Fox, established in 1986 and comparable in scope, by the 2000s, to the Big Three) are not the only players. Smaller networks, such as CW Network (established 2006, and owned by CBS and Warner Bros.), typically comprise small numbers of affiliate stations that may receive network programming for only parts of the day. They include Spanish-language or Hispanic networks (e.g. Univision) catering to the growing size and purchasing power of the Latino/a population.

The Big Three Model

The Big Three sustained the traditions of their radio predecessors that had been established by the 1934 Communication Act, and transitioned from radio to television on the basis of those earlier structures. These comprised nuclei of network owned-and-operated stations based in the nation's principal markets, and larger clusters of affiliate stations, independently owned or owned by chains, that took most of their programming and advertising from the net-works while adding local news (and advertising) and some other content. Local television news in 2008 was watched regularly by over half of the US population. A typical late newscast reached 12% of viewers watching television in a given market (but down from 21% in 1998) (Stelter 2008). News repre-sented about 40% of the average local station's revenue, contributing – at least until the economic downturn of 2008 – to the very high rates of annual return (sometimes 50%) on television investment, and accounting for the competi-tive influence of local television news on television news gathering generally.

Together the networks represented a model of broadcasting ownership, control and operation that was commercial, plural (though tending toward oli-gopolistic) and dependent for almost all revenue on advertising. In this way, the constitution of U.S. broadcasting policy represented a diametrically differ-ent approach to that of most of Europe, Asia, Africa and the Middle East (Latin America was mixed) where, for the first few decades of broadcasting, govern-ments adopted either of two models: (1) outright State-controlled and often State-financed monopolistic systems, or (2) "public" broadcasting systems, as in Western Europe, financed indirectly by the state, by license fee or by some other, generally non-commercial, measure intended to sustain a 'Chinese wall' between the State and the broadcaster. These systems were generally not dependent, at least initially, on advertising. In many such countries there has been increasing convergence since 1990 towards the US model namely, towards a plurality of commercial stations, diminishing State involvement, and increased dependence on advertising.

From the opposite direction, and less dramatically, there has been a mea-sure of convergence in the US towards the "public," and, we might say, "public sphere" European model. First, there were stipulations built into the 1934 Communications Act and subsequent legislation that broadcasters should serve (an ill-defined) "public interest." Criteria of "public interest" were established on a case-law basis. The news divisions of the major networks provided a public spirited face to an otherwise highly commercial operation. Their primetime evening newscasts were typically fronted by patriarchal white male anchors whose performances projected authoritative but avuncular, judicious impartiality within a framework of loyalty to nation and the flag. Morning shows were generally lighter mixes of information and entertainment, featuring more teamwork. The first evening woman co-anchor was Barbara Walters, paired with Harry Reasoner on ABC in 1976; Connie Chung was appointed co-anchor to Dan Rather on CBS in 1993. Neither of these matches was happy. Katie Couric was the first female appointed as sole anchor, in 2006, for CBS. She was joined by Diane Sawyer for ABC in 2009, leaving one male, Brian Williams, on NBC.

The 1996 Telecommunications Act in effect redefined public interest in terms of market competition, which it stimulated primarily by permitting access for telephony operators into television distribution and vice versa. Regulatory developments from the 1980s, up to and including the 1996 Telecommunications Act, removed many 'public interest' conditions that had been imposed subsequent to the 1934 Communications Act. These included the 'fairness doctrine', whose purpose was to ensure a balance of viewpoint in matters of controversy. (Surviving 'equal time' regulations require that the voices of competing electoral candidates be heard in the measure to which their parties had gained voters' support in previous comparable elections). The 'syn-fin' rules restricted the freedom of networks to syndicate their original programming. Other regulations had restricted (1) the share of the national market that any network could capture with the stations that it owned; (2) the number of television stations any network could own outright (network owned-and-operated stations constitute small proportions, less than 20%, of the entire networks, and are concentrated in the large markets); and (3) multiple ownership of media properties, and cross-ownership of print and broadcasting outlets in the same markets. The 1996 Act lifted such restraints more than a notch, although later FCC attempts at further relaxation were successfully resisted by Congress (Alexander et al. 2003; Croteau and Hoynes 2005).

US Public Broadcasting

The US 'public' broadcasting tradition was established by successful passage of the Public Broadcasting Act of 1967, which set up the Corporation for Public Broadcasting (CPB). Supported mainly from state and nonprofit local sources, the CPB developed, but did not own, a public broadcasting network in radio (including National Public Radio, NPR) and television (Public Broadcasting

Service, PBS). PBS, launched in 1970, grew to 354 affiliate stations by the 2000s (larger than any of the Big Three or Fox). These exercise collective ownership of the network.

PBS owns no stations. Many PBS stations are nonprofit enterprises, attached to such entities as state, health or educational (University) institutions. Unlike commercial networks whose affiliates depend heavily on network programming, PBS stations take most of their content from third party suppliers. Stations pay for both PBS and third party feeds. A PBS policy of 'common carriage' requires most member stations to adhere to the national prime time programs on a common schedule. All content is created by or in conjunction with third parties, including member stations, although PBS retains television distribution rights. CPB, which part funds both local stations and suppliers, obtains 15–20% of annual operating revenue from federal sources, 25–29% from state and local taxes, and 53–60% from pledge drives, donations and grants (including a substantial corporate sponsorship). In 2005, CPB received $464 m from Congress and $650 in donations from individual Americans.

The 1967 Act required strict PBS adherence to objectivity and balance, and prohibited federal interference in or control of programming content. Who should define what these principles mean in practice, or how government could guarantee them without simultaneously contravening them, are unresolved. CPB chair Kenneth Tomlinson (2003–2005) attempted to use CPB resources to eliminate what he perceived to be a liberal bias. He forced the resignation in 2005 of Bill Moyers, celebrated anchor of 'Now with Bill Moyers', although Moyers soon returned for the 'Bill Moyers Journal'. Already countering the weight of Bill Moyers, however, was conservative commentator Tucker Carlson and, for a while, the 'Journal Editorial Report', anchored by an editor of the Wall Street Journal's editorial page (who subsequently moved to the right-wing Fox News channel). Leading prime-time public affairs programming from PBS include 'Frontline', 'NOW on PBS', 'The Newshour with Jim Lehrer', 'The Charlie Rose Interview show', and 'Nightly Business Report'. (Engelman 1996)

CNN

The development of cable and satellite television has had major implications for both the business and content of television news. Cable News Network (CNN), the world's first 24-hour television news channel, was founded in 1980 by Atlanta station owner Ted Turner who in 1976 had uploaded his local Atlanta station (WTCG-TV-Channel 17) to satellite, making it available for multiple downloads by cable operators. This occurred a decade following the launch of the world's first commercial satellite, Early Bird, by COMSAT in 1965, one year after HBO became the first nationally-syndicated cable channel, and three years ahead of C-SPAN, ESPN and Nickelodeon. In 2009, CNN is owned by the Turner Broadcasting Systems division of the media conglomerate Time Warner. Its two major products are CNN for domestic news consumers and CNNI for international consumers. Alongside the main domestic channel, Turner launched the Headline News channel in 1982, originally under the title CNN2. This provided a 24-hour cycle of 30 minute news broadcasts. From 2005 this became Headline Prime, featuring prime time opinion anchors such as Glenn Beck and Nancy Grace. CNN facilitated the development of round-the-clock coverage of high intensity, high ratings news stories, such as the Shuttle Challenger disaster of 1986, the Jessica McClure toddler-in-the-well story of 1987, the 1991 Gulf War (an incomparable boost for CNN domestically and world-wide, offering the only television coverage of the war from inside Baghdad), the Los Angeles riots of 1992 and the O.J. Simpson trial for murder in 1995. Where CNN went, the networks followed. ABC, CBS, and NBC coverage of Simpson eclipsed coverage of significant foreign events such as the war in Bosnia (Kellner 2003). The business model for television news had transitioned from one based on high-minded public interest principles to a market model driven by consumer interest, ratings and advertising. This transformation was stimulated principally by competing news sources through cable and satellite, and the discovery by local television stations during the 1980s of new wealth through tabloidization of local news.

High visibility CNN news programs in 2009 included 'American Morning', 'CNN Newsroom', 'The Situation Room' (with Wolf Blitzer), 'Lou Dobbs' Tonight', 'Campbell Brown', 'Larry King Live', and 'Anderson Cooper 360'. The web-site CNN.com was launched in 1995. Media watchdogs such as Fair and Media Matters (Liberal), AIM and MRC (conservative) inevitably disagree as to whether CNN leans left or right. A 'CNN effect' (Volkmer 2005; Cottle 2008) has been postulated to denote the possible impact of CNN on pressuring governments into humanitarian responses to catastrophes such as the abandonment of Shiites in Iraq in 1991, and western interventions in Somalia 1992 and Kosovo 1995. This may have lent a 'liberal' aura to CNN that may be true only by contrast to the predominantly conservative tone of most mainstream US television news. Thussu (2000) examined CNN coverage of NATO's bombing in 1999, an unprecedented NATO intervention in the domestic affairs of a sovereign state. He found the bombing was reported uncritically as 'humanitarian intervention', and tended to follow the agenda set by the US military. Ackerman (2001) found that CNN was only slightly more likely than other US networks to use the word 'occupation' with reference to Israeli occupation of Palestine. More than 90% of US network TV reporting on the occupied territories failed to report that the territories were occupied. The percentage was closer to

80% in the case of CNN. Voorhees et al. (2007) suggest that in coverage of Hurricane Katrina, CNN represented minorities in a negative light, ultimately reinforcing inequalities. Minorities were disproportionately cast as victims, passive or in need of help, and rarely in positions of power or expertise. Eke (2008) cites findings that coverage of the Darfur Genocide in 2005 by CNN, MSNBC and Fox News were quickly overwhelmed by competing, domestic infotainment stories.

CNN's response to the competitive threat of Fox News (which in 2009 enjoyed higher ratings than CNN but fewer unique viewers per month) has been to give higher profile to opinionated anchors and, in the judgment of this author, move rightwards on political-economic, though not necessarily on social, issues. With occasional exceptions such as Anderson Cooper's gentle outrage against Federal fecklessness in its response to Hurricane Katrina, the line-up of celebrity anchors could scarcely be described as "progressive." Some have been associated with conservative positions (e.g. Wolf Blitzer on the Israeli-Palestinian conflict; Lou Dobbs on immigration) or feature conservative anchors (e.g. Glenn Beck until he moved to Fox). Notwithstanding its coverage from Baghdad during the first Gulf War, including reports of US-inflicted carnage of civilians (e.g. the US bombing of hundreds of civilians in the el-Amiriyah air-raid shelter), it cannot be argued that CNN or CNNI has significantly opposed or critiqued US foreign policy interests. In 1999 CNN had fired foreign correspondent Peter Arnett (AP veteran of 1960s Saigon and CNN correspondent from Baghdad in Gulf War One, 1991), following the network's retraction of an Arnett report that investigated whether U.S. forces had used nerve gas in Laos during the Vietnam war (Scott, 2004)

Fox News

After CNN's debut in 1980, and the increasing carriage by cable operators of both free-to-air national networks and local stations, the next significant arrival to cable was Fox News (Whittemore, 1990). The Fox Network was established in 1986 when Rupert Murdoch (for News Corporation) and Marvin Davis (co-owner with Murdoch of 20th Century Fox Film Corp) agreed to buy six television stations that had previously belonged to Metromedia. This was the same year that Murdoch completed his purchase of 50% of Fox Filmed Entertainment, the parent company of 20th Century Fox Film Corporation. Ten years later, in 1996, Murdoch announced the creation of a 24/7 cable news channel, Fox News. He appointed Roger Ailes to head it up. Ailes, previously with 'America's Talking' (later part of MSNBC), had been a senior Republican advisor. Belying the new channel's 'fair and balanced' slogan, Ailes demonstrated that through strongly opinionated evening talk shows (including 'The O'Reilly Report', 'The Crier Report', 'Hannity and Colmes', and later shows featuring such anchors as Greta Van Susteren, Shepard Smith, Neil Cavuto, Glenn Beck) he could shift the center of television news gravity significantly rightwards and in doing so realize enviable profits and political impact. The rightwing character of Fox news was amply demonstrated by Glen Greenwald's 2004 documentary 'Outfoxed', and Al Franklin's book, *Lies and the Liers Who Tell Them*, and in copious research (e.g. Thussu 2007; Jaramillo 2009). Channel ratings were boosted by spectacularly gung-ho coverage of the invasion of Iraq in 2003, and coverage of the Republican National Convention in 2004. For most of the 2000s, Fox led the ratings among cable news channels (though not in cumulative audience). In October 2009, White House Communications Director Anita Dun told CNN that "Fox News often operates almost as either the research arm or the communications arm of the Republican Party" (quoted by Melber 2009)

Fox News was the first channel, following the demise of the 'fairness doctrine' in 1986, to leverage the ensuing opportunities for different ways of 'doing' news. Its disappearance removed even the necessity for 'pretence' at being 'balanced'. The move by President Reagan's FCC to kill the fairness doctrine presumed that with the onset of digitization, cable and satellite, the age of television 'scarcity' was over. This was merely one part of the Reagan Administration's effective abandonment of the principle of media regulation for the public interest. Television could now be openly propagandistic, even if claiming not to be. Fox News' seizure of the 'zeitgeist' occurred only a few years ahead of the collapse of the Soviet Union and Eastern Europe (1989–1990), the State capitalism 'turn' of China in the 1990s, and a frenzy of capitalist expansion, globalization, boom (and then bust).

Fox pushed other networks, both cable and terrestrial, in a similar though not as extreme a direction. The political center as a whole shifted (further) rightwards, assisted by 'liberal media's' uncritical buy-in to neoliberal ideology. In terms of a few social or lifestyle issues such as tolerance for racial diversity, sexual orientation and abortion, there may have been substance to the Republican attempt to paint all mainstream media as 'liberal'. But for the charge to have carried real weight, at least a part of that mainstream would have had to have been identifiably, persistently and aggressively against war and the defense industries and sympathetic to labor, progressive taxation, and measures of wealth redistribution such as free universal health care, affordable university education, regulation of Wall Street, and the dismemberment of oligopolies. I am aware of no evidence that such was the case. During most years of the Bush presidency from 2000 to at least 2006 (and, in most respects, during the subsequent Obama administration), indeed, there was nothing remotely 'left wing' about any part of the television news establishment, therefore no hope or expectation anywhere that the Bush administration would be rigorously, persistently and in timely fashion held to account for its many proven crimes and abuses. These included but were certainly not limited to the invasions and occupations (in whole or in part) of two sovereign countries (Afghanistan, Iraq), threats of invasion against a third, Iran, on the basis of dubious evidence, destabilization of Pakistan, use of unmanned drones as tools for assassination, removal of a democratically elected regime in Haiti, connivance at or participation in an attempted coup d'etat against a democratically elected regime in Venezuela, illegal spying on us citizens, removal of habeus corpus protections, and wide-scale rendition, torture and human rights abuses against both us and non-us citizens.

MSNBC

Nothing remotely resembling 'left-wing', occurred on MSNBC until a curious 'liberal' turn at MSNBC in 2006, which belatedly propelled anchorman Keith Olbermann ('Countdown with Keith Olbermann') to resurrect a more astringent version of CBS' Edward R. Murrow (who in 1954 had helped puncture the sleazy red-baiting of Senator Joseph McCarthy). Olbermann finally gave television voice – a literate, rational and passionate voice – to the accumulated outrage that opinion polls suggest was felt by at least half of the US population against the Bush Administration's era of extreme corporatism, an Administration that had hurled the country back to levels of social inequality not experienced since the 1900s, struck a dangerously cavalier pose in the face of global environmental catastrophe and the threat of nuclear war, and embarked on an imperial rampage through the Middle East and Central Asia that it ingenuously described as a 'war on terror'. Other 'liberal' faces of the network included Chris Matthews, David Gregory and Rachel Maddow. The channel's morning show, however, was anchored from 2007 by former Republican congressman (1994–2001) and 'traditional' conservative, Joe Scarborough. Olbermann himself was forced out of MSNBC in 2010 and transferred to Al Gore's new minority liberal channel, Current TV.

MSNBC, like Fox News, was established in 1996, in a partnership between Microsoft and General Electic's NBC (now NBC Universal). NBC Universal parents one of the three major 'free-to-air' news networks. In 2005, NBC Universal purchased a majority stake in the channel, leaving Microsoft with 18%. The two companies maintained a 50–50 partnership in their web-site, msnbc.com. In comparison with CNN, MSNBC stories were longer and more detailed but not evidently more 'liberal'. Conservative icon Ann Coulter appeared on one of the channel's first shows. One of its first legal analysts was Barbara Olson, who told John Dean that she hated the Clintons and used Republican talking points in her campaign for the impeachment of President Clinton. In 2003, the channel hired right-wing talk radio star Michael Savage to host a weekend show, but fired him for scandalous language. That same year, NBC and MSNBC fired Peter Arnett for saying in an interview with Iraqi Television that the U.S. war plan had 'failed'. And in another incident that year, veteran talk show host Phil Donahue was fired as host of a nightly debate program because he was allowing 'too many' antiwar voices on the air. Then MSNBC's top rated show, Donahue aired in the same time slot as Fox News' 'Bill O'Reilly'. Donahue explained that MSNBC had ordered there would have to be two conservatives for every liberal, and that he himself counted as two liberals (Democracy Now 2005)! Another incident occurred in 2007 when right-wing talk radio star Don Imus was simulcast on MSNBC and passed scandalous comment on Rutgers University Women's Basketball Team, prompting several advertisers to withdraw support. Additionally, a study of covert lobbying practices on network television by The Nation (Jones 2010) found that MSNBC was "the cable network with the most egregious instances of airing guests with conflicts of interest."

MSNBC's so-called left-leaning turn corresponds with the arrival of Phil Griffin, who assumed executive oversight in 2006 (and became the network's president in 2008). His policy seems to have been to turn MSNBC into the antithesis of Fox News. That it should have taken the network a decade to formulate such an obvious response smacks of undependable, corporate desperation, not principle. Main MSNBC news shows in 2009 included 'Morning Joe', 'Andrea Mitchell Reports', 'Hardball with Chris Matthews', 'The Ed Show' (with Ed Schultz), and 'Countdown with Keith Olbermann and Rachel Maddow'.

A Question of Complicity

The age of network news progressively entered into decline as cable and satellite delivery overtook terrestrial television, the remote control facilitated consumer choice of what to view, the number of channels available to most homes multiplied from a handful to several hundred, and television content could be downloaded to computers and mobile devices.

It had been a worthy age, inspired by a public service ethos. While also patrician and authoritarian, it was likely preferable to some of the opinionated, partisan slanging matches that pass for television news in the 2000s on cable news networks. But it was also routinely partisan on behalf of the power elite. Rarely did it question U.S. foreign policy until too late to make much difference. It faithfully beat the drums for (often dubious and/or illegal) imperial war through Korea, Vietnam, Panama, the two Gulf Wars, Kosovo, Afghanistan, Iraq, Iran and Pakistan and remained studiously innocent if not ignorant through the many covert US acts of regime destabilization including US direct responsibility for, or participation in, the military dictatorship of Greece 1967–74, the overthrow of democratically-elected leader of Guatemala, Jacobo Arbenz in 1954, the overthrow of democratically-elected leader of Iran, Mohammed Mossadaq in 1953, the overthrow of the popular leader of Iraq, Karim Kassem, in 1963 (in favor, eventually, of Saddam Hussein), the overthrow of democratically-elected leader of Chile, Salvador Allende, in 1973, continuing onwards through to the overthrow of Haiti's first democratically elected leader, Jean-Bertrand Aristidt, in 2000, and support for the attempted overthrow of democratically-elected leader of Venezuela, Hugo Chavez, in 2002 (Blum 2008).

Contrary to Pentagon post-war rationalization, television did not 'lose' the Vietnam War. Certainly the release of iconic, revealing photos and footage of war atrocities such as the 'napalm girl' in 1972, the street execution of a guerrilla fighter in 1968, the My Lai massacre in 1968 and Walter Cronkite's gloomy prognostication after the 1968 Tet offensive likely had a profound and critical impact on many Americans. But the media broadly supported the Vietnam war. As Herman and Schiller (1989) argue, US news media may have questioned the 'strategy' for war, but failed to hold America's leaders accountable for a war in which America had no legal presence and which it fought on the basis of an ever shifting series of false or contestable pretexts, extending their transgressions covertly into Laos and Cambodia, at hideous cost in terms of regime destabilization, human life and suffering. America's media, led by the broadcast networks failed to expose anything like the full fraud of the war until after Daniel Ellsberg's leak of the Pentagon Papers in 1971, by which time public opinion was turning solidly against the war.

Media complicity with the initial invasion and de facto occupation of Vietnam was the stimulus for Herman and Chomsky's celebrated propaganda model (first chapter of their 1989 book *Manufacturing Consent*), and for the works of Daniel Hallin (1986), and Norman Solomon (2007), among many others. Similar critical and compelling analyses are available of almost every US overseas military engagement (e.g. see Kellner 1992, 2003 on both the first and second Gulf Wars). Scholarly dissection of network television coverage of war, and of media coverage of war more generally, is copious (among many additional sources see Allan and Zelizer 2004; Hoskins 2004; Thussu and Freedman 2003). The work of Douglas Kellner (1992, 2003) on network coverage of both the first and the second Gulf Wars has been particularly insightful, and frequently scathing.

Kellner's (1992) study of US network coverage of the first Gulf War confirms and exemplifies many of the observations of Hallin's (1986), and Herman and Chomsky's 1989 study of media coverage of Vietnam. As in Vietnam there were obfuscations as to the 'causes' of war. Was it really about Iraq's threat to Kuwait (which had once been part of Iraq)? This was a threat whose importance US diplomats had seemed to downplay in communications with Hussein. Was it about cutting Iraq down to size following the defeat of Iran in the Iraqi-Iran war (the US had egged on Saddam and played both sides), softening it up for an eventual return of western oil interests to Iraq? Rather than adhering to skeptical, questioning, historically-aware self-distancing from US authority that the mythology of an independent press might suggest as appropriate, network anchors and journalists predictably undertook the role of cheerleading on behalf of US forces and the Administration. Networks uncritically endorsed most of the Administration's 'Big Lies'. These included the allegation that Hussein was preparing to invade Saudi Arabia (probably hatched to convince the Saudis to allow US troops on Saudi soil); the 'babies taken out of incubators' invention of Hill and Knowlton, a public relations company representing the Kuwaiti government in exile; the claim that the Iraqi air force and its scud missiles were annihilated on the first night of attack; assertions as to the efficiency of the very inefficient Patriot missiles; the claims that bombing atrocities of a Baby Milk plant and a civilian bomb shelter in Baghdad had been in fact legitimate targets; the myth of 'precision bombings' that were in fact generally imprecise and accounted for only a small proportion of all bombing; the claim that oil spills in the Gulf were effected by Hussein when they were in fact the result of US bombing.

Kellner attributed to networks the function of 'conduiting' – uncritical, unquestioning and frequent repetition of official Administration, Pentagon claims. It is demonstrated in Kellner's analysis of network coverage of both the 1991 and 2003 Gulf wars and of the war in Afghanistan (Kellner 1992, 2003) and in many other studies (including Hallin 1986 on Vietnam, and Jaramillo 2009 on Iraq). The networks afforded scant attention to sources that favored alternatives to war. The antiwar movement was rarely seen or heard on television even though in practice it was well organized, large and vocal. The war was personalized for mass consumption as being a battle of wills between President Bush and Hussein (who was more often referred to by his first name, Saddam, faintly resonant of 'Satan', while the president was rarely, if ever, called "George"). Hussein was regularly compared with Hitler, a far graver and more powerful threat to the western world. There was very little contextualization: the media did not ask why the US had not stepped in when Iran invaded Iraq in the eight-year Iran-Iraqi war; why it had not intervened when Israel invaded the Lebanon in 1988; why it tolerated Israeli occupation of Palestine; why it tolerated Israeli nuclear weaponry.

Most journalists who covered the war were organized into press 'pools' where selected correspondents reported the war on behalf of groups of media. They were largely dependent on the military for access and transportation and were subject to the guidance of 'minders'. Stories deemed problematic could be subject to lengthy delays while reviewed by military censors. Infotainment frames were adopted from pleasure-inducing Hollywood narrative and other dramatic strategies. Networks relied primarily on pro-Administration sources, including veteran military experts – an earlier manifestation of the phenomenon that came to prominence in the second Gulf War namely, retired generals masquerading as 'Television pundits', but, unknown to the audience, pre-approved and pre-briefed by the Pentagon, and sometimes doubling as defense consultants. The networks worked to create the illusion of real-time presence, while obscuring the realities of censorship and technology. Truth was often lost in (misleading) numbers of sorties, hits, troops killed and wounded, etc. The enemy was often accused of crimes of which the Americans were guilty, such as violations of the Geneva Convention. The horror of war was sanitized both through control of the image and through language: the enemy was 'engaged', bombs were 'dropped ordnance', civilian deaths were 'collateral damage', targets were 'assets', 'assets' were 'visited', 'acquired', 'taken out', 'suppressed'. War planes were 'force packages' whose routine engagements in wholesale and cruel slaughter over large areas were sanitized as 'carpet bombing'.

Many of these issues resurfaced in network coverage of the invasion of Afghanistan in 2001 and of Iraq in 2003, where the mildly complicit 'press pool' ceded to egregious military stage-management of coverage through the 'embed' system (Jaramillo 2009). The scandal of 'Pentagon television pundits' persisted, along with evidence of routine appearance of lobbyists, the identity of their employers hidden from viewers. Barstow (2008) chronicled how, before the US invasion of Iraq in 2003, the Pentagon nurtured retired generals as 'expert' consultants to television networks. The generals benefited from access to top sources and expense-free travel that they sometimes used in association with work for defense companies to whom they were also consultants. Television networks seemed incurious about the practice, even though their use of such sources dated back at least to the first Gulf War (Kellner 1992). A former CNN chief news executive acknowledged in 2003 that CNN allowed the Pentagon to vet its military analysts. A four-month investigation by *The Nation* (Jones 2010) found evidence of egregious abuse of public trust by the cable networks who routinely invited highly-paid lobbyists on to programs without disclosing their affiliation. Sometimes these lobbyists parleyed the opportunity to interview news sources into an occasion of pitching them with their corporate 'sell'.

> Since 2007 at least seventy-five registered lobbyists, public relations representatives and corporate officials--people paid by companies and trade groups to manage their public image and promote their financial and political interests--have appeared on MSNBC, Fox News, CNN, CNBC and Fox Business Network with no disclosure of the corporate interests that had paid them. Many have been regulars on more than one of the cable networks, turning in dozens – and in some cases hundreds – of appearances..... Since then, guests with serious conflicts of interest have popped up with alarming regularity on every network..... Frequent television news commentators are also often given access to policy-makers, who may find that they are meeting with not just a TV pundit but also a paid lobbyist.
>
> JONES 2010

These lapses suggest a collapse of rudimentary professional ethics and signify routine, unaccountable complicity between the networks and corporate, military and political interest that is routine. Whereas it was once possible to argue (Meyrowitz 2009) that the arrival of television demystified the Presidency and the political process, we might conclude that in the 2000s, television has obfuscated the nature and methods of real power in society. Many sources have chronicled and critiqued network failure to adequately present to American audiences an account of recent American wars. I will suggest only four, namely Chossudovsky (2005) on the Taleban, Griffin (2008, 2009) on 9/11 and Bin Laden, Scott (2008) on the war on terror, and the BBC documentaries of Adam Curtis (particularly *The Power of Nightmares*, 2006). From these and other sources, we can reasonably argue, among many other things that the networks failed to investigate the Administration's history of relations with the Taleban; the extent to which Afghanistan had been reconfigured by American and Pakistani support of the mujahadeen during the 1980s war against the Soviets; US corporate energy interests in oil and gas pipelines across Afghanistan from the Caspian; the complex relationship between US, Pakistani and Saudi intelligence, on the one hand, and Bin Laden, multiple Afghan warlords, and the partly-fictitious entity of Al Qaeda, on the other. They failed to interrogate the many unanswered and unsettling questions that surrounded 9/11. They failed to hold the Administration properly to account for the Bush Administration's startling 2002 doctrine of pre-emptive warfare. They failed to interrogate and expose in timely fashion the Administration's deliberate manipulation of media and public opinion to falsely leverage 9/11 as the justification for a long prepared attack on Iraq, and its peddling, on the basis of highly dubious sources, of a mythology of 'weapons of mass destruction'. They played along with the Administration's staged public relations events such as Bush's 'Mission Accomplished' speech, the destruction of the Saddam Hussein statue, the 'rescue' of Private Jessica Lynch. They reported some of the worst atrocities of their nation's history with all the bravery of liveried courtiers before their King: these ranged from the looting of historical artifacts, Bremer's reckless disbandment of the Iraqi army, brutal detention and killing of large numbers of Iraqis on flimsy or nonexistent pretexts, illegal rendition, the tortures of Abu Ghraib, Baghram Air Base and Guantanamo, the 'friendly fire' shooting death of sports hero Pat Tillman, the deaths of US servicemen from faulty electrical wiring at the hands of Halliburton, reckless killings of civilians by mercenary contractors such as Blackwater. Media frequently and misleadingly presented the US occupiers as a neutral hand protecting different Iraqi sects from one another. For far too long they maintained the façade of a puppet Iraqi regime as an 'independent' government. Patriots seeking to oust the occupiers were routinely described as 'insurgents'. Media failed to expose or give voice to legitimate public outrage against war profiteering, beginning with Bush family involvement with defense contractor Carlyle, through the obscene profits of no-bid hand-outs to contractors like KBR, to the CIA-linked, mercenary regime of Blackwater (later Xe, now Academi). In short, they shied timidly from the central controversies of their times. In Afghanistan even into 2009 they continued to support without qualification the debatable proposition (Griffin 2009) that Osama Bin Laden was a main culprit behind 9/11 (it is Khalid Sheikh Mohammed, after years of torture in US captivity, who is the one actually charged with being the mastermind and who, in 2010, still awaits trial for the crime) or that he was still alive, and media struggled fecklessly to find meaning in a war in which, even on the US military admission, Al Qaeda was no longer a significant presence (Reid 2009).

Trends of Change in the New Millennium

Growth of Infotainment
The US television broadcast and cable networks bear a unique responsibility for the development of market-driven "infotainment" television and its export around the world, a process that includes: physical export and dissemination of television documentary products (e.g. CNNI, The Discovery Channel, the

History Channel, the proliferation of 'reality' television shows); sale of pro-gram 'formats'; multinational advertising that pushes channel producers and mangers towards infotainment by enhancing the importance of ratings; US investment in the ownership of television channels and programs; and, increasingly, local imitation of US entertainment business practices.

Thussu (2007) has reviewed the rise of television news infotainment. He quotes a 1998 Project for Excellence in Journalism study of US mass media over two decades, tracking a shift towards 'lifestyle, celebrity, entertainment and celebrity crime/scandal', and away from government and foreign affairs. Stories about scandals rose from just 0.015% in 1977 to 15% in 1997. Human interest and quality of life stories doubled from 8% in 1977 to 16% of all stories in 1997. Thussu quotes Kovach and Rosenstiel's (1999) identification of four factors behind the rise of infotainment and its 'corrosive' impact on journalism: the 24/7 news cycle and its appetite for 'live' news; the proliferation of many new networks; growing sophistication of news management and 'spin'; and intensification of a ratings mind-set that prioritized the dramatic and the entertaining.

Pew Project for Excellence in Journalism Annual Reports

The gathering crisis of the 2000s is nowhere referenced in more detail than in the annual reports on the state of news media by the Pew Project for Excellence in Journalism, beginning in 2004 Each traces key trends of the previous year across different news media. The 2004 report set a tone for the decade. It noted the paradox of growing diversity of news outlets while audiences were shrink-ing, amidst evidence of increasing press manipulation (including the Jessica Lynch story), and investors' fetish for news dissemination over news collec-tion. The outlook for many outlets was bleak. The report doubted whether online news sites would prove a durable or sufficient compensation for loss of advertising in traditional media. Convergence was less of a threat.

The 2005 report noted a growth in available models of doing journalism, some of them partisan ('journalism of affirmation'), seemingly at odds with what most Americans said they wanted. The report proposed that journalism needed more transparency and expertise, through the roles of 'authenticator' or 'referee' – a 'show me' approach very different to the 'trust me' authority of the network age, some of whose doyen (e.g. Dan Rather or Peter Jennings) had recently died or retired. Mainstream media were investing too cautiously in building (even online) new audiences, leaving real innovation to Google, YouTube, and blogs. Profitability increasingly depended on cost-cutting tactics such as cheap unscripted news programs.

The 2006 report noted the paradox of more journalistic outlets yielding fewer stories, sameness of style, modest resources and smaller audiences.

Authorities could easily divert journalists away from real news. In newsrooms, 'accountants' had won their long battle against 'idealists'. Notions of 'public interest' were derided. 'Fragmentation' of product and platform, argued the 2007 report, was a response to too many organizations essentially doing the same thing – but not enough of the really important things, as demonstrated by deteriorating coverage of local government. The industry was becoming more aggressive in redeveloping its economic model, moving away from dependence on an advertising industry that was outgrowing its need for media. The 2007 report ruminated whether the investment community would look beyond news as a declining industry and redefine it as one in transition. Bravely, it asked whether the public corporation was a suitable framework for the kind of transition that newsrooms needed and whether private capital might be more effective. In content, the report noted a move from a journalistic culture of 'argument' to one of 'answers', offering solutions, certainty, crusades, yet not committed to giving the 'other side' equal play.

Content

The 2004 report noted a growing range of topics covered, but lighter treatment, more self-branding and commercials. There was pressure to run with stories more quickly, and concentration on 'blockbuster' stories. Cable news favored live interviews and reporter stand-ups rather than written and edited packages.

The 2005 report concentrated on media bias in coverage of Iraq and the 2004 election. Across all media, 25% of coverage was deemed negative towards US involvement in Iraq, 20% positive, 35% neutral. The three nightly newscasts and PBS were slightly more negative. Such recompense for media failure to expose false pretexts for war came too late, I would argue, to make a difference and ignored the ultimate "success" of the war – return of western majors to Iraqi oil development. Fox was twice as likely to be positive. CNN and MSNBC were evenly split. A high percentage (60%) of selected foreign news stories used anonymous sources, as against 50% of morning TV and 29% of newspaper front page stories, but only 9% of cable. In contrast to the free-to-air networks, cable news was more thinly reported, using fewer sources. Cable was more one-sided and opinionated, most notably so in the case of Fox. The broadcast evening newscasts on the other hand provided greater depth, through more edited packages (involving more planning and script).

The 2006 report observed that most media news was transitory, lacking in long-term consequence, with few top stories continuing to be covered two or three days after first appearance, too often drawing on a small number of sources. Some stories on national television, the report noted, "essentially relied on a single source, sometimes the same one on every channel." There was excessive repetition within the 24-hour news cycle.

News coverage in 2007 as in 2004, was dominated by Iraq and election topics consumed one third of the total news hole, thus contributing to a notable narrowing of the news agenda. Overall in 2007 U.S.-related foreign affairs accounted for 17% of coverage, followed by U.S. election and political coverage at 13%. Non-U.S. related foreign news coverage accounted for 11%. Other categories were crime 7%; government 6%; disasters 5%; health 5%; economics 4%; lifestyle 4%; and business 3%. There had been a precipitous decline in government coverage from 16% on the broadcast networks in 2003 to 6% in 2007; and from 29% on cable in 2003 to 7% in 2007. Important domestic subjects given only superficial attention included education (1% of the domestic news hole), transportation (0.8%), religion (0.7%), court/legal system (0.4%), development/sprawl (0.2%). These topics, said the report, 'bend', i.e. require constant coverage so that consumers will understand the significance of incremental changes.

'World' coverage was not really about the world but about 'some US interests abroad'. Only three countries received notable coverage: Iraq, Iran and Pakistan. Countries receiving scant attention included, surprisingly, Afghanistan, North Korea, Darfur, Russia, China and the Lebanon. Israel-Palestine accounted for 0.5% of the foreign news whole; nuclear negotiations with North Korea, 0.4%; violence in Darfur 0.2%; deteriorating relations with Russia 0.2%; China 0.5%. The report lamented the "remarkably short attention span" of what it called "drive by" coverage – the brief flooding of a hot news zone with instant coverage, followed by next to nothing. Also called 'hit-and-run', this was particularly notable on cable. Tabloid-style gossip and scandal was not a strong feature of broadcast networks, but came principally from cable. Older media (press and broadcast networks) were broader, more diverse and less likely to be dominated by mega-stories. Broadcast networks and newspapers focused least attention on the 'big' stories and carried the highest number of topic areas. Only newspapers included business, health and medical affairs among top priorities. Broadcast networks provided the most coverage of disasters and accidents. Cable devoted the most time to crime.

Transitioning from Network to Post-Network Age

Geoffrey Baym (2010) identifies three phases in the evolution of television news. The 'network age', protected by FCC policies that generally privileged incumbent players against newcomers, endured from the 1940s through to the emergence of cable as a significant competitor in the 1980s and was character-ized by an oligopoly of the 'Big 3': ABC, CBS, and NBC. News in this period was conceived as a professional avocation distinct from entertainment, and con-centrated on "rational-critical investigation of matters of assumed public interest." (Baym 2010, 54–70) On the downside, Baym cites James Carey (1993) to the effect that this approach to news "reduced the role of citizens, speaking at and for them but allowing them no role in the conversation except as the audience". This era was succeeded by the period of market-driven multi-chan-nel transformations coincident with the emergence of cable and satellite, and the removal of regulations that mandated news and public affairs program-ming as in the 1996 Telecommunications Act. This in turn has been succeeded by the 'post-network' age. It is the product not just of technology developments (principally VCR, CDS, DVD, Internet, DVR, personal computers, MP3 players, 3G mobile phones, Internet-enabled television), but also of shifts in political economy and culture, including the shift from national to global cultures, the corporatization of culture, and cultural hybridization (Baym 2010, 172–174). The dominant features of this age are as follows:

(i)   A shift of content from medium-specific to flows across multiple media channels
(ii)   Increased interdependence of communications systems
(iii) Multiple ways of accessing media content (anywhere, anytime conve-nience)
(iv)   More complex relations between top-down corporate media and bot-tom-up participatory experimentation
(v)   Experimentation
(vi)   Greater genre instability, including infotainment ("aestheticiztion of the political-normative sphere" and "politicization of the aesthetic-expres-sive sphere" as exemplified by the popularity of satirists who come to be regarded as significant sources of political news and comments, includ-ing Stephen Colbert ('The Colbert Report' started in 2005), Bill Maher and Jon Stewart ('The Daily Show' started in 2004)
(vii) Discursive integration of different and sometimes contradictory "styles, standards and assumptions."

The emergence of a post-network age in the 2000s has radically destabilized the business model of network television. The distinction between 'terrestrial' and cable/satellite television news has grown progressively blurred as a result of the mandatory shift from analogue to digital television in 2009 and the absorption of most commercial television suppliers within the major media conglomerates notably Disney, General Electric, Microsoft, Time Warner, and Viacom/CBS. These link together national/local terrestrial, cable and satellite networks with the Hollywood studios and distributors. Drawing from the analyses of Baym (2010) and Jenkins, (2006), I identify the principal roots of these trends:

(i)   relentless decades-long decline in audience ratings for the 'old' networks and achievement of only modest ratings for the 'new' networks

(ii)   aging audience

(iii) diffusion of total advertising revenue across more and more outlets, including online sites and social network media, leaving less to spend on traditional television. Advertisers showing greater independence of media content altogether as they explore new methods of direct access to their preferred customers

(iv)   increasing opportunities for audiences to access news content without exposure to advertising, reduces advertiser interest in supporting traditional television

(v)   increasing audience resistance, especially among younger audiences, to being tied down to a particular time to watch news

(vi)   more competition for audience leisure time, including the Internet and video-games

(vii) collapse in the perceived 'authority' of news, coincident with (a) the rise of opinionated journalism, (b) infotainment, (c) the inability of television news programming to hold the powerful to convincing account for abuses that have included the launch of wars on false pretext, (d) susceptibility to gross manipulations of information and logic by powerful lobbyists "turning public information into marketing the purpose of manufacturing public perception" (Baym 2010, 22).

In line with Baym, Lotz (2009) chronicles a move from the 'network' era through the 'multi-channel' transition of the 1980s–1990s, to the 'post-network' era. The network era was characterized by minimal viewer choice and control under conditions of high concentration or monopoly of supply (justified, as Uricchio, 2009, notes, by the logic of 'scarcity' – a logic that had a lot less to do with the limitations of spectrum, as commonly claimed, and much more to do with the politics of allocation), predictable schedules, clustered advertising packages (not sponsored programs as in the early days of television), family viewing, non-offensive homogeneous content, and expensive news operations that bought the sympathy of policy-makers. The model was also characterized by commitment to public service. All these features are transitioning in the post-network era towards heightened audience control and choice from multiple sources of anytime-anywhere television, financed by sponsorship and subscription as well as clustered advertising, with more heterogeneous, segmented or customized content, supported by weaker, less-profitable news operations whose news sometimes migrates to other categories of programming, including comedy (Blondheim and Liebes 2009). Although market logic appears to have vanquished that of the public sphere as determinant of content, Lunt finds evidence of a new kind of public service by which popular television genres "reflect a normative social order oriented to self-regulation and development in which expertise is constituted as an aid to everyday living...a site of social control, mobilizing individuals in processes of rationalization (the adoption of psychological discourse), self-surveillance, and confession (Lunt 2009, 172)".

Conclusion

US Network television is not in imminent threat of annihilation, but is in danger of gradual evaporation from a thousand cuts, many of which I have reviewed in the preceding pages:

- the loss of an audience willing to watch at fixed hours of day or night;
- competition from others sources of information and entertainment, including electronic books and video-games;
- an overwhelming loss of younger viewers with sufficient knowledge and news skills to appreciate anything more than extremely simplified, selective and misleading content
- growing consumer preference for 'anywhere, anytime' viewing which opens the door to secondary providers and/or spreads the available advertising expenditure across a broader range of outlets, including online news services of both traditional print and traditional broadcast organizations, mobile outlets, YouTube and Hulu.
- greater desperation for advertising revenue, scratching down Chinese walls that once separated editorial from advertising;
- the continuing loss of news 'quality' in the sense of services that offer news that is authentic, independent of and truly critical of power, both trustworthy and of relevance to people's real needs as opposed to the manufactured and inauthentic wants imposed on them by media conglomerates in their bid to sell larger numbers of viewers to advertisers.

In this chapter I have reviewed the development of the original 'network' structure of US television news, noting the considerable degree to which this has been contested by the arrival of cable and satellite providers. These in turn helped to transform the field towards one of channel abundance, in news as in most other genres, within a context of industry concentration and conglomeration. Since this connects to issues of power, I have considered the extent to which the Republican charge of 'liberal media' holds up in the case of the three original 'terrestrial' channels and the three newer 'cable' channels. I have found little evidence to support that charge in the context of what is perhaps the gravest controversy of all, US overseas military engagements, and quite a lot of evidence that suggests that mainstream US television is principally a conduit for authoritative pronouncement from agents of the State and the corporatocracy. The transition from the network era to a 'post-network' era of poorly-resourced news abundance and anytime/everywhere television, has not eluded the deadening and orthodox hand of US conglomerate capitalism, but it does contain such potential for rupture and fragmentation that may make it increasingly difficult for the State to successfully and comprehensively impose on media its hegemonic accounts of world affairs through the lenses of neo-liberal capitalism and imperial interest.

References

Ackerman, Seth. 2001. Al-Aqsa Intifada and the U.S. Media. *Journal of Palestine Studies* 30 (2): 61–74.

Alexander, Alison, James Owers, and Rod Carveth. 2003. *Media Economics: Theory and Practice*. London: Routledge.

Allan, Stuart and Barbara Zelizer. 2004. *Reporting War: Journalism in Wartime*. London: Routledge.

Auletta, Ken. 1992. *Three Blind Mice: How the TV Networks Lost Their Way*. New York: Vintage.

Barkin, Steve. 2003. *American Television News: The Media Marketplace and the Public Interest*. New York: M.E. Sharpe.

Barnouw, Erik. 1968. *A History of Broadcasting in the United States*. New York: Oxford University Press.

Barstow, David. 2008. Behind TV Analysts: Pentagon's Hidden Hand. *New York Times*, April 20. http://www.nytimes.com/2008/04/20/us/20generals.html?pagewanted=all &_r=0 (accessed April 20, 2008).

Baym, Geoffrey. 2010. *From Cronkite to Colbert: The Evolution of Broadcast News*. Boulder: Paradigm.

Blondheim, Menahem and Tamar Liebes. 2009. Television News and the Nation: The End? *The Annals of the American Academy of Political and Social Science* 625 (September): 182–195.

Blum, William. 2008. *Killing Hope: u.s. Military and c.i.a. Intervention Since World War II.* Common Courage Press.

Carey, James. 1993. The Mass Media and Democracy: Between the Modern and the Postmodern. *Journal of International Affairs* 47 (1): 1–21.

Chossudovsky, Michel. 2005. *America's 'War on Terrorism'.* Nishayuna: Global Research.

Collins, Scott. 2004. *Crazy Like a Fox: The Inside Story of How Fox News Beat cnn.* New York: Portfolio.

Cottle, Simon. 2008. *Global Crisis Reporting.* Milton Keynes: Open University Press.

Croteau, David and William Hoynes. 2005. *The Business of Media: Corporate Media and the Public Interest.* Thousand Oaks: Pine Forge Press.

Curtis, Adam. 2006. *The Power of Nightmares.* London: British Broadcasting Corporation.

Eke, Chinedu. 2008. Darfur: Coverage of Genocide by Three Major u.s. Networks on their Evening News. *International Journal of Media and Cultural Politics* 4 (3): 277–292.

Engelman, Ralph. 1996. *Public Radio and Television in America: A Political History.* Thousand Oaks: Sage Publications.

Epstein, Jay. 2000. *News From Nowhere: Television and the News.* Washington: Ivan R. Dee.

Goldenson, Leonard and Wolf, Marvin. 1991. *Beating the Odds: The Untold Story Behind the Rise of abc.* New York: Scribners.

Greenwald, Glen. 2004. *Outfoxed: Rupert Murdoch's War on Journalism.* IWantMedia Inc.

Griffin, David. 2008. *The New Pearl Harbor Revisited: 9/11, the Cover-Up, and the Expose.* Northampton: Olive Branch Press.

Griffin, David. 2009. *Osama Bin Laden: Dead or Alive.* Northampton, ma: Olive Branch Press.

Hallin, Daniel. 1986. *The 'Uncensored War:' The Media and Vietnam.* New York: Oxford University Press.

Hoskins, Andrew. 2004. *Televising War: From Vietnam to Iraq.* London: Bloomsbury Academic.

Jaramillo, Deborah. 2009. *Ugly War, Pretty Package: How cnn and Fox News Made the Invasion of Iraq High Concept.* Bloomington and Indianapolis: Indiana University Press.

Jenkins, Henry. 2006. *Convergence Culture: Where Old and New Media Collide.* New York: New York University Press.

Jones, Sebastien. 2010. The Media-Lobbying Complex. *The Nation*, March 1. http://www.thenation.com/doc/20100301/jones/single (accessed March 3, 2010).

Lotz, Amanda. 2009. What is U.S. Television Now? *The Annals of the American Academy of Political and Social Science* 625 (September): 49–59.

Lunt, Peter. 2009. Television, Public Participation, and Public Service: From Value Consensus to the Politics of Identity. *The Annals of the American Academy of Political and Social Science* 625 (September): 128–138.

Katz, E. and P. Scannell. 2009. The end of television? Its impact on the world (so far). *The Annals of the American Academy of Political and Social Science*, Vol. 625, September, pp. 49–59.

Kellner, Douglas. 1992. *The Persian Gulf TV War*. New York: Westview Press.

Kellner, Douglas. 2003. *Media Spectacle*. New York: Routledge.

Kovach, Bill. and Tom Rosenstiel. 1999. *Warp Speed: America in the Age of Mixed Media*. New York: The Century Foundation Press.

Melber, Ari. 2009. New White House Line Against Fox: It's War. *Huffington Post*, October 12. http://www.huffingtonpost.com/ari-melber/will-obamas-new-anti-fox_b_3169 83.html (accessed October, 2009).

Meyrowitz, Joshua. 2009. We Liked to Watch: Television as Progenitor of the Surveillance Society. *The Annals of the American Academy of Political and Social Science* 625 (September): 32–48.

Paper, Lewis J. 1987. *Empire: William S. Paley and the Making of CBS*. New York: St. Martin's Press.

Preston, William Jr., Edward S. Herman and Herbert I. Schiller. 1989. Hope and Folly: The United States and UNESCO, 1945–1985. Univ. Of Minnesota Press: USA.

Reid, Robert H. 2009. Al-Qaida Showing Smaller Presence in Afghanistan. *Huffington Post*, June 10. http://www.huffingtonpost.com/2009/10/07/al-qaida-showing-smaller _n_311985.html (accessed March 2014).

Scott, Peter. 2008. *The Road to 9/11: Wealth, Empire and the Future of America*. University of California Press.

Solomon, Norman. 2007. *Media Love, Got War: Close Encounters with America's Warfare State*. Sausalito: Polipoint Press.

Stelter, Brian and Bill Carter. 2010. Network News at a Crossroads. *New York Times*, February 28. http://www.nytimes.com/2010/03/01/business/media/01network.html ?scp=1&sq=Steler%20and%20Carter&st=cse, (accessed, May, 2010).

Thussu, Daya. 2000. Legitimizing Humanitarian Intervention? CNN, NATO and the Kosovo Crisis. *European Journal of Communication* 15 (3): 345–362.

Thussu, Daya. 2007. *News as Entertainment: The Rise of Global Infotainment*. London: Sage.

Thussu, Daya and Freedman, Desmond. 2003. *War and the Media: Reporting Conflict 24/7*. London: Sage.

Uricchio, William. 2009. Contextualizing the Broadcast Era: Nation, Commerce, and Constraint. *The Annals of the American Academy of Political and Social Science* 625 (September): 60–73.

Volkmer, Ingrid. 2005. *News in the Global Sphere: A Study of CNN and its Impact on Global Communications*. London: John Libbey.

Voorhees, Courte, John Vick and Douglas Perkins. 2007. Came Rain or High Water: The Intersection of Hurricane Katrina, the News Media, Race and Poverty. *Journal of Community and Applied Social Psychology* 17: 415–429.

Weaver, David, Randal Beam, Bonnie Brownlee, Paul Voakes and Wilhoit G. Cleveland. 2007. *The American Journalist in the 21st Century: U.S. News People at the Dawn of New Millennium.* Mahway: Lawrence Erlbaum Associates.

Whittemore, Hank. 1990. *CNN: The Inside Story: How a Band of Mavericks Changed the Face of Television News.* New York: Little Brown.

CHAPTER 9

Corporate Social (Ir)Responsibility in Media and Communication Industries[1]

Marisol Sandoval

Introduction

Microsoft is the most socially responsible company in the world, followed by Google and The Walt Disney Company – at least according to the perceptions of 47,000 people from 15 countries that participated in a survey conducted by the consultancy firm Reputation Institute.[2] Based on the results of this survey the Reputation Institute compiled a ranking of 100 companies with the best CSR reputation worldwide. The top 3 companies in this ranking belong to the media and communication sector: Microsoft (rank 1), Google (rank 2), and The Walt Disney Company (rank 3) (Reputation Institute 2012, 19).

Considering the apparent success of the CSR strategies of leading media and communication companies it is surprising that the corporate social responsibilities of this sector have thus far been neglected as a research topic both in CSR research and in media and communication studies: Within the debate on CSR, media are often only discussed in regard to their role of raising awareness and enabling public debate about corporate social responsibility (Dickson and Eckman 2008, 726; Dyck and Zingales 2002, 5; EC 2011, 7). What is lacking are theoretical and empirical studies about the corporate social (ir)responsibility of media and communication companies themselves.

This paper contributes to overcoming this blindspot. In a first step I discuss possible theoretical approaches to CSR in media and communication companies (section 2). Subsequently I take a closer look at the corporate social (ir)responsibility of the three companies that were ranked to have best CSR reputation worldwide (section 3). I show that the actual practices of Microsoft, Google and The Walt Disney Company do not correspond to their reputation.

---

1   Reprinted with the permission of EURICOM from Javnost – The Public.

2   *France, Germany, Italy, Russia, Spain, United Kingdom, Australia, China, India, Japan, South Korea, United States, Canada, Brazil and Mexico Source: Reputation Institute. 2012. CSR is Not Dead, It is just Mismanaged. Retrieved from* http://www.reputationinstitute.com/thought -leadership/csr-reptrak-100?/thought-leadership/2012-corporate-social-responsibility *on February 14, 2013.*

In the conclusion (section 4) I therefore highlight the limitations of CSR and suggest an alternative concept.

Theories of CSR in Media and Communication Industries

One of the first theorists of CSR was Howard Bowen's who defined the *Social Responsibilities of the Businessman* (1953) as "the obligations of businessman to pursue those policies, to make those decisions, or to follow those lines of action which are desirable in terms of the objectives and values of our society" (Bowen 1953, 6). The idea that businessmen should serve society instead of only pursuing the interests of shareholders contradicted the dominant economic view according to which the purpose of the corporation is to maximize profits.

In 1962 the influential liberal economist and winner of the Nobel Memorial Prize in Economic Sciences Milton Friedman therefore called CSR a "fundamentally subversive doctrin" (Friedman 1962/1982) and later argued that the only responsibility of corporations is "to make as much money as possible"(Friedman 1970/2009, 75). Today CSR seems much less controversial: In 2011, 95% of the 250 largest global companies[3] reported about their CSR activities (KPMG 2011, 7). However, the question remains how CSR theories deal with these two different goals that are ascribed to the corporation. How do theories of CSR relate the traditional corporate goal to maximize profit and the goal to act socially responsible?

A systematic description of different approaches to the relation between the corporate and the social can be based on Wolfgang Hofkirchner's (2003, 2013) distinction of four possible ways of relating two phenomena with different degrees of differentiation: Reductionism, projectionism, dualism and dialectics (Hofkirchner, 2003, 133): Reductionism reduces the higher differentiated phenomenon to the lower differentiated one. Projectionism in contrast projects the higher degree of differentiation on the lower differentiated side. Dualism separates both phenomena from each other and does not recognise any interrelations. Dialectical thinking on the contrary considers how both sides mutually shape each other.[4] Based on this typology reductionist, projectionist and dualist approaches to CSR can be described as follows:

---

3   Based on the Fortune Global 500 List: http://money.cnn.com/magazines/fortune/global500/.

4   In regard to profit goals and social goals of media companies, the former can be considered as the lower and the latter as the higher differentiated phenomenon: Profit is a goal of a single corporation within the economic sub-system of society. Caring for social issues on the contrary means contributing to the functioning of society as a whole and not just to the

- Reductionism reduces the social responsibilities of the corporation to a means for advancing profit goals. Acting socially responsible is regarded as a means for avoiding government regulation (e.g. Almeder 1980, 13), for opening up new markets and business opportunities (e.g. Drucker 1984) or for improving corporate image and reputation and creating good relationships with stakeholders (e.g. Jones 1995).
- Projectionism on the contrary projects ethical principles or a social consciousness onto the profit goals of corporations. This approach does not question the profit motive as such but highlights that profit should be generated in a socially responsible way. According to the projectionist view this is possible by subjecting profit generation to the expectations of society (e.g. Frederick 1960, Carroll 1979), equal respect for the interests of all stakeholders (e.g. Freeman 1994), government regulation (e.g. McInerney 2007), or democratic control (Scherer and Palazzo 2007).
- Dualism treats economic and social goals of the media as disjunctive and argues that media companies should simultaneously achieve both, being economically successful and acting socially responsible. In a dualist manner the concept of philanthropy for example postpones socially responsible behaviour to a point after profit goals have already been achieved (e.g. Carnegie 1889).
- A dialectical perspective considers mutual interrelations between profit goals and social responsibilities and therefore describes the relation between the corporate and the social as inherently conflictual. This approach puts forward a critique of dominant CSR theories (Banerjee 2008, 73; Fleming and Jones 2013, 6; Corlett 1998, 103, Sklair and Miller 2010). It is based on the insight that profit generation necessarily means exploitation, injustice and inequality. A dialectical approach highlights that understood as voluntary corporate self-regulation, CSR strengthens corporate power rather than limiting it. It therefore stresses that CSR should not be reduced to a managerial question but be discussed on a political level.

In the following I apply this typology to theories of CSR in media and communication industries (sections 2.1–2.4).

Reductionism: Social Responsibility as Strategic Advantage

Reductionist accounts of the social responsibility of the media highlight how social issues can be approached in ways that benefit business interest. In this

---

success of one of its parts. Doing social good and contributing to the well-being of society can thus be described as a more complex and higher differentiated goal than generating profit and contributing to the well-being of the corporation.

manner, Anke Trommershausen (2011) tries to show how addressing emerging challenges in the area of communication and culture can be turned into strategic opportunities for companies (Trommerhausen 2011, 27). Based on Carsten Winter's (2006) concept of the TIME (telecommunication, information, media, and entertainment) industries, she analyzed Corporate Social Responsibility in telecommunication, information and media (TIM) companies.

Trommershausen (2011, 30) argues that the particular "social" about the responsibility of TIM(E) companies lies in the realm of communication and culture. She stresses that the challenges related to the emergence of digital network media could be turned into strategic advantages if corporate responsibility strategies focus on the core business of a company (Trommershausen 2011, 181): the challenge of ensuring access would for create potentials for entering new markets (Trommershausen 2011, 171–174); the challenge of changing stakeholder relations would entail the potential of successfully managing stakeholders by individualizing relations to stakeholders through digital media (Trommershausen 2011, 174–178); the challenge of enabling the constitution of a public sphere would yield long term strategic potentials if TIM(E) companies ensure a secure and fair access to digital media products and services (Trommerhausen 2011, 179–181); the challenge of corporate responsibility management could result in competitive advantages if professional corporate responsibility management and control strategies are established (Trommershausen 2011, 182).

Trommershausen's approach to CSR in media and communication companies is based on a corporate logic according to which business goals are more important than social responsibilities. She argues that realizing competitive advantages requires a strategic approach to CSR"Only that way it becomes possible to exploit strategic potentials and test them with respect to a Return on Corporate Responsibility based on the Business Case" (Trommershausen 2011, 182 translation MS[5]). The notion of a "Return on Corporate Responsibility" reduces the idea of social responsibility ad absurdum – instead of contributing to the common good, responsible behaviour is supposed to yield a financial return.

Apart from its instrumentality, another limitation of Trommershausen's approach is its exclusive focus on the media's responsibilities for communication and culture. She argues that media convergence has lead to the emergence of digital network media, which include hardware such as PCs, notebooks, mobile phones as well as web 2.0 media such as weblog and wikis

---

5 "Nur so können die strategischen Potenziale tatsächlich genutzt und hinsichtlich eines Return on Corporate Responsibility durch den Business Case geprüft werden." (Trommershausen 2011, 182).

(Trommershausen 2011, 33). The hardware industry is an example that perfectly illustrates that working conditions and environmental destruction are important issues for the media and communication sector.[6] Trommerhausen ignores these issues when arguing that the particular social about the responsibility of TIM(E) companies is their responsibility for communication and culture and thus fails to grasp the whole range of social responsibilities of the media and communication sector.

CSR strategies that are based on such a reductionist approach are likely to be highly selective and will ignore social problems if addressing them contradicts business goals. The main beneficiaries of a reductionist approach to the social responsibility of the media are the owners and shareholders of media corporations.

Projectionism: Ethics in a Commercial Media System

Projectionist approaches are based on the assumption that in order to be socially responsible, media should meet the expectations of society. Following this view responsible media, despite their commercial organization, need to embody certain moral values. Projectionist approaches become manifest in ethics codes for journalism and media.

Already in 1956 Siebert, Peterson and Schramm described a social responsibility theory of the press as one of *Four Theories of the Press*, which is based on the assumption that the commercial organization of media needs to be balanced by a strong ethical awareness. It therefore points at the necessity of establishing ethical codes that ensure that the press works for "the public good" (Siebert, Peterson and Schramm 1956, 76f).

Early examples of such codes are the code by the American Society of Newspaper Editors (1923) and the recommendations made in the report *A Free and Responsible Press* (1947) by the Commission on the Freedom of the Press (1947), known as the Hutchins Commission. The aim of ethics codes is that media, despite their commercial organization, meet their social responsibilities. They "provide working journalists with statements of minimums and perceived ideals" (Elliott-Boyle, 1985/1986, 25). These standards specify ideal journalistic behaviour in respect to ethical issues of journalistic practices, which include "freedom, objectivity, truth, honesty, privacy" (Belsey and

---

6 The European project makeITfair for example has shown in numerous reports that on the one hand unacceptable working conditions exists in the supply chain of media hardware companies and that on the other hand the improper disposal of electronic products creates fundamental threats for human health and the environment. See: http://makeitfair.org/en?set_language=en.

Chadwick 1994, xiii). Himelboim and Limor argue that journalistic ethics codes are designed to define the role of journalists in society (Himelboim and Limor 2011, 76).

Irrespective of their particular content a main problem regarding voluntary ethics codes is, that they contain guidelines for journalists without sufficiently considering how economic realities hamper the implementation of these guidelines. Market pressures often constrain the work of journalists. McQuail for example points out that codes of ethics provide some normative guidelines, which however cannot always be applied in actual journalistic practices (McQuail 2010, 172). Codes that simply demand from journalists to protect sources, be truthful and fair (Laitila 1995), to ensure integrity truth and, objectivity (Jones C. 1980, 83), or to commit to the public's right to know (Himelboim and Limor 2011, 82) treat ethical behaviour as an individual responsibility of journalists.

Awareness of journalists for their role in society is certainly important. It is however doubtful that ethical commitments of journalists are enough for achieving a socially responsible media system. Some contributors to the field of media ethics recognize this shortcoming. McManus for example stresses: "Major American journalism ethics codes, however, not only fail to examine the corporate profit motive, most don't even recognize its existence"(McManus 1997, 13). Similarly Richards highlights: "At a theoretical level, one of the major weaknesses in many analyses of journalism ethics is the failure to accommodate the realities of corporatism"(Richards 2004, 123). The projectionist belief that commercial media can become socially responsible through imposing on them guidelines for ethical behaviour is both individualistic and idealistic and likely to overlook existing economic pressures and necessities. In a commercial media system journalism is a business and media companies that strive for a profit have to abide the demands of the market, which can contradict journalistic ethics.

Dualism: Commercial Success and Ethical Behaviour

Dualist approaches to CSR treat economic interests and social responsibilities of the media as separate from each other. Altmeppen's (2011) concept of "media social responsibility" exemplifies this approach. It is based on a distinction between journalism and the media. According to Altmeppen, journalism selects topics and creates content that can be distributed via the media. In Altmeppen's view journalism is no business model. It would depend on media organizations that ensure its funding and distribute its products (Altmeppen 2011, 249). Media organizations on the contrary would generate money trough the distribution of content, which allows them to pay for journalism and the production of media content (Altmeppen 2011, 249).

According to Altmeppen (2011, 257–259) the responsibility of journalism is related to its societal role, which would consist in the production of socially important information The main social responsibility of media companies would on the contrary lie in providing the necessary resources for journalistic production. Treating media and journalism as structurally and functionally different entities establishes a dualism between economic goals and social responsibility: Media generate profit, journalism is ethical.

The analytical distinction between journalism and media for identifying social responsibilities is questionable. In fact both are operating together, journalistic production requires financial resources, and media organizations cannot make money without journalism. Neither of the two is able to operate without the other, which creates strong mutual dependencies. A dualism between content (journalism) and organizational form (media) that assumes that media is a business model while journalism is not, runs danger of regarding journalism as independent from market pressures. Furthermore Altmeppen's claim that journalism would be no business model is questionable. He himself argues that "media 'pay' a 'price' to journalism for its creation of informative, topical content" (Altmeppen 2011, 258 translation MS[7]). This shows that the business model of journalism is selling media content to media companies. Media companies receive money from advertising clients. Those who pay for journalism in fact are advertisers. What Altmeppen conceptualizes as media is just the administrative intermediary that organizes the sale of advertisements. It is exactly this double role of media content companies as at the same time both profit-oriented economic entities and providers of media content, which challenges the media's ability to meet its social responsibilities. An approach that is based on a distinction between media and journalism misses this double role and resulting challenges.

Dialectics: The Social Irresponsibility of Commercial Media

Dialectical approaches stress that economic goals and social responsibilities of the media mutually shape each other. From this perspective economic success and profitability of media companies have consequences that impair their social responsibility. At the same time socially responsible media that resist commercial mechanisms and market pressures are likely to suffer from a lack of resources and visibility.

Streams of media studies that – without referring to the notion of CSR – have always stressed the importance of considering interrelations between the

---

7   "Medien 'zahlen' dem Journalismus einen 'Preis' für die Lieferung informativer, aktueller Inhalte" (Altmeppen 2011, 258).

economic organization of media and their social and cultural roles and responsibilities are critical theory and political economy of media and communication.

Already Karl Marx pointed out that the press has the important social role of serving as a public watchdog. According to Marx the press should be "the public watchdog, the tireless denouncer of those in power, the omnipresent eye, the omnipresent mouthpiece of the people's spirit that jealously guards its freedom"(Marx 1849/1959, 231[8]). He at the same time recognized that in order to fulfil its important social role, the press needs to be organized in a non-commercial way: "The primary freedom of the press lies in not being a trade"(Marx 1842/1976, 71[9]).

Following Marxian thinking, critical political economy of media and communication departs from the insight that media have a double role in society: they on the one hand are profit oriented corporations and on the other hand have certain special social and cultural responsibilities. Murdock and Golding point out "that the mass media are first and foremost industrial and commercial organizations which produce and distribute commodities" (Murdock and Golding 1997, 3f). However, they at the same time stress that media production also has an important ideological role, "which gives it its importance and centrality and which requires an approach in terms not only of economics but also of politics" (Murdock and Golding 1997, 4f). Similarly Oscar Gandy stresses: "The media are seen to have an economic as well as an ideologic dimension" (Gandy 1997, 100).

Based on this recognition of the double role of media and communication, critical political economy highlights that understanding the media's effects in society requires studying them within the wider context of capitalism. Mosco argues that critical political economy decentres the media: "Decentering the media means viewing systems of communication as integral to fundamental economic, political, and other material constituents" (Mosco 2009, 66). Herman and McChesney point at the necessity of considering global capitalism for understanding the social role of media (Herman and McChesney 1997, 10). Similarly Garnham emphasized that understanding the capitalist mode of production is essential for the study of cultural practices (Garnham 1998, 611). Knoche points out that analysing the relationship between media and capitalism is among the basic questions of a critical political economy (Knoche 2002, 105)

---

8 Translation: Marxists.org: http://www.marxists.org/archive/marx/works/1849/02/07.htm accessed on March 5, 2011.

9 Translation: Marxists.org: http://www.mlwerke.de/me/meo1/meo1_066.htm accessed on March 5, 2011.

These statements illustrate that studying interrelation between the economic dimensions of media and communication on the one hand, and their social and cultural responsibilities on the other hand is at the heart of a critical political economy of the media. Based on this orientation critical political economists highlight how economic mechanisms and pressures that are at play in a commercial media system, impair the ability of media to meet their social responsibilities: They (a) show how generating private profit based on media and communication requires the exploitation of media producers, audiences and prosumers (Fuchs 2011a, 2010, Garnham 1986/2006, 224; Smythe 1977/1997, 440). Critical approaches to the role of media in society (b) highlight that producing media as commodities leads to the subsumption of culture under market principles and commercial pressures, which fosters uniformity, conformism (Horkheimer and Adorno 1947/1997) and ideological media content (Schiller 1997, McChesney 2004; Herman and Chomsky 1988). A critical political economy perspective (c) shows that the circulation of media and communication products as commodities has as a consequence that access to these goods is restricted. A commercial media system turns media into "a source of private profit rather then [...] to provide information widely and cheaply to all" (Garnham 1983, 19f). The fact that in a corporate media system media access becomes structured by income, fetters the empowering potential of media and communication (Murdock and Golding 2002, 124), and threatens the democratic process (Schiller and Schiller 1988, 154).

Based on this brief overview over the research field of critical political economy of communication, one can conclude that a dialectical perspective on the social responsibilities of the media emphasizes that business interests of media companies tend to undermine the creation of a socially responsible media system: In order to be economically successful, corporate media need to produce media and communication products as commodities that are based on the exploitation of labour power of employees and/or media users; need to produce media content that meets the preferences of the majority and that creates advertising friendly climate; and need to enforce the exclusion from media and communication products in order to be able to accumulate profit. Commercial media are thus creating a media culture that is based on exploitation, conformity and exclusion.

The ideas advanced by dialectical approaches to the social responsibility of the media are embodied in the concept of public service broadcasting as an alternative to the commercial media model. The idea of public broadcasting is based the insight that in order to be able to serve the public interest, broadcasting needs to be freed from market pressures and the need to be financially successful (Seaton 2003, 112f; McQuail 2010, 178). However, since the 1980s the deregulation of the media markets has increasingly put public broadcasting under pressure (McChesney 1997, Murdock and Golding 1999, 125). Public broadcasting stations in Europe today have to compete with numerous private radio and television companies and are thus no longer free from market pressures.

With the decline of the public service broadcasting model the success of the commercial media becomes complete. The question, how commercial mechanisms affect the social responsibilities of the media in their everyday operations, and which consequences this has for media and communication in the 21st thus becomes ever more pressing.

Corporate Social (Ir)Responsibility in Media and Communication Companies

I began this chapter with a reference to the CSR reputation ranking complied by the Reputation Institute, according to which Microsoft, Google and The Walt Disney Company are the three companies with the best CSR reputation worldwide. In the previous section I argued that in order to assess corporate social (ir)responsibilities it is necessary to consider interrelations between a company's economic goals and its social responsibility. Based on such a dialectical perspective on CSR I will in the following discuss in how far the actual practices of these companies correspond to their reputation.

Microsoft – Knowledge Monopoly?

People around the globe are using Microsoft's proprietary software: In September 2011 the operating system MS Windows had a worldwide market share of 86.57%.[10] Given this dominant market position, it is not surprising that Microsoft is economically highly successful: In 2011 it was the largest software company and the 42nd largest company in the world.[11] In the financial year 2012 Microsoft's net profits were almost 17 billion USD, its revenues amounted to 73.7 billion USD and its total assets were 121.2 billion USD (Microsoft SEC-Filings, 10-k form 2012).

---

10   NetMarketshare. 2011. Top Operating System Share Trend. Retrieved from http://www
      .netmarketshare.com/os-market-share.aspx?qprid=9 on October 14, 2011.

11   Forbes Magazine. 2012. The World's Biggest Public Companies. Retrieved from http://
      www.forbes.com/global2000/list/#p_1_s_ao_Software%20&%20Programming_All%20
      countries_All%20states_ on February 15, 2013.

Microsoft is however not only an economically successful company, but also committed to CSR. Since 2003 the company published nine CSR reports. In its most recent Citizenship report Microsoft highlights "Our citizenship mission is to serve globally the needs of communities and fulfil our responsibility to the public"(Microsoft 2013, 2).

Despite this commitment to CSR, Microsoft has been strongly criticised for its business practices. In the late 1990 the company was criminally convicted both in the United States and in Europe[12] for maintaining "its monopoly power by anti-competitive means."[13]

Apart from these violations of anti-trust law, critics highlight that even on a more basic level Microsoft's business model is socially irresponsible. Microsoft's business success is based on proprietary software and thus on software patents: Until September 2011 Microsoft has registered 22,501 patents at the U.S. Patent and Trademark Office.[14]

Civil society initiatives such as the Free Software Foundation's End Software Patents in the United States and No Software Patents in Europe highlight that software patents are problematic in several respects: Their main arguments against software patents include that software patents create advantages for large corporations and lead to monopolization; hinder innovation; privatize and restrict access to knowledge; threaten the freedom of information; create artificial scarcity and that software consists of mathematical formulas and abstract ideas, which are not patentable.[15,16] Open Source Watch stresses that "For many in the open source community, the company [Microsoft] represents all that is troubling about closed source software development" (OSS Watch 2011).

Microsoft is aware of the fact that patents are a fetter to creativity and innovation. Bill Gates in 1991 stressed that patents hamper technological

---

12   The Guardian. 2006. EU Hits Microsoft 280.5 m Antitrust Fine. By Mark Tran on July 12, 2006. Retrieved from http://www.guardian.co.uk/business/2006/jul/12/europeanunion .digitalmedia on October 3, 2011.

13   United States of America vs. Microsoft Corporation. 2000. Conclusions of Law. Retrieved from http://news.cnet.com/html/ne/Special/Microsoft/conclusions_of_law_and_order .html on October 3, 2011.

14   U.S. Patent and Trademark Office. List of Microsoft Patents. Retrieved from http://patft .uspto.gov/netacgi/nph-Parser?Sect1=PTO2&Sect2=HITOFF&p=1&u=%2Fnetahtml%2F PTO%2Fsearch-bool.html&r=0&f=S&l=50&TERM1=microsoft&FIELD1=ASNM&co1=AN D&TERM2=&FIELD2=&d=PTXT on September 28, 2011.

15   End Software Patents. Why Abolish Software Patents. Retrieved from http://en.swpat.org/ wiki/Software_patents_wiki:_home_page on October 6, 2011.

16   No Software Patents. The Dangers. Retrieved from http://www.nosoftwarepatents.com/ en/m/dangers/index.html on October 6, 2011.

innovation: "If people had understood how patents would be granted when most of today's ideas were invented, and had taken out patents, the industry would be at a complete standstill today" (Gates 1991). Microsoft's business practices thus deprive society from the best possible software. Making all software source codes publicly available would allow other programmers to further adapt, develop, and improve software. Collectively, the chances are higher that software is developed that matches the various needs of individuals and society.

Microsoft, through patenting software and requiring users to purchase a license in order to be allowed to use it, makes software scarce. This creates access barriers and thus fosters digital exclusion. In its CSR communication Microsoft highlights that the digital divide hampers the realization of the full potentials of technology: "Technology is a potent force that can empower millions of people to reach their goals and realize their dreams – but for many people around the world, the Digital Divide keeps that power out of reach"(Microsoft 2003, 23). Microsoft repeatedly made a "comprehensive commitment to digital inclusion, and to help address inequities" (Microsoft SEC-Filings. 10-k forms 1994–2012, 48). For that purpose Microsoft initiated programs that are intended to confront the digital divide, such as the Unlimited Potential (UP) program in which Microsoft makes donations to community centres libraries and schools in third world countries (Microsoft 2003, 23); the Partners in Learning programme, which for example consist in equipping school PCs with Windows operating system (Microsoft 2003, 23f), and most recently the Microsoft YouthSpark Initiative that aims at "helping the next generation use technology to make a real impact for a better tomorrow"(Microsoft 2013, 1).

These programs do not change the fact that proprietary software as such hampers access to software and fosters exclusion. Quite on the contrary the company's programmes rather strengthen the dependence on Microsoft products. Students acquire the skills for using Microsoft's software, instead of being trained how to use available open source alternatives. These initiatives thus help Microsoft in establishing new markets for its proprietary software. Microsoft's supposed attempt to reduce digital inequality further promotes it.

Microsoft's business interests conflict with the common good: Instead of allowing the collective capacities of the human intellect to develop the best possible software for society and making it universally accessible. Microsoft – the company with the worldwide best CSR reputation – patents software and monopolizes access to knowledge in order to create the highest possible profits for the company.

Google – Evil Spy?

Google controls 84.77% of the global search engine market.[17] According to the Alexa Top Sites Ranking Google.com is the most frequently accessed website on the Internet.[18] The company's profits between 2001 and 2010 on average grew by 103% each year and reached 8.5 billion USD in 2010 (Google SEC-Filings, 10-k forms 2004–2010). This income is almost entirely based on advertising: In 2010 Google's revenues were 29.3 billion USD, 96% of which was generated through advertisements (Google SEC-Filings, 10-k form 2004–2010).

Users can access all of Google's services free of charge. While using these services users produce a huge amount of information. This data ranges from demographic user information, to technical data and usage statistics, to search queries and even the content of emails. Google turns this data into a commodity in order to generate profit: Instead of selling its services as a commodity to users, its business model consists in selling user data as a commodity to advertisers.

Google considers this business model as socially responsible. Its famous corporate credo is "You can make money without being evil."[19] The company describes its business model as beneficial for both advertisers and users. Advertisers would benefit from personalized marketing opportunities while users would receive relevant ads: "We give advertisers the opportunity to place clearly marked ads alongside our search results. We strive to help people find ads that are relevant and useful, just like our results."[20]

However, critics highlight that Google's business model is more problematic than this description suggests. Scholars (e.g. Fuchs 2010, Fuchs 2011b, Vaidhyanathan 2011, Tene 2008) as well as corporate watchdogs (GoogleWatch. com[21] Privacy International 2007, Google Monitor 2011) highlight that Google's business model of selling user data to advertisers constitutes a fundamental invasion of user privacy. Google Monitor for example stressed: "Google's targeted advertising business model is no 'privacy by design' and no 'privacy by default'"(Google Monitor 2011). Likewise Vaidhyanathan argues that Google's privacy policy is "pretty much a lack-of-privacy policy"(Vaidhyanathan 2011, 84)

---

17   NetMarketshare. 2012. Search Engine Market Share. Retrieved from http://netmarket share.com/report.aspx?qprid=4&qptimeframe=M&qpsp=145 on January 19, 2012.

18   Alexa.com Top Sites. Retrieved from http://www.alexa.com/topsites on November 17 2011.

19   Google. Philosophy. Retrieved from http://www.google.cn/intl/en/about/company/philosophy/ on February 15, 2013.

20   Google. Competition. About Ads. Retrieved from http://www.google.com/competition/howgoogleadswork.html on November 18, 2011.

21   GoogleWatch. Retrieved from http://www.google-watch.org/bigbro.html on January 21, 2012.

and Maurer et al. stress that"Google is massively invading privacy"(Maurer et al. 2007, 5).

These critics show that the commodification of user data entails the threat of surveillance and invades the rights of Internet users. The use of user data for advertising purposes requires the creation of databases that contain huge amounts of information about each Google user and to make information about individuals available to private companies. The information stored in databases can be combined in different ways in order to identify different consumer groups that might be susceptible to certain products. For Internet users it becomes impossible to determine, which of their data is stored in which databases and to whom it is accessible. The fact that this information is available could at some point in the future have negative effects for an individual user. The available data could for example support discriminatory practices (Gandy 1993, 2) by allowing to identify which individuals have a certain sexual orientation or political opinion or suffer from a certain disease.

An example that illustrates how widespread the use of information stored in Google's databases can be and how difficult it is for users to maintain control over their personal information is the so-called Prism programme of the US National Security Agency (NSA). In 2013 documents were revealed that show that the NSA can access the systems of Google and other Internet companies such as Facebook[22] and collect and store a variety of data about Internet users including search histories, content of emails, or live chats.[23] Google officially refutes these allegations,[24] even though US President Barack Obama confirmed the existence of the surveillance scheme.[25]

Furthermore extensive advertising does contribute to the commercialization of the Internet. As a consequence of an advertising-based business model, which characterizes not only Google, but most web 2.0 companies (Sandoval 2012), users are permanently confronted and annoyed with ads for consumer goods and services.

---

22   The Guardian. 2013. NSA Prism Program Taps in to User Data of Apple, Google and Others. By Glenn Greenwald and Ewen MacAskill on June 7, 2013. Retrieved from http://www .guardian.co.uk/world/2013/jun/06/us-tech-giants-nsa-data on July 19, 2013.

23   TheGuardian. 2013. NSA Prism Program Taps in to User Data of Apple, Google and Others. By Glenn Greenwald and Ewen MacAskill on June 7, 2013. Retrieved from http://www .guardian.co.uk/world/2013/jun/06/us-tech-giants-nsa-data on July 19, 2013.

24   Larry Page. 2013. What The...? Google Official Blog on June 7, 2013. Retrieved from http:// googleblog.blogspot.co.uk/2013/06/what.html on July 19, 2013.

25   The Guardian. 2013. Facebook and Google Insist they did not Know of Prism Surveillance Program. By Dominic Rushe on June 8, 2013. Retrieved from http://www.guardian.co.uk/ world/2013/jun/07/google-facebook-prism-surveillance-program on July 19, 2013.

Google's philosophy is based on the principle of not being evil. The inventor of this famous motto, Paul Buchheit stressed in an interview that this slogan was intended to demarcate Google from its competitors which "were kind of exploiting the users to some extent" (Buchheit 2008, 170). However, Google's business model is also based on the exploitation of users (Fuchs 2010, 2011b) as it turns data, which Google users produce while using their services, into its property that is then sold as a commodity to advertisers.

Google provides services that are highly valued by most Internet users. However, if they want to use these services they have no other choice than consenting to Google's terms of services and the usage of their data for advertising purposes. This gives Google a high amount of power over deciding about how user data are used and to whom they are made available. The free accessibility of Google's services thus comes at high costs: the renunciation of the right to determine the use of personal information.

Google's history of tax avoidance further shows that in the end the company's profit interest outweigh its commitment to do business that benefits society and is not evil: A report published by the UK Public Accounts Committee (PAC) revealed that between 2006 and 2011 Google's revenue based on UK operations amounted to 18 billion USD, while during that period the company only paid 16 million USD in UK corporation tax (PAC 2013, 5). By avoiding taxes Google fails to fulfil one of its basic responsibilities to society

The Walt Disney Company – Nightmare Factory?

In 2011 The Walt Disney Company was ranked number 141 in Forbes list of the 2000 biggest corporations worldwide. Between 2000 and 2010 Disney's profits on average grew by 15% each year (The Walt Disney Company. SEC-Filings. 10-k forms 1997–2012). In 2012 Disney's total revenues amounted to 42,3 billion USD, which consist of income from media networks (46%), parks and resorts (30.5%), studio entertainment (13.8%), consumers products (7.7%) and interactive services (2%) (The Walt Disney Company. SEC-Filings. 10-k forms 1997–2012). These data show that the media content business still makes up the largest part of Disney's revenues. However, 38.2% of the revenues from the Walt Disney Company are derived from theme parks and consumer products. The Walt Disney Company in its CSR communication prides itself of being "the world's largest licensor" of manufactured goods (The Walt Disney Company 2008, 5; The Walt Disney Company 2010, 5)

Disney has developed a strategy to exploit the popularity of its movie characters through Disney theme parks, Disney books, Disney toys, Disney furniture, Disney clothes, etc. Disney brought the strategy of cross-promotion to perfection. Janet Wasko in her book "Understanding Disney" (2001) states:

"Indeed, the Disney company has develop the strategy so well that is represents the quintessential example of synergy in the media/entertainment industry. 'Disney synergy' is the phrase typically used to describe the ultimate in cross-promotional activities" (Wasko 2001, 71).

In its 2012 Citizenship Targets Disney states that it wants to "Act and create in an ethical manner and consider the consequences of our decisions on people and the planet"(The Walt Disney Company 2012, 2). Disney presents itself as a socially responsible company, also in respect to working conditions in its supply chain: In its 2008 CSR report the company for example stressed: "We strive to foster safe, inclusive and respectful workplaces wherever we do business and wherever our products are made" (The Walt Disney Company 2008, 11).

However, during the last 15 years NGOs have continuously criticized Walt Disney for violating labour laws and its own Code of Conduct. In 1996, the National Labor Committee (NLC) revealed violations of labour laws and human rights in Haitian supplier factories of North-American companies such as Walt Disney and Wal-Mart. In a factory licensed by Disney, workers producing "Mickey Mouse" and "Pocahontas" pyjamas were paid only 12 cents per hour, which was far below the legal minimum (NLC 1996). After these conditions in Disney's Haiti-based supplier factories became public, Disney not only adapted its Code of Conduct for Suppliers and established the International Labor Standards (ILS) Program, but also relocated its production to China (China Labour Watch 2010a, 6), where violations of human rights and labour standards continued to exist

During the last years labour rights activists have documented a large number of corporate wrongdoings regarding working conditions in Disney's supplier companies. Criticism was voiced by several watchdog organizations such as China Labour Watch, Student and Scholars Against Corporate Misbehaviour and Students Disney Watch. These organizations report about sweatshop-like working conditions in Disney's supplier factories. The problems detected based on interviews with workers relate to:

· Non-compliance with minimum wage regulations (SACOM 2005, 14–19; SACOM 2006, 11–13; China Labour Watch, 2010a).
· Excessive and compulsory overtime work (SACOM and NLC 2005, 7; Students Disney Watch 2009, 1f),
· Poor living conditions in factory dormitories (SACOM 2006, 16), high work pressure (SACOM and NLC 2005, 11),
· Unsafe working environments, chemical hazards or high level of dust or noise without protection equipment (SACOM 2005, 6–13; China Labour Watch 2009, 2; Students Disney Watch 2009, 1f).

- No or only insufficient labour contracts (SACOM 2006, 10; Students Disney Watch 2009, 1f) and denial of health or pension insurance (SACOM and NLC 2005, 14)
- In some of Disney's supplier factories even child labour was detected (China Labour Watch 2009, 3; China Labour Watch 2010b 11, 19).

The Disney brand is famous for creating exciting worlds of happiness – unfortunately for thousands of factory workers the reality cannot live up to this fantasy. Students Disney Watch states: "Disney strives very hard to create a theme park and culture featured with fantasy and happiness. Nevertheless, Disney does not have any interest in the well-beings of the workers who produce Mickey Mouse in the sweatshops"(Students Disney Watch 2009, 2).

Workers in Disney's supplier factories are producing toys, books, clothes, and furniture. These merchandizing products for Disney's children's program, family movies, TV shows, and series symbolize a world of fun, joy, fantasy, and happy endings. It is sad irony that the day-to-day working reality of the mostly young workers in Disney's factories is opposed to joyful fantasy worlds Disney creates in its TV and film productions.

Conclusion

The examples described in the previous section illustrate the limitations of CSR: Despite the fact that the companies discussed here have a good CSR reputation; their actual practices are socially irresponsible. Their profit interests make socially responsible behaviour impossible: Microsoft's profits depend on software patents, which turn knowledge into a scarce good and thus contradict the possibility of establishing open and accessible knowledge resources. Google needs to commodify user data in order to generate profit and thus contributes to the commercialization of the Internet and the surveillance and exploitation of Internet users. The extreme exploitation of workers in the supply chain of the Walt Disney Company ensures to keep production costs los and profit margins high.

The debate on CSR largely focuses on voluntary corporate self-regulation. CSR often serves as an argument for legitimizing neoliberal deregulation and privatization: corporations are supposed to voluntarily adopt responsible behaviour rather than being obliged to it by law. The examples discussed here however reveal a fundamental contradiction between corporate interests in profit maximization on the one hand and socially responsible conduct on the other hand. It is unlikely that corporations will voluntarily refrain from irresponsible behaviour if this undermines their profit interests. This therefore points at the limits of voluntary CSR. The idea of voluntary corporate self-regulation is deeply flawed: it strengthens rather than limits corporate power, it depoliticises the quest for a responsible economy, and it ideologically mask how corporate interests, competition and power structures are related to irresponsible conduct.

Nevertheless the increased quest for CSR shows that there is a desire within society for an economy that is socially responsible. Largely constrained by the premise that corporate conduct can be rendered socially responsible through voluntary self-regulation, it however fails to realize this goal. Establishing a socially responsible media and communication system requires going beyond CSR. For that purpose one can employ a technique that Marx suggested for discovering the "rational kernel" in Hegel's idealist understanding of dialectics. Marx argued that Hegel's dialectics "is standing on its head. It must be inverted, in order to discover the rational kernel within the mystical shell" (Marx 1867/1990,103). The same holds true for CSR. In order to discover its "rational kernel" within the "mystical shell," CSR must be turned from its head to its feet – turned from its head to its feet, Corporate Social Responsibility (CSR) turns into the Responsibility to Socialize Corporations (RSC).

RSC is the logical continuation of a dialectical approach to CSR that considers conflicts between the profit motive and social responsibility: in order to become truly social, capitalist corporations need to be socialized, so that private wealth turns into common wealth. Socializing the media means to replace the privately controlled commercial media system with a socially controlled non-commercial media system

Rather than relying on corporate self-regulation, RSC points at the need to expand democratic social control over corporate conduct and to restrict corporate power. This can be achieved through government regulation on the one hand and pressure form civil society groups on the other hand. As the discussion of Microsoft's, Google's and Disney's corporate social irresponsibilities (see section 3) illustrates, corporate watchdogs have an important role in exposing corporate misconduct that reveals the failure of corporations to live up to their own codes of conducts, CSR policies and promises of self-regulation. RSC furthermore points at the need to strengthen non-commercial alternatives in the media and communication system. Only freed from the need to accumulate and to maximize private profits, media and communication can realize their full potentials and contribute to the common good. This requires political reforms that improve the structural conditions for establishing alternative media projects and that foster the transformation from a commercial towards a commons based media and communication system.

References

Almeder, Robert. 1980. The ethics of profits: Reflections on corporate social responsibility. In *Business and Society* 19(2), 7–14.

Altmeppen, Dieter. 2011. Journalistische Berichterstattung und die Verantwortung von Medienunternehmen: Über die doppelte Verantwortung von Medienunternehmen. In: *Handbuch CSR*, 247–266, edited by Juliana Raupp, Stefan Jarolimek and Friederike Schultz. Wiesbaden: vs.

American Society of Newspaper Editors. 1923. *Code of Ethics or Canons of Journalism.* Retrieved from http://ethics.iit.edu/indexOfCodes-2.php?key=18_113_1262 on March 6, 2011.

Banerjee, Subhabrata Bobby. 2008. Corporate social responsibility. The good the bad and the ugly. In *Critical Sociology 34*(1), 51–79.

Belsey, Andrew and Ruth Chadwick. 1994. Preface. In *Ethical Issues in Journalism and the Media*, xi-xii, edited by Andrew Belsey and Ruth Chadwick. London: Routledge.

Bowen, Howard. 1953. *The Social Responsibility of the Businessman.* New York: Harper.

Buchheit, Paul. 2008. Interview (interviewed by Jessica Livingston). In *Founders at Work: Stories of Startups' Early Days*, 181–172, edited by Jessica Livingston. NewYork: Springer.

Carnegie, Andrew. 1889. Wealth. In *The North American Review* 148(391), 653–665.

Carroll, Archie B. 1979. A three-dimensional conceptual model of corporate social performance. In *Academy of Management Review* 4, 497–505.

China Labour Watch 2009. *Shattered Dreams: Underage Worker Death at Factory Supplying to Disney, Other International Brands.* Retrieved from http://chinalaborwatch .org/pro/proshow-106.htmlon August 29, 2011.

China Labour Watch. 2010a. *Code of Conduct Is No More than False Advertising. Disney Suppliers Continue Exploiting Chinese Workers.* Retrieved from http://www .chinalaborwatch.org/upfile/2011_1_19/201119143318163.pdf on August 29, 2011.

China Labour Watch 2010b. *Investigation Report of Two Walt Disney Factories.* Retrieved from www.chinalaborwatch.org/investigations/2010_11_10/C00403E.pdf *on August 29, 2011.*

Commission on Freedom of the Press. 1947. *A Free and Responsible Press.* Retrieved from http://www.archive.org/stream/freeandresponsib029216mbp/freeandresponsib 029216mbp_djvu.txt on March 6, 2011.

Corlett, Angelo J. 1998. A Marxist approach to business ethics. In *Journal of Business Ethics* 17, 99–103.

Dickson, Marsha A. and Molly Eckman. 2008. Media portrayal of voluntary public reporting about corporate social responsibility performance: does coverage encourage or discourage ethical management. In *Journal of Business Ethics* 83, 725–743.

Drucker, Peter. 1984. The new meaning of corporate social responsibility. In *California Management Review 16*(2), 53–63.

Dyck, Alexander and Luigi Zingales. 2002. *The Corporate Governance Role of the Media*. Retrieved from http://papers.ssrn.com/sol3/Delivery.cfm/SSRN_ID335602 _code021101510.pdf?abstr actid = 335602&mirid = 1 on March 12, 2011.

Elliott-Boyle, Deni. 1985/1986. A conceptual analysis of ethics codes. In *Journal of Mass Media Ethics* 1(1), 22–26.

European Commission 2011. *Communication from the Commission. A Renewed Strategy 2011–2014 for Corporate Social Responsibility*. Retrieved from http://eur-lex.europa .eu/LexUriServ/LexUriServ.do?uri=COM:2011:0681:FIN:EN:PDF on September 5, 2012.

Fleming, Peter and Marc Jones 2013. The End of Corporate Social Responsibility Los Angeles: Sage.

Frederick, William. 1960. The growing concern over business responsibility. In *California Management Review* 2, 54–61.

Freeman, Edward. 1994. The politics of stakeholder theory. Some future directions. In *Business Ethics Quarterly* 4(4), 409–421.

Friedman, Milton. 1962/1982. *Capitalism and Freedom*. Chicago: University of Chicago Press.

Friedman, Milton. 1970/2009. The social responsibility of business is to increase its profits. In *Business Ethics. Case Studies and Selected Readings*, 75–80, edited by Marianne M. Jennings. Mason: South Western.

Fuchs, Christian. 2010. Labor in informational capitalism and on the Internet. In *The Information Society* 26(3), 179–196.

Fuchs, Christian. 2011a. *Foundations of Critical Media and Information Studies*. New York: Routledge.

Fuchs, Christian. 2011b. A contribution to the critique of the political economy of Google. In: *Fast Capitalism* 8(1).

Gandy, Oscar H. 1997. The political economy approach: a critical challenge. In *The Political Economy of the Media Volume 1*, 87–106, edited by Peter Golding and Graham, Murdock. Cheltenham/Brookfield: Elgar.

Gandy, Oscar. 1993. *The Panoptic Sort. A Political Economy of Personal Information*. Boulder: Westview Press.

Garnham, Nicholas. 1983. Public service versus the market. In *Screen* 24(1), 6–27.

Garnham, Nicholas 1986/2006: Contribution to a political economy of mass-communication. In *Media and Cultural Studies. KeyWorks* edited by Meenakshi Gigi Durham and Douglas Kellner, 201–229, Malden, Oxford, Carlton: Blackwell.

Garnham, Nicholas. 1998. Political Economy and Cultural Studies: Reconciliation or Divorce. In *Cultural Theory and Popular Culture*. A Reader, John Sorey, 600–612. Edinburgh: Pearson.

Gates, Bill. 1991. *Challenges and Strategy*. May 16, 1991. Retrieved from http://www.std .com/obi/Bill.Gates/Challenges.and.Strategy September 28, 2011.

Google SEC-Filings. 10-k forms 2004–2010. In Edgar Database. Retrieved from http:// www.sec.gov/cgi-bin/browse-edgar?action=getcompany&CIK=0001288776& type=10-k&dateb=&owner=exclude&count=40 on January 16, 2011.

Google Monitor. 2011. Google's No Privacy by Design Business Model. Retrieved from http://googlemonitor.com/2011/googles-no-privacy-by-design-business-model/ on January 21, 2012.

Herman, Edward S. and Noam Chomsky. 1988. *Manufacturing Consent. The Political Economy of the Mass Media*. London: Vintage Books.

Himelboim, Itai and Yehiel Limor. 2011. Media institutions, news organizations, and the journalistic social role worldwide: A cross-national and cross-organizational study of codes of ethics. In *Mass Communication and Society* 14(1), 71–92.

Hofkirchner, Wolfgang. 2003. A new way of thinking and a new world view. On the Philosophy of Self-Organisation I. *Causality, Emergence, Self-Organisation*, 131–149, edited by Arshinov, Vladimir and Christian Fuchs. Moskau: NIA-Parioda.

Horkheimer, Max and Theodor W. Adorno. 1947/1997. *Dialectic of Enlightenment*. London, New York: Verso.

KPMG. 2011. *KPMG International Survey of Corporate Responsibility Reporting*. Retrieved from   http://www.kpmg.com/Global/en/IssuesAndInsights/ArticlesPublications/ corporate-responsibility/Documents/2011-survey.pdf on August 2, 2012.

Jones, Clement. 1980. *Mass Media Codes of Ethics and Councils. A Comparative International Study of Professional Standards*. UNESCO Reports and Papers on Mass Communication. Paris: UNESCO Press.

Jones, Thomas M. 1995. Instrumental stakeholder theory: A synthesis of ethics and economics. In *Academy of Management Review* 20(2), 402–437.

Knoche, Manfred. 2002. Kommunikationswissenschaftliche Medienökonomie als Kritik der Politischen Ökonomie der Medien. In *Medienökonomie in der Kommunikationswissenschaft. Bedeutung, Grundfragen und Entwicklungsperspektiven. Manfred Knoche zum 60. Geburtstag*, 102–109, edited by Gabriele Siegert. Münster: Lit.

Laitila, Tiina. 1995. Journalistic codes of ethics in Europe. In *European Journal of Communication* 10(4), 527–544.

Marx, Karl. 1842/1976. Debatten über Preßfreiheit und Publikation der Landständischen Verhandlungen In *MEW Volume 1*, 28–77. Berlin: Dietz.

Marx, Karl. 1849/1959. Der erste Preßprozess der "Neuen Rheinischen Zeitung" In *MEW Volume 6*, 223–239. Berlin: Dietz.

Marx, Karl 1867/1990. *Capital Volume I*. London: Penguin.

Maurer, Hermann, Tilo Balke, Frank Kappe, Narayanan Kulathuramaiyer, Stefan Weber and Bilal Zaka. 2007. *Report on Dangers and Opportunities Posed by Large Search Engines, Particularly Google*. Retrieved from http://www.iicm.tugraz.at:8080/ Ressourcen/Papers/dangers_google.pdf on January 21, 2012.

McChesney. 1997. The Mythology of Commercial Broadcasting and the Contemporary Crisis of Public Broadcasting. The 1997 Spry Memorial Lecture. Retrieved from http://www.ratical.com/co-globalize/RMmythCB.html on March 8, 2011.

McChesney, Robert W. 2004. *The Problem of the Media. U.S. Communication Politics in the 21st Century*. New York: Monthly Review Press.

McInerney, Thomas 2007. Putting regulation before responsibility: Towards binding norms of corporate social responsibility. In *Cornell International Law Journal* 40, 171–200.

McManus, John H. 1997. Who's responsible for journalism. In *Journal of Mass Media Ethics* 12(1), 5–17.

McQuail, Dennis. 2010. *Mass Communication Theory*. 6th edition. London: Sage.

Microsoft 2003. Citizenship Report. Retrieved from http://www.microsoft.com/about/corporatecitizenship/en-us/reporting/ on September 26, 2011.

Microsoft. 2013. Citizenship Report. Retrieved from http://www.microsoft.com/about/corporatecitizenship/en-us/reporting/ on February 14, 2013.

Microsoft SEC-Filings. 10-k forms 1994–2012. In Edgar Database. Retrieved from http://www.sec.gov/cgi-bin/browse-edgar?action=getcompany&CIK=0000789019&owner=exclude&count=40 on October 5, 2011.

Mosco, Vincent. 2009. *The Political Economy of Communication*. London: Sage.

Murdock, Graham and Peter Golding. 1997. For a political economy of mass communication. In *The Political Economy of the Media Volume I*, 3–32, edited by Peter Golding and Graham Murdock. Cheltenham, Brookfield: Elgar.

Murdock, Graham and Peter Golding. 1999. Common markets: corporate ambitions and communication trends in the UK and Europe. In *Journal of Media Economics* 12(2), 117–132.

Murdock, Graham and Peter Golding. 2002. "Digital Possibilities, Market Realities: The Contradictions of Communications Convergence". Socialist Register, 38: 111–129.

NLC. 1996. *The U.S. in Haiti. How to get Rich on 11 Cents an Hour.* Retrieved from http://www.globallabourrights.org/reports?id=0178 on September 1, 2011.

OSS Watch 2011. *Microsoft: An End to Open Hostility*. Retrieved from http://www.oss-watch.ac.uk/resources/microsoft.xml on September 27, 2011.

PAC. 2013. Tax Avoidance – Google. Nith Report of Session 2013–2014. Retrieved from http://www.publications.parliament.uk/pa/cm201314/cmselect/cmpubacc/112/112.pdf on July 26, 2013.

Privacy International. 2007. Consultation Report. Race to the Bottom? Retrieved from http://www.privacyinternational.org/issues/internet/interimrankings.pdf on January 21, 2012.

Reputation Institute 2012. Is CSR Dead or Just Mismanaged. Retrieved from http://www.reputationinstitute.com/thought-leadership/complimentary-reports-2012 on February 14, 2013.

Richards, Ian. 2004. Stakeholders vs shareholders: Journalism, business and ethics. In *Journal of Mass Media Ethics* 19(2), 119–129.

SACOM. 2005. *Looking for Mickey Mouse's Conscience – A Survey of the Working Conditions of Disney's Supplier Factories in China.* Retrieved from *sacom.hk/wp -content/uploads/2008/07/disney.pdf on September 1, 2011.*

SACOM. 2006. *A Second Attempt in Looking for Mickey Mouse's Conscience –* A Survey of the Working Conditions of Disney's Supplier Factories in China. Retrieved from http://sacom.hk/wp-content/uploads/2008/09/7-disney-research-2006.pdf on September 1, 2011.

SACOM and NLC 2005. *Disney's Children's Books Made with the Blood, Sweat and Tears of Young People in China. Retrieved from* http://www.woek-web.de/web/cms/upload/ pdf/aktion_fair_spielt/publikation/sacom_national_labor_committee_ 2005_disneys _childrens_books.pdf on September 1, 2011.

Sandoval, Marisol. 2012. Consumer surveillance on web 2.0. *Internet and Surveillance,* edited by Christian Fuchs, Kees Boersma, Aders Albrechtslund and Marisol Sandoval. New York:Routledge.

Scherer, A.G. and Palazzo, G. 2007. Toward a political conception of corporate responsibility. Business and society seen from a Habermasian perspective. In *Academy of Management Review* 32, 1096–1120.

Schiller, Herbert. 1997. Manipulation and the packaged consciousness. In *The Political Economy of the Media Volume I*, Peter Golding and Graham Murdock, 423–437. Cheltenham, Brookfield: Elgar.

Schiller, Herbert and Schiller Anita. 1988. Libraries, public access to information, and commerce. In *The Political Economy of Information*, 146–166, edited by Vincent Mosco and Janet Wasko. Madison: The University of Wisconsin Press.

Seaton, Jean. 2003. Broadcasting history. In: *Power Without Responsibility*, 6th edition, 107–234, edited by James Curran and Jean Seaton. London: Routledge.

Siebert, Fred S., Theodore Peterson and Wilbur Schramm. 1956. *Four Theories of the Press*. Urbana: University of Illinois Press.

Sklair, Leslie and David Miller. 2010. Capitalist globalization, corporate social responsibility and social policy. In *Critical Social Policy* 30(4), 472–495.

Smythe, Dallas W. 1977/1997: Communications: Blindspots of western Marxism. In *The Political Economy of the Media Volume I*, 438–464, edited by Peter Golding and Graham Murdock. Cheltenham, Brookfield: Elgar.

Students Disney Watch. 2009. *Mickey Mouse is No Longer Lovely*. Retrieved from http://sacom.hk/wp-content/uploads/2009/12/sdw-labour-report_summary.pdf on August 31, 2011.

Tene, Omar. 2008. *What Google Knows: Privacy and Internet Search Engines*. Retrieved from http://works.bepress.com/omer_tene/2 on January 21, 2012.

The Walt Disney Company 2008. *Corporate Responsibility Report*. Retrieved from http:// corporate.disney.go.com/files/FINAL_Disney_CR_Report_2008.pdf on September 1, 2011.

The Walt Disney Company 2010. *Corporate Citizenship Report*. Retrieved from http://corporate.disney.go.com/citizenship2010/downloads/ on September 1, 2011.

The Walt Disney Company. SEC-Filings. 10-k forms. 1997–2012 In Edgar Database. Retrieved from http://www.sec.gov/cgi-bin/browse-edgar?action=getcompany&CIK=0001001039&type=10-k&dateb=&owner=exclude&count=40 on September 5, 2011.

Trommerhausen, Anke. 2011. *Corporate Responsibility in Medienunternehmen*. Köln: Halem.

Vaidhyanathan, Siva. 2011. *The Googlization of Everything (And Why We Should Worry)*. Berkeley: University of California Press.

Wasko, Janet. 2001. *Understanding Disney*. Cambridge: Polity.

Winter, C. 2006. Einleitung: TIME-Konvergenz als Herausforderung für Management und Medienentwicklung [Preface: TIME convergence as a challenge for management and media development]. In M. Karmasin & C. Winter (Eds.), Konvergenzmanagement und Medienwirtschaft – ein Lehrbuch [Convergence management and media economics – A text book] (pp. 13–53). Wilhelm Fink-Verlag (UTB): Munich.

CHAPTER 10

Media Spectacle and the North African Arab Uprisings

Some Critical Reflections[1]

Douglas Kellner

> With the development of capitalism, irreversible time is unified on a world scale.... Unified irreversible time is the time of the world market and, as a corollary, of the world spectacle.
>
> GUY DEBORD (1967)

In the past decades, media spectacle has become a dominant form in which news and information, politics, war, entertainment, sports, and scandals are presented to the public and circulated through the matrix of old and new media and technologies.[2] By 'media spectacles' I am referring to media constructs that present events which disrupt ordinary and habitual flows of information, and which become popular stories which capture the attention of the media and the public, and circulate through broadcasting networks, the Internet, social networking, cell phones, and other new media and communication technologies. In a global networked society, media spectacles proliferate instantaneously, become virtual and viral, and in some cases becomes tools of socio-political transformation, while other media spectacles become mere moments of media hype and tabloidized sensationalism.

Dramatic news and events are presented as media spectacles and dominate certain news cycles. Stories like the 9/11 terror attacks, Hurricane Katrina, Barack Obama and the 2008 U.S. presidential election, and in 2011 the Arab Uprisings, the Libyan revolution, the UK Riots, the Occupy movements and other major media spectacles of the era, cascaded through broadcasting, print, and digital media, seizing people's attention and emotions, and generating complex and multiple effects that may make 2011 as memorable a year in the history of social upheaval as 1968.

---

1 This study is extracted from my forthcoming work *Media Spectacle 2011: From the Arab Uprisings to Occupy Everywhere!*

2 In this chapter I expand my concept of media spectacle developed in a series of previous books. See Kellner (1992, 2001, 2003a, 2003b, 2005, 2008).

In today's highly competitive media environment, 'Breaking News!' of various sorts play out as media spectacle, including mega-events like wars, 9/11 and other spectacular terrorist attacks, extreme weather disasters, or, in Spring 2011, political insurrections and upheavals. These spectacles assume a narrative form and become focuses of attention during a specific temporal and historical period, that may only last a few days, but may come to dominate news and information for extended periods of time, as did the O.J. Simpson Trial and the Clinton sex/impeachment scandal in the mid-1990s, the stolen election of 2000 in the Bush/Gore presidential campaign, or natural and other disasters that have significant destructive effects and political implications, such as Hurricane Katrina, the BP Deepwater Horizon Oil Spill, or the Fukushima-Daiichi nuclear catastrophe. Media spectacles can even become signature events of an entire epoch as were, arguably, the 9/11 terrorist attacks which inaugurated a historical period that I describe as Terror War.[3]

During the spring of 2011, media spectacles of the North African Arab Uprisings in Tunisia, Egypt and Libya emerged, followed by uprisings throughout the Middle East, produced transformative events that are having major consequences. The global Arab cable broadcasting channel and Internet site Al-Jazeera, located in Doha, referred to these events collectively as "The Arab Awakening," a historical event which suggested that a new era of political struggle and insurrection was emerging in parts of the world that had been ruled for decades by oppressive dictatorships often supported by Western neo-colonial and imperialist powers. Indeed, the overthrow of dictatorial regimes in Tunisia and Egypt in Spring 2011 inspired insurrectionary movements in Libya, Yemen, Bahrain, and Syria, which are ongoing and taking dramatic and unpredictable forms. Further, the North African Arab Uprisings inspired the Occupy movements which erupted, first, in the United States in September 2011 and then throughout the world.

The media spectacles of the Arab Uprisings thus generated tumultuous global spectacles of political struggles throughout the Middle East and other parts of the world, in which political upheaval and revolution were circulated, promoted, and took a multitude of forms. I will argue that a significant dimension of globalization involves the circulation of images of popular political uprisings and insurrections. Of course, globalization continues to reproduce neo-liberal market economics and intensifying global economic crisis, but

---

3   For my account of the O.J. Simpson Trial and the Clinton sex/impeachment scandal in the mid-1990s see Kellner (2003a). The stolen election of 2000 in the Bush/Gore presidential campaign is described in Kellner (2001). An analysis of the 9/11 terrorist attacks and their aftermath is contained in Kellner (2005).

globalization also has a significant political and cultural dimension that involves the circulation of discourses of human rights, international law, and democratic resistance – as well as terrorism and other darker phenomena. Globalization is thus highly contradictory and ambiguous, and is increasingly a terrain of political and social struggle.[4] This study will look at the North African Arab Uprisings through the prisms of their circulation as global media spectacles and after describing my concept of media spectacle and will draw some preliminary conclusions concerning the role of media spectacle in the Arab Uprisings and contemporary history. First, however, I want to establish a historical context for what I see as the emergence of media spectacle as a dominant form of culture, media, and now political struggle.

The Rise and Triumph of Media Spectacle

> In societies dominated by modern conditions of production, life is presented as an immense accumulation of *spectacles*. Everything that was directly lived has receded into a representation.
>
> GUY DEBORD (1967)

The emergence of media spectacle as a dominant form of "Breaking News!" that came to construct major news cycles arose as a central mode of news and information in the U.S. with the development of 24/7 cable and satellite news channels which broadcast news and opinion 24 hours a day, 7 days a week. With the rise of global media based on cable and satellite television and the Internet, the spectacle has become global. Major examples include Gulf War 1, the first live TV war; the 9/11 and associated Al Qaeda terrorist attacks; the Iraq war of 2003; and, most recently, the Arab Awakening and Uprisings of 2011.[5]

The infrastructure of media spectacle that generates its proliferation is global cable and satellite television which emerged in the 1980s era of neoliberalism and deregulation, and increased media monopoly and competition between different media corporations and media technologies. The period marks the rise of cable news networks that broadcast news 24/7 and used media spectacle to capture viewers. In the 1990s, new media and politicized

---

4   For my earlier analyses of globalization, continued here, see Kellner (2002) and also Kellner and Best (2001).

5   For my engagement with Gulf War 1 see Kellner (1992). 9/11 and associated Al Qaeda terrorist attacks are described in Kellner (2003b). The Iraq war of 2003 is discussed in Kellner (2005), while the Arab awakening and uprisings of 2011 are considered in Kellner (2012).

forms of media proliferated including Talk Radio, Fox News and other highly partisan and explosive talk shows. Highly politicized mainstream media exemplified today in the u.s. in the battles between Fox News and MSNBC cable news channels, as well as within the Internet which has become a contested terrain used by left, right, and everyone in-between.

The epoch of neoliberalism also exhibited the rise of infotainment, with the implosion of news and entertainment like the O.J. Simpson trial, Clinton sex scandals, and various celebrity scandals. Fierce competition for ratings and advertising led information and news to become more visual and engaging, bringing codes of entertainment into journalism. News accordingly became more narrative and tabloid, with scandals and ever-multiplying segments on fashion, health, entertainment, and items of personal interest. In this media environment, hard politics and international news are now declining on the major u.s. television networks like ABC, CBS, and NBC, while the cable news networks are dominated by media spectacle and often partisan political talk shows.

The 1990s was an era in which media spectacle accelerated in the fields of sports, entertainment, fashion, and consumer culture, which were always a domain of the spectacle. In addition, the 1990s witnessed the spectacle of globalization and anti-globalization movements, the global commodity spectacle such as the McDonald's and Nike spectacle, NBA basketball, the World Cup, and other global sports spectacles. This was also a period in which spectacle came to play an even greater role in Hollywood film during the blockbuster era.

In the 2000s, blogs, wikis, Facebook, MySpace, and other new media and social networking sites, such as YouTube and Twitter, further proliferated the ubiquitous and omnipresent media matrix. Hence, the political economy and communications technology infrastructure of media spectacle have generated a proliferation of cable and satellite television, followed by the dramatic eruption of new technologies like the Internet and social networking media. The Internet made it possible for everyone to voice opinions and to circulate news and information through ever-expanding new media and social network sites, in which Facebook, MySpace, I-Phones and I-Pads, and other new technologies enable everyone to become part of the spectacle (if you can afford and know how to use the technology). Hence, today, everyone, from Hollywood and political celebrities to Internet activists in Egypt and Tunisia, or terrorists like Al Qaeda, can create their own media spectacles, or participate in the media spectacle of the day – as the Occupy movements are dramatically demonstrating on a global scale as I write.

Media spectacles traditionally have an aesthetic dimension and often are dramatic, bound up with ritual events and competition like the Olympics, World Cup, Superbowl, or Oscars that feature compelling images, montage, and stories, and which engage mass audiences and generate discussion and debate throughout the media.[6] Spectacles have a theatrical dimension and dramatize key issues and conflicts of a given society, as the O.J. Simpson murder trial and Clinton sex scandals in the 1990s were spectacles in which key battles concerning gender, sexuality, race, celebrity, power, and the justice and political system played out. The spectacles take a narrative form becoming stories around which the society is constructed at a given moment and which can be contested and used for various social and political ends (such as the 9/11 terror attacks and ensuing Terror War. Hence, media spectacle in the contemporary era encompasses both news and information and sports and entertainment, and in the following studies I will focus on how news media, social networking and new media, and popular forms of entertainment and culture helped circulate the struggles in the North African Arab Uprisings.

The length, duration, and import of media spectacles, of course, varies. Certain media spectacles like the O.J. Simpson trial may dominate news cycles until they are replaced by a new media spectacle, such as the Clinton sex scandals. The September 11, 2001, spectacles of terror have helped generate an era of Terror War with global terror networks fighting local, national, and global security and military networks, and it may be that this historical era is coming to an end as the 2011 Arab Uprisings, Occupy movements, and other popular struggles proliferate; of course, it is likely that both cycles of media spectacle will continue and overlap for some time.

Hence, new forms of political struggle and insurrection are emerging as a potent and fecund field of media spectacle. In this study, I will explore the emergence of the new forms and strategies of struggle that erupted in 2011 in the North African Arab Uprisings. But, first, let me further explicate and illustrate my concept of media spectacle, and how it differs from Guy Debord, whose book *The Society of the Spectacle* has had a major impact on post-1960s critical theory and shaped my own work in multiple ways.

Guy Debord and the Society of the Spectacle

When the real world changes into simple images, simple images become real beings and effective motivations of a hypnotic behavior.

---

6   Here I am only discussing media spectacle as major socio-political events of the contemporary moment and their impacts on journalism and politics. For analyses of a diversity of types of media spectacle including a historical genealogy of the spectacle going back to Greek, Roman, and Middle Eastern cultures see Kellner (2003a).

> The spectacle as a tendency 'to make one see the world' by means of various specialized mediations.
>
> GUY DEBORD

To clarify my concept of media spectacle, I will next indicate some differences between my use of media spectacle from French theorist Guy Debord's 1960s classic, *The Society of the Spectacle* and the concept of the 'society of the spectacle' developed by Debord and his comrades in the Situationist International, which has had major impact on a variety of contemporary theories of society and culture.[7]

Debord's conception of the society of the spectacle, first developed in the 1960s, continues to circulate through the Internet and other academic and subcultural sites today. It describes a media and consumer society, organized around the production and consumption of images, commodities, and staged events. For Debord, spectacle "unifies and explains a great diversity of apparent phenomena" (Debord 1967, #10), describing media events and programming, advertising and the display of commodities, stores, malls, and other sites of consumption in the media and consumer society.

Hence, for Debord, spectacle constituted the overarching concept to describe the media and consumer society, including the packaging, promotion, and display of commodities and the production and effects of all media. Using the term 'media spectacle', I am largely focusing on various forms of technologically-constructed media productions that are produced and disseminated through the so-called mass media and now new media and social networking as well, ranging from radio and television to the Internet and the latest wireless gadgets and social networking. Every medium, from music to television, from news to advertising, has its multitudinous forms of spectacle, involving such things in the realm of music as the classical music spectacle, the opera spectacle, the rock spectacle, and the hip hop spectacle. Spectacle forms evolve over time and multiply with new technological developments.

---

7   Guy Debord's *The Society of the Spectacle* (1967) was published in translation in a pirate edition by Black and Red (Detroit) in 1970 and reprinted many times; another edition appeared in 1983 and a new translation in 1994. Thus, in the following discussion, I cite references to the numbered paragraphs of Debord's text to make it easier for those with different editions to follow my reading. The key texts of the Situationists and many interesting commentaries are found on various Web-sites, producing a curious afterlife for Situationist ideas and practices. For further discussion of the Situationists see Chapter 3 in Best and Kellner (1997) as well as Best and Kellner (2003a), and Kellner (2001). On Debord's life and work see Kaufmann (2006). On the complex and highly contested reception and effects of Guy Debord and the Situationist International, see Marcus (1990), McDonough (2002), and Wark (2008).

As we proceed into an era of ever-proliferating spectacle, multiple media are becoming more technologically dazzling and are playing expanding and intensifying roles in everyday life. Under the influence of a multimedia image culture, seductive spectacles fascinate the denizens of the media and consumer society and involve them in the semiotics of an ever-expanding world of entertainment, information, and consumption, which deeply influence thought and action. In Debord's words: "When the real world changes into simple images, simple images become real beings and effective motivations of a hypnotic behavior. The spectacle as a tendency 'to make one see the world' by means of various specialized mediations (it can no longer be grasped directly), naturally finds vision to be the privileged human sense which the sense of touch was for other epochs" (ibid., #18).

Experience and everyday life are thus shaped and mediated for Debord by the spectacles of media culture and the consumer society. For Debord, the spectacle is a tool of pacification and depoliticization; it is a "permanent opium war" (ibid., #44) that stupefies social subjects and distracts them from the most urgent task of real life – recovering the full range of their human powers through creative practice. Debord's concept of the spectacle is integrally connected to the concept of separation and passivity, for in submissively consuming spectacles, one is estranged from actively producing one's life. Capitalist society separates workers from the products of their labor, art from life, and consumption from human needs and self-directing activity, as individuals inertly observe the spectacles of social life from within the privacy of their homes (ibid., #25, #26). The Situationist project, by contrast, involved an overcoming of all forms of separation, in which individuals would directly produce their own life and modes of self-activity and collective practice, illustrated today by the Occupy movements.

The correlative to the spectacle for Debord is the spectator, the reactive viewer and consumer of a social system predicated on submission, conformity, and the cultivation of marketable difference. The concept of the spectacle therefore involves a distinction between passivity and activity, and consumption and production, condemning lifeless consumption of spectacle as an alienation from human potentiality for creativity and imagination. The spectacular society spreads its wares mainly through the cultural mechanisms of leisure and consumption, services and entertainment, ruled by the dictates of advertising and a commercialized media culture.

This structural shift to a society of the spectacle involves a commodification of previously non-colonized sectors of social life and the extension of bureaucratic control to the realms of leisure, desire, and everyday life. Parallel to the Frankfurt School conception of a 'totally administered', or 'one-dimensional', society (Horkheimer and Adorno 1972; Marcuse 1964), Debord states that: "The spectacle is the moment when the consumption has attained the 'total occupation' of social life" (Debord 1967, 42). Here exploitation is raised to a psychological level; basic physical privation is augmented by "enriched priva- tion" of pseudo-needs; alienation is generalized, made comfortable, and alienated consumption becomes "a duty supplementary to alienated produc- tion" (ibid.).

Hence, Debord's work is totalizing, with spectacle reproducing the entirety of capitalist media/consumer society, so that for Debord everything is part of the spectacle. By contrast, I analyze specific media spectacles and types of media spectacle like political spectacles and spectacles of terror, such as the 9/11 attacks and the acts of domestic terrorism and school shootings that I describe in my book Guys and Guns Amok (Kellner 2008). Thus, while Debord presents a rather generalized and abstract notion of spectacle, I engage spe- cific examples of media spectacle and how they are produced, constructed, circulated, and function in the present era. In addition, I am reading the pro- duction, text and effects of various media spectacles from a standpoint within contemporary u.s. and global society in order to help illuminate and theorize its socio-political dynamics and culture, and more broadly, globalization and global culture. Debord, by contrast, was analyzing a specific stage of capitalist society, that of the media and consumer society organized around spectacle. In addition, Debord deploys a French radical intellectual and neo-Marxian per- spective, while I employ a multiperspectivist model, using Frankfurt School critical theory, British cultural studies, French postmodern theory, and many other theoretical constructs (Kellner 1995, 2003a, 2003b, 2008, 2010).

In sum, Debord's concept of the spectacle is monolithic and overpower- ing. For Debord, the society of the spectacle generates a system of domina- tion enforcing passivity, obedience, consumerism, and submission. To be sure, Debord opposes the passive spectator of spectacle and valorizes the active creator of situations, and offers strategies for forms of resistance to the spectacle that have been influential on subsequent politics and continue to be influential in an era of new media and social networking. Yet Debord's conception of creating situations tends to valorize artistic and subcultural activity, while I am arguing that media spectacle itself is a contested terrain that can be as a force of opposition and resistance, as well as domination and hegemony – and can be a site of contestation, reversal, and even revolution as I argue in this chapter.

Further, I analyze the contradictions and reversals of the spectacle, whereas Debord tends to project a unitary and hegemonic notion of the soci- ety of the spectacle, although he and his comrades sketched out various models of opposition and struggle and in fact inspired in part the rather spectacular May'68 events in France. For an example of the reversal of a media spectacle, or at least its contradictions and contestation, the Clinton sex scandal became a contested arena in which, surprisingly, Clinton's popularity rose as the scandal unfolded and the Republicans began carrying out impeachment (Kellner 2003a). While the 2003 Iraq war was initially presented as a triumph for the Bush/Cheney administration and Pentagon, it was contested and soon became an unpopular war (Kellner 2005). Barack Obama arguably won the Democratic Party primary because he was the only major Democratic candidate who opposed the Iraq war in the beginning, although Obama was also a master of media spectacle, which enabled him to win the presidency and become a world-class celebrity.[8] Yet in a situation of an intensively polarized u.s. society, the Obama spectacle has itself become sharply contested as his opponents attempt by all possible means to undermine his presidency.

Finally, Debord's analysis of the spectacle is denunciatory, developing a neo-Marxian attack on consumer capitalism. My concept, by contrast, is diagnostic, analyzing social problems, conflicts, and key events and transformations of the contemporary era. Debord's notion of the society of the spectacle theorizes the emergence in the post-World War II era of the media and consumer society and continues to be relevant in analyzing today's social formations and politics. Both his social critique and models of radical politics continue to be of utmost importance for critical social theory and radical politics today. Yet the emergence of new media, new forms of global capitalism, and new models of political struggle call for updating of Debord's concepts in a transformed socio-economic, political, and cultural context. These new forms of global struggle are illustrated in the North African Arab Uprisings and the Occupy movements, the former of which I engage in this study.

The North African Arab Uprisings

There are decades in which nothing happens and there are weeks when decades happen.

V.I. LENIN

---

8   I have previously argued that Barack Obama won the presidency in part because he mastered media spectacle; see Kellner (2009, 2010).

With the Spring 2011 North African Arab Uprisings in Tunisia, Egypt, and Libya, we see that political insurgencies and hoped for revolutions have been unfolding as media spectacles that circulate images and discourses of revolt, freedom and democracy through global media. These insurrections – which erupted in late January 2011 and have continued to shake the world and reconstitute the political landscape of North Africa and the Middle East during Spring and through 2011 and into the foreseeable future – may be seen in retrospect as inaugurating a new epoch of history, in which political uprisings and insurrections radicalize entire regions of the world and drive out corrupt and entrenched dictatorships.

To begin, however, I should open with some caveats and cautionary warnings. While Al-Jazeera, CNN, and most U.S. media networks at first repeatedly used the term 'revolution' to describe the events in Tunisia, Egypt, and Libya, since we do not know if a thorough transformation of the these societies will take place or not, I'm using the more modest term 'North African Arab Uprisings' to describe the important media spectacles and political insurrections of the Arab Spring which may yet be looked back upon as world-historical and transformative events.[9]

Reflecting upon the dramatic uprisings in North Africa in the Arab Spring, it is, to be sure, 'revolutionary' to overthrow military regimes and corrupt dictators who have been oppressing their people for decades. It is 'revolutionary' to put aside a government and political system and to construct another freer and more democratic one. It is tremendous that self-organizing people can produce a democratic upheaval that hopefully will fundamentally alter their political fate and future. These events are clearly astonishing examples of people's power, of the masses becoming a force in history who throw off decades of oppression and fundamentally alter the forces of sovereignty in specific societies.

But we do not yet know if North African Uprisings will produce a revolution proper, as we do not know the form the military government in Egypt, for example, will take in the immediate future, what kind of constitution the

---

9   After initially using the discourse of "revolution" to describe the overthrow of dictatorships in Tunisia and Egypt, Al-Jazeera and other global networks then used terms like 'Libya's Uprising', 'Egypt's New Era', and 'Tunisia in Transition', followed by terms like 'The Arab Spring', 'The Arab Awakening', or 'The Arab Uprising' to describe the events engaged in this chapter. Curiously, Wikipedia has its pages on the events under the rubric of 'Tunisian revolution', '2011 Egyptian revolution', and '2011 Libyan Civil War'. By 'revolution', I follow Herbert Marcuse's concept of revolution as a rupture with the previous social order that develops new forms of economy, politics, culture and social relations (Kellner 1984).

Egyptians will produce, the quality and results of their promised elections, the amount of popular participation and other goals that would constitute a fundamentally different social order, and thus a revolutionary break from the Mubarak era. Hence, it is premature to pronounce the '18 Days That Shook the World' in Egypt a 'revolution' at this time – nor can we predict the form that the insurrections will ultimately take in Tunisia, Libya, Yemen, Bahrain, Syria, and other Middle Eastern states that were challenged by their people in the Arab Spring that has blossomed into a Year of Upheaval, 2011.

To be sure, if the Egyptians throw out the corrupt leaders and functionaries of the past three decades, this would be remarkable, but if the same people are governing in similar ways in Egypt the word 'revolution' wanes in significance, so I am using the term 'Uprising'. In addition, I am advocating multicausal analysis, arguing that media spectacles such as presidential elections, wars, and political uprisings and upheaval have multiple causes and are caught up in a complex matrix of events. For instance, there is not just one cause that generated the Bush/Cheney intervention into Iraq in 2003. While the official reason that the U.S. went to war in Iraq to eliminate Saddam Hussein's 'weapons of mass destruction' was obviously bogus, there were multiple hidden agendas which led the U.S. to invade and occupy Iraq.[10] These included control of Iraqi oil and establishing bases in the Middle East for future interventions; the tremendous amount of money made by war contractors often closely related to the Bush/Cheney Gang; and a wealth of geopolitical factors.

Arguably, the Bush/Cheney Iraq intervention was organized as a media spectacle that would present U.S. military power as dominant in the world today and would help establish new U.S. military bases in the Middle East near the world's largest oil supplies. A successful intervention into Iraq would also help with the re-election of the Bush/Cheney Gang. The Iraq (mis)adventure embodied the fantasies of George W. Bush and a cabal of neo-con ideologues who envisaged a New American Century and emergence of Western-style 'democracies' throughout the region. And George W. Bush imagined that he was battling the forces of 'evil', and could succeed in destroying a force of evil that his father had failed to eliminate. Thus, while the official justification of seizing Saddam Hussein's 'weapons of mass destruction' was clearly a fake excuse, it would also be a mistake to see the Iraq invasion simply as a grab for oil, or any other single primary cause.

Major events like the Bush/Cheney administration Iraq intervention and the North African Arab Uprisings are thus overdetermined, and have multiple causes. The dynamics in each specific country are dissimilar, although there

---

10   This analysis of the multiple causes of the Iraq war is further developed in Kellner (2005).

may be common goals, aspirations, and tactics of struggle. Hence, I do not want to argue that media spectacle is the primary cause of current events and world history today, but suggest that it is a form in which political insurrections and struggles are represented and circulated that can become causal factors in an overdetermined matrix of events. For instance, the Tunisian Uprising could have helped inspire an Egyptian Uprising which apparently helped inspire uprisings in Libya and throughout the Middle East. In all cases of the Arab Uprisings, you had masses of people which had long been oppressed suddenly rising up and demanding radical change and democratic freedoms.

The North African Uprisings thus constituted a break and rupture with their previous totalitarian governments and in turn inspired Uprisings and a cycle of struggles throughout North Africa and the Middle East. Media spectacle became the form of the Uprisings which were circulated via Al-Jazeera and other television networks, new media like Facebook and YouTube, and various social networking groups. In each case, there were unprecedentedly large demonstrations in oppressive societies that had not allowed freedom of speech and assembly, state authoritarian governments fought back against the demonstrators, often killing many who henceforth became martyrs. In turn, demonstrations often erupted at the martyr's funerals, and continued to intensify with radical demands for the dictators and their regimes to go and for power to the people. In many cases, participants in the struggles took their own videos of state violence against the protestors which were circulated via Twitter, Blackberries, and cell phone networks on the Internet, and in some cases through global cable TV networks. The people were participating in the creation of the spectacles of the Arab Awakening and Uprising, not only in that their bodies were part of the democratic masses. Further, individuals within the masses found their own voices and helped construct the spectacle through their own DIY ('Do It Yourself') media artifacts sent to the Internet, circulated throughout social networking, and in some cases disseminated through global television networks like Al-Jazeera.

Looked at globally and historically, I would suggest that the recent North African Arab Uprisings can be read as a set of interconnected spectacles with many parts, as were the anti-Communist uprisings in 1989 that led to the collapse of the Berlin Wall and Soviet Empire, and then to the fall of the Soviet Union itself, world-historical events that provide an anticipatory parallel to the media spectacles in the Middle East. In the 1980s, demonstrations in Poland from the Solidarity Movement were visible in Hungary via television and other media which helped inspire demonstrations in that country which in turn were visible in other Eastern bloc countries like East Germany (DDR) and Czechoslovakia. The powerful images of people uprising against the communist regimes, demanding freedom and a new society, produced a chain of movements, insurrections, and overthrowing of communist regimes, much like the Arab Uprisings, and producing the collapse of bureaucratic state communism. In this complex historical matrix, the then dominant broadcasting media of television circulated images and forms of struggle via television that were seen throughout the Soviet bloc countries, helping to produce multiple uprisings and the delegitimation of autocratic communist regimes, leading to the collapse of Soviet empire in eastern Europe, culminating in the fall of the Berlin wall and Velvet Revolution in Czechoslovakia in 1989.[11] These dramatic events of 1989 eventually lead to the collapse of the Soviet regime in the U.S.S.R, driving some people to see 1989 as beginning a new epoch in history.[12]

Images of the spectacle of uprisings against repressive state communist governments and social systems resonated with citizens of other oppressed countries in the Soviet bloc, and these resonant and viral images spread through the global broadcasting and news networks and inspired people in neighboring Soviet bloc countries, helping to motivate people to hit the streets

---

11   To be sure, there were organized opposition movements to the Soviet regimes within the Eastern Central Europe Soviet bloc countries and within the Soviet Union itself. These oppositional movements had been for decades writing critiques of the regime, sometimes clandestinely circulated, and had organized opposition to the Soviet system. On the other hand, certainly the cascading collapse of one communist regime after another, seen throughout Europe and the communist bloc on television, and discussed on radio, newspapers, and other media, helped to mobilize massive crowds that led to the overthrow of the communist regimes. For first person witness of these events, see the narrative and concise analysis by Ash (1993), republished with a new Afterword in 1999. Among other themes, Garton Ash describes the role of the media in making images of the oppositional movements visible to various publics and the struggle for media access of the oppositional movements. In a key summary judgment, Garton Ash wrote: "In Europe at the end of the twentieth century all revolutions are telerevolutions" (1993, 94). In the Prague Velvet Revolution, Garton Ash wrote: "television is now clearly opening up to report the revolution," signalling that Václav Havel and the oppositional movement had won the revolution (ibid., 101).

12   Francis Fukuyama (1992) famously argued that the collapse of Soviet Communism in the 1990s marked the triumph of Western Ideas of Freedom and Democracy, and thus the end of major political conflicts. With the 9/11 terror attacks on the U.S. and the resulting era of Terror War, Fukujama's ideas were widely discredited (Kellner 2003b). To some extent, though, the Ideas of Freedom and Democracy are indeed part of the struggle in the North African Arab Uprisings, which revealed that many more enemies of a free society had to be eliminated before one could seriously argue that we had entered the realm of freedom dreamed of by liberals and Karl Marx.

and demonstrate for change themselves. Hence, throughout the Eastern Bloc state communist nations, there were uprisings and struggles, governments resigning, or being overthrown, and the democratic revolutions thus inspired a whole cycle of struggle in 1989 – just as we are now seeing in the Middle East and North African Arab Uprisings.

Although such events are complex and overdetermined, and media spectacle alone is but one factor in the complex matrix of history, yet it is certainly a significant one, even an increasingly important factor as media spectacles proliferate globally through new media and social networking. Indeed, broadcasting and new media have become ubiquitous throughout the Middle East, as they have become part of a new global media ecology.[13] In the following sections, I will discuss the role of Al-Jazeera, new media and social networking, and media spectacle in the Arab Awakening and Uprisings during the Arab Spring of 2011, but will also be concerned with providing contextual and multicasual analysis of these events, beginning with Tunisia and then turning to Egypt.[14] While my argument is that media spectacle is the form in which the Arab Awakening and Uprising have circulated throughout North Africa and the Middle East, media spectacle itself is not the cause of the cascading insurrections, and each country needs to be addressed in terms of their own history, society, culture, and political regimes, which I will do below.

Sparks in Tunisia

When people decide to live, destiny shall obey, and one day...the slavery chains must be broken.

TUNISIAN POET ABU AL-QASIM AL-SHABI

The rapid cycle of North African Arab Uprisings began when a young 26-year-old Tunisian man Mohamed Bouazizi, who could not find work and was reduced to selling produce from a cart in the street, set himself on fire in front of the local governor's office on December 17, 2010 in Bouzid, an impoverished agricultural town, helping spark Tunisian and then Egyptian and Libyan uprisings. Bouazizi's family and friends recount that he took these

---

13   On the new media ecology that the Internet and other new technologies have produced, see Poster, (1995) and Kahn and Kellner (2008, 22–37).

14   For reasons of space, I am not engaging the upheavals in Libya which mutated from an Uprising to what has been described as both a Civil War and a revolution, events that I engage in detail in Kellner (2012).

desperate measures because he had become unbearably angry after he had been repeatedly mistreated by police, who tried to get him to pay bribes or close down his cart.[15]

On February 19, 2011, 60 Minutes broadcast an episode titled 'The Spark' which described how following the self-immolation protest, activists in Tunisia began circulating images of Bouazizi, made him into a martyr, organizing marches commemorating him and protesting the oppressive Tunisian regime. The protests escalated as Tunisian forces shot at protestors, leading to yet bigger demonstrations that were energized on January 24, 2011 when dictator Zine el-Abidine Ben Ali who had been in power twenty-three years fled the country.[16]

I might note that the man who set himself on fire was emulating Buddhist monks in Vietnam, whose widely broadcast and discussed self-immolations helped generate a world-wide antiwar movement in the Vietnam era. The global nature of spectacle was also highlighted in the 60 Minutes episode 'The Spark' which interviewed Tunisian Internet activists who helped mobilized the insurgency and who were connected to Egyptian Internet activists who would use similar tactics in Egypt, suggesting the rise of a Youth International of Internet Activists.[17]

While there were claims that the Tunisian Uprising was the 'first WikiLeaks revolution' because oppressive features of the regime in Tunisia was documented by WikiLeaks which presented notes of American diplomats discussing the corruption of the President Ben Ali and his family, it is also believed that people already knew that their regime was oppressive and corrupt (Dickinson, 2011)[18] Further, Al-Jazeera and other Arab networks covered the Tunisian Uprising and circulated protests and critiques of the Ben Ali regime.

---

15   For an account of previous self-immolations that helped mobilize protest movements, see Wirth (2011). The 'Werther effect' refers to mass suicides in 18th century Europe after Goethe's hero Werther committed suicide in a popular novel, and there were a wave of suicides throughout the Middle East after Bouazizi's immolation although none of the other suicides appeared to have provided sparks for a revolution.

16   See Mackey (2011) which recounts how "the desperate act of the vendor, Mohamed Bouazizi, led to protests in the town, which were recorded in video clips posted on YouTube. By the time he died on Jan. 4, 2011, protests that started over Mr. Bouazizi's treatment in Sidi Bouzid had spread to cities throughout the country."

17   In addition to the 60 Minutes Report, see also. Kirkpatrick and Sanger (2011).

18   The text was widely circulated on the Internet. Dickinson (2011) wrote: "Tunisians didn't need any more reasons to protest when they took to the streets these past weeks – food prices were rising, corruption was rampant, and unemployment was staggering. But we might also count Tunisia as the first time that WikiLeaks pushed people over the brink. These protests are also about the country's utter lack of freedom of expression – including when it comes to WikiLeaks."

Hence, I am not arguing that media spectacle is the key causal force of the Tunisia Uprising, as, obviously, there were many factors that alienated the Tunisians which led them to take to the streets, including the autocratic and corrupt nature of the regime. Factors in Tunisia which led to the uprising, included the economic situation, with declining jobs and job possibilities, rising food prices, and worker unrest that all contributed to the Tunisian upheaval that drove out Ben Ali, his family, and some of the regime's corrupt associates.

Ben Ali came into power as he ascended to the office of President on November 7, 1987, after attending physicians to the former president Habib Bourguiba declared that he was medically incapacitated and unable to fulfill the duties of the presidency. Ben Ali, previously Prime Minister, achieved power through a 'soft coup d'etat' and preserved Tunisia's republican tradition, keeping power through winning two elections. The Ben Ali regime pursued neo-liberal economic policies, dismantling a heavily statist economy and winning praise from the IMF and World Bank. While the GNP grew in recent years, unemployment skyrocketed and educated youth were having trouble finding jobs.[19] At the same time, Ben Ali's family and regime became more and more blatantly corrupt, and Ben Ali became increasingly authoritarian, alienating vast sectors of the society.

The Tunisian Uprising against the Ben Ali regime exhibited the rise of the masses against a totalitarian dictatorship in a popular struggle with no apparent leaders, no dominant parties, and no discernible hierarchy, with individuals from diverse classes, ages, religion and ways of life fusing together into a collective mass whose power frightened the corrupt dictator Ben Ali to flee, after the military made it clear that they were not going to fire on the masses of protestors. Demonstrators included older people, professional men and women, students, workers and the unemployed. No one predicted this momentous insurrection, and so far, to my knowledge, few have adequately described its genealogy and prehistory.[20]

Indeed, the Tunisian Uprising has multiple origins and forces who participated in the struggles from workers to students, intellectuals, and women. As Kevin Anderson (2011) noted:

> Although not widely reported at the time, the mass strikes of 2008 in Gafsa were one indicator of the underlying social tensions in Tunisia. This phosphate-mining region, long a center of labor unrest, has in recent

---

19   See Callinicos (2011) on Tunisia's economy.
20   On the background and trajectory of the Tunisian Uprising, I am drawing on Anderson (2011).

decades been wracked by mass unemployment due to mechanization. In January 2008, the Gafsa phosphate miners rose up after a rare instance of taking on new hires at the mines showed that those hired were the beneficiaries of corruption and nepotism. The revolt lasted six months, after which several of its leaders were imprisoned. Gafsa strikers were not supported by the UGTT [General Union of Tunisian Works], then still tied closely to the state. The workers did gain the support of dissident bloggers and Facebook users, however, who launched a campaign on behalf of those imprisoned.

Robin Morgan describes how in Tunisia's relatively secular and progressive society, women had earlier gained rights of contraception, divorce, and relative equality within the society. In the Tunisian Uprising, women sought more democratic power and rose up against continued inequality. In Tunisia's 'Jasmine revolution', a blogger Lina Ben Mhenni, known to the world as 'tunisian girl', was one of the first to alert the world to the Tunisian Uprising and called for women to join in the demonstrations. Hence, in Robin Morgan's words: "Women flocked to rallies – wearing veils, jeans, and miniskirts – young girls, grandmothers, female judges in their court robes. They ousted a despot and inspired a region" (Morgan 2011b, 21). In addition, as feminist scholar Nadia Marzouki noted:

> At all the major demonstrations leading to Ben Ali's flight from the country, men and women marched side by side, holding hands and chanting together in the name of civil rights, not Islam. The national anthem, not 'Allahu akbar,' was the dominant rallying cry, and the women were both veiled and unveiled. The tone of the protests was rather one of reappropriating patriotic language and symbols: Women and men lay in the streets to spell 'freedom' or 'stop the murders' with their bodies and worked together to tear down and burn the gigantic, Stalin-style portraits of Ben Ali on storefronts and street corners.
>
> MARZOUKI cited in ANDERSON, 2011

Demonstrations intensified, and when the General Union of Tunisian Works (UGTT) broke away from the ruling apparatus, joined the demonstrators, were part of a blockade against the Interior Ministry, and supported a general strike, the military saw that the regime could not be defended, refused to fire on demonstrators, and supported Ben Ali's ouster. Al-Jazeera also reported over the weekend of January 8–9, that 2,000 members of the police, who had been on the frontline of repressing demonstrations, joined the protestors. While Ben Ali desperately announced that he would not run for another term on January 13, 2011 and pledged to improve the economy and allow freedom of the press, while also declaring a state of emergency, protesters responded with a massive demonstration, demanding that he resign and on January 14, he fled the country.[21]

On Saturday January 15, it was announced that Ben Ali was seeking asylum in Saudi Arabia, that Tunisian Prime Minister Mohamed Ghannouchi declared temporary rule and promised elections for the fall, leading exultant Tunisians to explode with joy while people throughout the Middle East looked on with wonder. Tunisians were suspicious of the new caretaker government which was dominated by members of Ben Ali's party, the Constitutional Democratic Party (CDP), and eventually all members of the party were eliminated from the new coalition government, which included Tunisian blogger Slim Amamou, aka Slim404, who had helped organize the Tunisian Uprising and was made minister of youth and sport in the post-revolutionary government.

Underground music scenes and subcultures had also contributed to the Uprising, including Skander Besbes, aka Skhder, described as a "luminary of Tunisia's electro and dance scene, and in clubs and rave nights used the explosive sound system to present attacks on the government and prepare youth for the uprising" (Morgan 2011a). Andy Morgan notes that electro music was relatively safe as a protest form in Tunisia because it was instrumental, and "metal and rock were partially protected by English lyrics which the police didn't understand" (ibid.). Yet, Morgan explains:

> it took a rapper to galvanise Tunisia's youth, whose frustration had been fuelled by years of government corruption, nepotism, ineptitude and general state-imposed joylessness. Until a few months ago, Hamada Ben Amor, aka El Général, was just a 21-year-old wannabe MC in a Stussy hoodie, leather jacket and baseball cap. He lived with his parents and elder brother in a modest flat in a drab seaside town south of Tunis called Sfax, where his mother runs a bookshop and his father works in the local hospital. El Général didn't even register on the radar of Tunisian rap's premier league which was dominated by artists such as Balti, Lak3y, Armada Bizera or Psyco M. It was a community riven by the usual jealous spats and dwarfed by the more prolific rap scenes of Morocco and France.
> IBID.

Morgan recounts how on November 7, 2010, El General "uploaded a piece of raw fury called 'Rais Le Bled' (President, Your Country) on to Facebook" (ibid.). The lyrics contained a resounding political attack:

---

21   For a detailed account of the crisis in Tunisia as it unfolded see The Guardian (2011) and Le Monde (2011).

"My president, your country is dead/
People eat garbage/
Look at what is happening/
Misery everywhere/
Nowhere to sleep/
I'm speaking for the people who suffer/
Ground under feet."

Morgan describes how

> within hours, the song had lit up the bleak and fearful horizon like an
> incendiary bomb. Before being banned, it was picked up by local TV sta-
> tion Tunivision and al-Jazeera. El Général's MySpace was closed down,
> his mobile cut off. But it was too late. The shock waves were felt across the
> country and then throughout the Arab world. That was the power of pro-
> testing in Arabic, albeit a locally spiced dialect of Arabic. El Général's
> bold invective broke frontiers and went viral from Casablanca to Cairo
> and beyond.
>
>   IBID.

This example points to how there is an Arab public sphere that operates across
diverse media and borders, in which music, poetry, art, and other cultural forms
function to circulate forms of cultural resistance that came together in the Arab
Uprising.[22] While U.S. media had very little coverage of the Tunisian Uprising,
Al-Jazeera closely covered the events, as it had in the demonstrations in Iran in
2009 and would continue to cover and circulate the Arab Awakening and
Uprisings. The synergy of global media television coverage, Internet and social
networking documenting and promoting the Uprisings, the fusion of many artists and cultural critics with the movement, and the coming together of multiple organizations and social strata helped circulate the Tunisian Uprising to
Egypt and then the Eyptian Uprising to the entire Middle East and beyond.

Upheaval in Egypt

Democracy is the solution.

            ALAA AL ASWANY 2011

---

22   On the Arab public sphere see Lynch (2006) and Ayish (2008). On the Arab hip hop public
      sphere see Ulysses (2011).

Egypt has been one of the great historical civilizations and traditional major political and cultural influence in the Middle East, but had suffered for more than thirty years under the corrupt and dictatorial rule of Hosni Mubarak who ascended to the presidency in 1981 after the assassination of Anwar al-Sadat. While Mubarak ostensibly introduced a system of 'democratic' elections, they were farces with Mubarak winning 99.99% of the vote in elections of 1987, 1993, 1999, and 2005. While Mubarak himself was old and sick, he and his cronies were pushing for his son Gamal to succeed him, setting up a family dynasty. The Mubarak regime was one of the most corrupt and repressive in the region and was increasingly hated by its people, and was thus rife for an Upheaval.[23]

As for the Egyptian Uprising, there were a series of anticipatory events, circulated via the Middle Eastern and global media, which inspired the tumultuous and significant 2011 insurrection against the hated Mubarak regime. These events included a revolt of textile workers in the city of El Mahalla el Kubra, who demonstrated against Mubarak in 2008, where demonstrators stomped on Mubarak's picture, police shot into the crowd killing two, and the event and two murdered workers were made martyrs on YouTube and Facebook (Phelps 2011, A1). As Joel Benin has argued, Egypt's workers had been steadily organizing independent trade unions, outside of the state union movement dominated by the Mubarak government, had been successfully been making economic and political demands, and were an important part of the movement that overthrew Mubarak (Benin 2011).[24]

---

23   For meticulous and detailed analyses and documentation of the corruption and totalitarian repression in the Mubarak regime, see Elaasar (2009). Elaasar, however, does not foresee the Egyptian Uprising and tends to overlook democratic forces within Egypt itself. Egyptian writer Alaa Al Aswany (2011), author of the acclaimed Egyptian novel, The Yacoubian Building and an excellent story collection Friendly Fire, provides in his essay collection On the State of Egypt a wonderful set of short essays that present problems and struggles in Egypt that predate the Uprising, with each essay ending with the statement 'Democracy is the solution', a phrase that serves as the epigram for this section and the hope for a better Egyptian future. Al Aswany opens his collection with an Introduction On Tahrir Square that documents his own participation in the Uprising, preceded by an analysis of why Egyptians had not rebelled in a mass uprising previously.

24   Benin claims that workers movements had very progressive aims from the beginning of the Uprising: "At the appropriate moment, workers did not hesitate to fuse economic and political demands. On February 9, Cairo transport workers went on strike and announced that they would be forming an independent union. According to Hossam el-Hamalawy, a well-informed blogger and labor journalist, their statement also called for abolishing the emergency law in force for decades, removing the ruling National Democratic Party (NDP) from state institutions, dissolving Parliament (fraudulently elected in 2010), drafting a new Constitution, forming a national unity government, prosecuting corrupt

While Mubarak had ruled Egypt with an iron hand since assuming power, there were many democratic forces mobilized against him from all sectors of society. In a series of short essays from 2005 up to the uprisings, Egyptian writer Alaa Al Aswany documented many critiques, protests, and emergence of forces of opposition in Egypt during the previous decade (Al Aswany 2011). Actors in these events included intellectuals, politicians, students, and many others throughout Egyptian society. Concerning the important role of women, Robin Morgan notes that despite decades of dictatorship, "a long-established feminist movement has survived there. Women had been key to the 1919 revolution against the British, but after independence were ignored by the ruling Wafd Party (Morgan 2011, 21). Documenting specific events that helped spark the Uprising, Shahin and Juan Cole note that:

> In Egypt, the passionate video blog or 'vlog' of Asmaa Mahfouz that called on Egyptians to turn out massively on January 25th in Tahrir Square went viral, playing a significant role in the success of that event. Mahfouz appealed to Egyptians to honor four young men who, following the example of Mohammed Bouazizi in an act which sparked the Tunisian uprisings), set themselves afire to protest the Mubarak regime.
>
> Although the secret police had already dismissed them as 'psychopaths,' she insisted otherwise, demanding a country where people could live in dignity, not 'like animals.' According to estimates, at least 20% of the crowds that thronged Tahrir Square that first week were made up of women, who also turned out in large numbers for protests in the Mediterranean port of Alexandria. Leil-Zahra Mortada's celebrated Facebook album of women's participation in the Egyptian revolution gives a sense of just how varied and powerful that turnout was.
>
> COLE and COLE 2011

Hence, the Egyptian Uprising can be read as a fusing of workers, students, women, and individuals from a diversity of popular movements.[25] A PBS *Frontline Report*, Revolution in Cairo (Benin 2011), described how a group of

---

officials and establishing a basic national minimum wage of 1,200 Egyptian pounds a month (about $215)" (Benin 2011, 8).

25   Joel Benin (2011) writes: "the events of January-February followed a decade of escalating mobilizations among many different sectors of Egyptian society – committees in solidarity with the Palestinian people and in opposition to the U.S. invasion of Iraq; the Kifaya (Enough) movement for democracy; doctors, judges, professors; and, above all, industrial and white-collar workers" (ibid.).

young students and professionals had for the past three years been organizing an April 6 Youth Movement, commemorating a 2008 labor demonstration and developing a web-site and Facebook page documenting the crimes of the Mubarak regime and organizing protests.[26]

After the murder by Mubarak thugs of Khalid Said, a young Egyptian who was beaten to death by police in June 2010, Google executive Wael Ghonim helped to establish a Facebook site We are all Khalid Said to commemorate the martyr. The Facebook page eventually had more than 1,500, 000 followers and was used by activists to educate Egyptians and others about the horrors of the Mubarak regime and to developing democracy movements. As Linda Herrera (2011) describes it in Egypt's Revolution 2.0: The Facebook Factor (2011),

> The events leading to Khaled's killing originated when he supposedly posted a video of two police officers allegedly dividing the spoils of a drug bust. This manner of citizen journalism has become commonplace and youth are getting more emboldened to expose the festering corruption of a police force that acts with impunity. On June 6, 2010, as Khaled Said was sitting in an internet café in Alexandria, two police officers entered and asked him for his I.D.. He refused to produce it and they proceeded to drag him away and allegedly sadistically beat him to his death as he pleaded for his life in the view of witnesses. The officers claimed that Khaled died of suffocation after swallowing a packet of drugs. His family released a photograph to an activist of the broken, bloodied, and disfigured face from Khaled's corpse. This photo, and a portrait of the gentle soft skinned face of the living Khaled, went viral. The power of photographic evidence combined with eyewitness accounts and popular knowledge of police brutality left no doubt in anyone's mind that he was senselessly and brutally murdered by police officers, the very people who are supposed to act in the interest of public safety.

Ahmed Maher, Ghonim and other Egyptian Internet activists used the Khalid Said Page and other Internet tools to organize a January 25, 2011 demonstration titled "January 25: Revolution against Torture, Corruption, Unemployment and

---

26   Author and journalist David Wolman (2011a) was present at the failed 2008 anti-Mubarak demonstration and wrote an article on Egyptian Internet activism that featured Ahmed Maher and his April 6 Youth movement comrades. Wolman also stayed in touch with Maher and returned to Egypt as the anti-Mubarak uprising exploding, writing an e-book on the event.

Injustice" in Tahrir Square, also billed as a 'Day of Rage'.[27] Thousands appeared at the demonstration which became focused on overthrowing the Mubarak regime and for the next 18 days a growing movement centered in Tahrir Square which would lead to the end of Mubarak's rule.

There were therefore arguably multiple genealogies and anticipations of the Egypt Uprising. Robin Morgan describes the role of women in Tahrir Square where according to Amal Adbel Hady of the New Women Foundation "all generations and social classes were represented." While Hady noticed that much more media attention was focused on men rather than women, Morgan notes that on January 18, 2011, a woman "whom Egyptians now call 'Leader of the revolution'...uploaded a short video to YouTube and Facebook in which she announced, 'Whoever says women shouldn't go to protests because they will get beaten, let him have some honor and manhood and come with me on January 25'. The video went viral. The planned one-day demonstration became a popular phenomenon" (Morgan 2011, 21).[28]

In addition, there had been heavy media coverage of the Iran demonstrations and calls for regime change after an allegedly stolen election in 2009. Indeed, for years Al-Jazeera has been promoting democracy in the Middle East, and has regularly produced critiques of corrupt regimes, presented demonstrations and calls for change, and debated Middle East politics.[29] Commentators noted how Al-Jazeera "has emerged as a full-fledged political actor because it reflects and articulates popular sentiment. It has become the new Nasser. The leader of the Arab world is a television network" (Agha and Malley 2011, A01). In addition to Al-Jazeera, an oppositional Internet culture, as noted, had been steadily developing in Tunisian and Egypt, including connections between youth in these countries, who also had external help from hacker groups abroad: "In Operation Egypt and Operation Tunisia, Anonymous and other groups coordinated to restore citizens' access to websites blocked by the government. The efforts extanded beyond the Internet, with faxes used to communicate vital information as a means of last reort. (In class 'lulzy' style. Cyberactivists also caused havoc by ordering enormous quantities of pizza delivered to Egyptian and Tunisian embassies) (Penny 2011).

---

27   See Wolman 2011b.

28   For another account of how a YouTube video was used to assemble young women and men to join the demonstrations against Mubarak see Wall and El Zahed (2011, 1333–1343).

29   On the role of Al-Jazeera in Middle East politics see Miles (2005), Lynch (2006), and Zayani (2005).

There were also in Egypt thirty years of a corrupt dictatorship in Egypt, the Mubarak Thug Regime, which had totally alienated the people and made them ripe for revolt (as had the Soviet regime in the 1980s). Likewise, the economic situation was bad in Egypt, especially for educated young people who could not get good jobs. Yet it appears to be Internet activists and young people who began the revolt in Egypt and continued to support it throughout the struggle. As was well publicized, Wael Ghonim, a former Google manager, admits that after the Tunisian uprising and regime change, he and other young people used Facebook and Twitter to organize demonstrations in four different squares of Cairo, unleashing the massive protests and coining the phrase 'Revolution 2.0' (Parker 2011). I myself received an email from a young scholar Bahaa Gamil Ghobrial whom I met at a conference in the U.S. in December, 2010, and he sent me the following email documenting the role of new media and social networking:

> The demonstration started on Jan 25th and the call for it was done mainly through Facebook. Because of the government's heavy control over all the traditional media, the Internet is the only available option for all opposition parties and movements.
>
> The youth who called for the first demonstration on Jan 25th belong to upper middle class in Egypt and most of them, if not all, have Internet access. So, I agree with the argument that information technology and socialnetworks, such as Facebook contributed greatly to the uprising – propelling it forward and enabling Egyptians to self-organize. Facebook is the second most visited website in Egypt (around 5 million Facebook users) and it is followed by YouTube (the third most visited website). Twitter is ranked 21 among the most visited websites in Egypt, but I believe that it will be soonin the top fifteen most visited websites after the uprising in Egypt. Kindly find attached two images regarding the increase of tweets after Jan 25th.
>
> Also, last Wednesday the new prime minister decided to unblock the Internet after 5 days of shutting it down; so we started to use it to mobilize citizens and encourage them to participate in the demonstrations. As you might know, sometimes these demonstrations are not safe; so, as soon as we reach Tahrir Square, we take photos of the demonstration and upload them to our Facebook profiles to tell our friends that we are participating and encourage them to come over.
>
> In addition, we currently have two teams in Egypt, anti-Mubarak and pro-Mubarak; so, we are using new media tools, such as Facebook and YouTube, to show pro-Mubarak people what the regime did to protesters.

Many of the pro-Mubarak people were convinced that Mubarak should step down after watching these videos.

In the survey that I conducted for my thesis that was about the impact of new media on political communication in Egypt with a special focus on the Egyptian Presidential election in 2011 at http://dar.aucegypt.edu:8080/jspui/handle/10526/738.

GHOBRIAL 2011

There is no question that social networking and new media contributed to the Egyptian Uprising, but to the issue whether the events can be interpreted as a 'Twitter revolution', or a revolution using Twitter, I would argue that Twitter, Facebook, new media, and social networking are only part of the story and am against technological determinism and exaggerating the causal force of new media, as I am hesitant at this point to use the term 'revolution'. To be sure, Facebook pages commemorated martyrs who had been killed by police in the current and previous demonstrations and, according to my Egyptian colleague cited above, YouTubes and Facebook communiqués concerning repression of Egyptians helped turn pro-Mubarak demonstrators into anti-Mubarak ones, or ones who realized his regime was finished.

Yet it is perhaps the global cable networks that broadcast 'Revolution' live, as events were unfolding 24/7 on Al-Jazeera and various Arab networks, as well as CNN and BBC. The often-saturation coverage on global TV networks, and especially Al-Jazeera, made the struggle in Egypt a world-historical event of global interest helping in turn to incite people to pour into the street to take part in the momentous upheaval, as live TV footage and interviews were circulated through global media. While there have not yet appeared scholarly investigations of the role of Al-Jazeera and other television networks in inspiring and mobilizing the North African Arab Uprisings, it is highly likely that the images of demonstrations, uprisings, and the overthrow of regimes in Tunisia and then Egypt inspired protestors throughout the world.[30]

---

30   On this point, Miriyam Aouragh and Anne Alexander note that online viewership of Al-Jazeera English reached record growth rates during the demonstrations in Egypt (2,500%) (2011, 1348). For specific data on Egypt, see http://www.alexa.com/topsites/countries/EG and for its overall growth rates, see http://www.alexa.com/siteinfo/aljazeera.net. The authors also provide an excellent account of how Internet activists in the Egyptian revolution used various new media in different phases of the struggle. They recognize the importance of Al-Jazeera and global television networks as well, and argue that the Egyptian revolution presents fresh insights in the connections between new media, satellite television networks, and political struggle.

Indeed, Al-Jazeera has been covering and circulating protests and critiques of the various Middle East regimes since its origins in the mid-1990s.[31] During the Bush/Cheney administration, Al-Jazeera was vilified as 'anti-American', and their broadcasting facilities were bombed in Afghanistan (see Kellner 2005). Yet in subsequent years, both its Arabic and English networks have been widely praised as providing first-rate reporting and a diversity of opinion. If the Gulf War was the 'moment of CNN', when its images from Iraq and the Gulf region were broadcast throughout the world, the North African Arab Uprisings were the 'moment of Al-Jazeera',[32] where hits to its web-television site received a record number of viewers, and Al-Jazeera English was played on various PBS and other news channels and cable systems throughout the world, and was available on the Internet, making it an indispensible source of news and information and a material force in promoting and encouraging the democratic uprisings through positive representations of the demonstrators and negative ones of the repressive regimes being demonstrated against. In fact, Hillary Clinton conceded during a Q&A session before the U.S. Foreign Policy Priorities Committee on Information War that: "Al-Jazeera has been the leader in that [it is] literally changing people's minds and attitudes. And like it or hate it, it is really effective" (Hall 2011)[33]

---

31   In an interesting article, Barkho (2011) provides examples of internal guidelines and news production practices of Al-Jazeera and the BBC in relation to the Israel-Palestine conflict. Barho's study does not touch on the issues engaged in this study. My own studies (Kellner 2012) focus on how Al-Jazeera-English functioned in the Arab Uprisings and other momentous struggles and spectacles of 2011. Barkho notes that there are differences between Al-Jazeera Arabic and English, as well as overlapping issues, but as far as I know there are no scholarly studies of the differences between Al-Jazeera English and Arabic in covering the Arab Uprisings. For my studies, I have been confined to the Al-Jazeera English channel and web-site.

32   Marc Lynch argues that "the period from 1997–2002 well deserves the much-abused title of 'the Al-Jazeera Era'. Building on its successful coverage of Iraq, as well as the second Palestinian Intifada and its exclusive access to Afghanistan after 9/11, Al-Jazeera dominated Arab public discourse for these crucial years" (2006, 128). While this is arguably true, I would say that during the North African Arab Uprisings Al-Jazeera became not only a global media force, but also became a voice and a primary influence on the dramatic uprisings of the period. Hence, while the 'CNN moment' marked the time that CNN became the dominant source of news, images, and opinion during the Gulf War of 1991, Al-Jazeera became a globally recognized source of news and opinion during the North African Arab Uprisings and arguably a major force in inciting the insurrections (an argument made by the Qaddafi regime and government officials from other countries).

33   Scandalously, many cable systems in the U.S. do not carry Al-Jazeera, although some, like my Los Angeles Time-Warner system, play its news programs on some PBS channels, and, of course, it is available through the Internet.

Hence, perhaps television was as influential as the Internet in inciting and intensifying the Egyptian Uprising spectacle, since the live events on TV were so dramatic and engrossing (although to some extent the distinction between television and Internet collapses since Al-Jazeera, BBC, CNN, and other major global television networks are accessible on the Internet). Television presents a 'you-are-there' spectacle of history in the making as major events are covered 24/7 by cable networks, and now the Internet. Whenever there is a significant media spectacle, global media pour into the spot, whether it is New York after 9/11, Iraq during the 2003 Bush-Cheney Iraq war, the Gulf coast during and after Hurricane Katrina, Haiti after the 2010 earthquake, and now Egypt after the uprisings (although with the eruption of the Libyan Uprising in late February 2011, global media quickly refocused its attention on the new spectacle of the Libyan Uprising).

The global media often take the positions of the opposition movements, or victims of extreme weather events or terrorist attacks, because they come to empathize with the people who they are covering. The spectacles are punctuated by 'Breaking News', and major events like the 9/11 terror attacks, the Gulf War, and now North African Arab Uprisings gain massive rapt audiences. The Big Stories are made compelling and involving, and the proliferating feeding of images, action scenes, opinions from the street, 'expert analyses', and, in the case under investigation, masses of people risking their lives for their country, present exciting live television at its best. Big Stories like the North African Arab Uprisings grip entire regions and become the major spectacle of their era.

As the Egyptian Uprising unfolded, while there were people killed during the demonstrations, the army appeared neutral and people kept pouring into the streets and squares of Cairo and other Egyptian cities, getting increasingly radicalized and becoming the stars of a global media spectacle which was energizing oppositional consciousness throughout the Middle East. On the third day of the protests, the Muslim Brotherhood leadership told its members to support the demonstrations, as young members of the Brothers already had. The Brothers began providing security for the demonstrators and bringing in food and medical supplies.[34]

Not only were women very involved in participating in the Egyptian Uprising, but they were also instrumental "in much of the nitty-gritty organisation that turned Tahrir Square from a moment into a movement. Women were

---

34   For a balanced view of the Muslim Brotherhood and their role in the uprising see the PBS Frontline episode The Brothers (broadcast February 22, 2011). BBC Reports, however, presented a more unsettling report on the Brotherhood, highlighting their radical Islam roots and current orientation. For a scholarly examination see Pargeter (2010).

involved in arranging food deliveries, blankets, the stage and medical help" (Rice et al. 2011).[35] Robin Morgan (2011) points out that "soon, unsung protest coordinator Amal Sharaf – a 36-year-old English teacher, single mother and member of the the organizers April 6 Youth Movement – was spending days and nights in the movement's tiny office, smoking furiously and overseeing a crew of men. Google employee Wael Ghonim, who privately administered one of the Facebook pages that were the movement's virtual headquarters, would later become an icon – but after he was arrested, young Nadine Wahab, an Egyptian American expert on new media advocacy, took over, strengthening the online presence (Morgan, 2011, 21).

In addition, youth cultures and artists were involved in the movement and massive protests. As in Tunisia, the rap music community became very involved, and Andy Morgan noted that:

> Karim Adel Eissa, aka A-Rush from Cairo rappers Arabian Knightz, stayed up late into the night of Thursday 27 January recording new lyrics for the tune 'Rebel', which he was determined to release on Facebook and MediaFire. 'Egypt is rising up against the birds of darkness," spat the lyrics. "It was a direct call for revolution,' Karim says. 'Before, we'd only used metaphors to talk about the corrupt system. But once people were out on the streets, we were just like, 'Screw it.' If we're going down, we're going down.'
>
> He and his crew just about managed to upload the new version of the song before Karim was called away to help with the vigilante security detail who were down in the streets keeping his neighbourhood free of looters and government thugs.
>
> IBID., 21

Further, Andy Morgan points out how a diversity of musicians, ranging from older popular artists to young performed daily for crowds and invigorated the participants with their music, some of which was composed for the Uprising:

> After the uprising of 25 January, Cairo's Tahrir Square resounded to the traditional Egyptian frame drum or *daf*, which pounded out trance-like beats over which the crowd laid slogans full of poetic power and joyful hilarity. As the Egyptian people rediscovered what it felt like to be a nation, united and indivisible, they reverted to the raw power of their

---

35   See also Leil-Zahra Mortada's (2011) Facebook page which documents a diversity of activities.

most basic musical instincts to celebrate their mass release from fear –
traditional drumming and chanting and patriotic songs from the glory
days of yore when Egypt trounced the forces of imperialism in 1956 or
took Israel by surprise in 1973.

IBID., 21

In the following days, ever greater numbers of people congregated in Tahrir
Square, renamed 'Liberation Square', in Cairo and global media poured in to
make the spectacle global. On Day Nine, things turned nasty with Mubarak
sympathizers and thugs going after demonstrators and the global media themselves. Organized thugs were bused in and attacked protestors with knives,
machetes, and other weapons; Horse and Camel riders also assaulted the protestors, many of whom were knocked off the horses and camels and beaten up.
Foreign media personnel were threatened and hit by thugs in front of the cam-
era which caught the episode; other global media workers were arrested and in
some cases held blind-fold overnight, assuring that foreign media would continue to be critical of the Mubarak regime and be sympathetic to the
demonstrators.

There were pitched fights all day February 2 between protestors and
Mubarak thugs; hundreds of Molotov cocktails were thrown; both groups
picked rocks from the streets to throw at opponents; buildings were set on fire;
some reporters were attacked and detained by Mubarak thugs, then released,
making February 2 and 3 days of intense drama and spectacle, broadcast live
over global media networks like CNN, BBC, and Al-Jazeera.

Events continued to be intensely dramatic on Day Ten, as hundreds of thousands of anti-Mubarak demonstrators gathered in Tahrir Square, which
emerged as Ground Zero for the insurgency. Crowds also appeared at other
sites throughout Egypt, with demonstrators calling for a 'Day of Departure'.
During the following days, the occupation of Tahrir Square continued to
expand, demonstrations continued to unfold throughout the country, the army
remained neutral, and the Mubarak regime began to make concessions.
Mubarak appeared on television claiming he would not run for president again
and then nominated chief of intelligence Omar Suleimen as Vice-President,
with whom he would share power during the build-up to promised elections in
September.

Mubarak's concessions were perceived as too little, too late, and the demonstrations continued unabated, calling for Mubarak to surrender the presidency.
On Days 14 and 15 workers joined in with strikes throughout the country,
and on Day 17, it was rumored that Mubarak would step down with the military
organizing a new government (a claim reiterated by CIA Chief Leon Panetta).

Tremendous anticipation grew as it was announced that Mubarak was coming to speak on television. In his long rambling speech, however, he appeared not to yield and the crowds roared their disapproval.

As commentators unparsed Mubarak's ambiguous speech, it became apparent that he said he was transferring power to Vice President Omar Suleimen who came on after Mubarak and told the crowd to go home. The people in Freedom Square, however, went wild, shouting "Leave, Leave, Leave!," waving their shoes at the cameras, a gesture of utter contempt in the Arab world. The Western press described Mubarak's stunt as a 'Right Feint' and an Egyptian-American commentator on Al-Jazeera summed it up: 'We was Punked!' In fact, the arrogant Mubarak was obviously unaware of the depth of the hatred of his people and thought he could play verbal games with them, holding onto power.

Mubarak's speech prompted President Barack Obama to respond that "the Egyptian people have been told that there was a transition of authority, but it is not yet clear that this transition is immediate, meaningful or sufficient," and for the first time Obama made it clear to Egyptian officials that Mubarak must go (Warrick, 2011). According to an anonymous American source, the Obama administration had been "trying to walk a fine line between retaining support for Mubarak while trying to infuse common sense into the equation (ibid.). By the end of the day, it was clear the situation was no longer tenable (ibid.).[36]

On February 12, Mubarak left Cairo for his resort home in Egypt, and reports said that the protest in Cairo's Tahrir Square had spilled out into surrounding streets following Friday Prayers. Protesters were now also massed outside Egypt's state television headquarters and the presidential palace in the Heliopolis district of the Egyptian capital and, significantly, the Army turned their cannons on their tanks away from the people. Then Vice-President Suleiman came on Egyptian state television to say that Mubarak had dissolved his government and handed over power to the military and Egypt and perhaps much of the rest of the Arab world exploded with joy. As *The Associated Press* reported on February 12, 2011:

> President Hosni Mubarak of Egypt resigned his post and turned over all power to the military on Friday, ending his nearly 30 years of autocratic rule and bowing to a historic popular uprising that has transformed politics in Egypt and around the Arab world.

---

36   Gardner (2011) provides an excellent account of Mubarak's last days, the behind-the-scene gyrations of the u.s. government, and a detailed historical account of u.s. relations with the Nasser, Sadat, and Mubarak regimes in 2011.

The streets of Cairo exploded in shouts of 'God is Great' moments after Mr. Mubarak's vice president and longtime intelligence chief, Omar Suleiman, announced during evening prayers that Mr. Mubarak had passed all authority to a council of military leaders.[37]

ROGERS 2011

Of course, the struggle for democracy and freedom was only starting in Tunisia and Egypt, and long, tumultuous, and unpredictable struggles lay ahead for these bellwethers of the Arab Uprising which were beginning the transition to democracy after decades of dictatorship. Yet we do know that demonstrations intensified right after the success of the Egyptian Uprising in Yemen, Bahrain, Iran, and, most dramatically, Libya, inaugurating months of intense struggle that ultimately led to the victory of the anti-Qaddafi forces and the death of Qaddafi and one of his sons, and arrests of his other sons, including his heir-apparent Saif-al Islam.

The global media had circulated images of uprisings in Tunisia and Egypt which drove out dictators who had ruled with an iron fist for 23 and 32 years, and then gave up power when they saw that great masses of their own people were against them, while creating tremendous excitement throughout the Arab world and the global public sphere. The spectacle of the Arab Uprisings broadcast live on Al-Jazeera and other global networks had inspired publics throughout North Africa and the Middle East to challenge their societies, to voice their grievances, to militate for radical social transformation, and to demonstrate against corrupt regimes.

Tumult in the Arab World 2011: From the Arab Spring to Bloody, Summer, Fall and Winter

You rose up, oh Egypt. And after patience and the night came victory. Egypt, you rose up, and your son succeeded and he waved your flag high.

Popular Egyptian song by ADEL-HALIM HAFEZ

Throughout the Middle East, after the Friday prayers demonstrations erupted during the Arab Spring in Bahrain, Yemen, Egypt, Syria, and other Arab

---

37   See Tony Rogers (2011) for a comparative overview of how major media outlets presented Mubarak's overthrow. For illuminating accounts of the experience of Egyptian intellectuals in Tahrir Square during the last days of Mubarak and transition to a new regime see Yasmine El Rashidi (2011a, 2011b).

countries in what was becoming a weekly ritual as the people of the region sought democracy and freedom (Goodman 2011). In Egypt, on February 6, after former Prime Minister Ahmed Shafik resigned following boisterous demonstrations that called for his removal because of his closeness to Mubarak, Shafik was replaced by the popular former transportation minister Essam Sharaf who had quit his cabinet position in 2006 and had joined the demonstrators to oust Mubarak. When he went to Tahrir square on March 4 to celebrate the change, he was hoisted upon demonstrators shoulders and received a tumultuous greeting, broadcast live on Al-Jazeera.

There were reports that Egypt was undertaking a thoroughgoing 'de-Mubaraking' of Egypt's public spaces, replacing all signs and names of spaces citing Mubarak with alternatives, such as replacing the Mubarak subway station sign with "Marrtyrs [sic] of the January 25, Revolution" (Al-Jazeera 2011). Criminal investigations are being undertaken against Mubarak and other of his ministers, including the once-powerful and feared Interior Minister, Habib el-Adly. Yet critics claimed that arbitrary arrest and torture were continuing, and that government officials were burning documents that would indicate their complicity in Mubarak era crimes (el Dahshan 2011).[38]

Moving against the former state security apparatus, demonstrators in Alexandria burned down the hated state security headquarters, while a group in Cairo stormed the office and found officials burning documents. Some documents were taken out of the office, which contained information documenting the extent to which the Mubarek regime spied on and kept files on ordinary citizens, according to one of the demonstrators interviewed by Al-Jazeera (March 5, 2011). On March 7, there were reports on Al-Jazeera that eight floors of underground cells were found in the Cairo state security headquarters where opponents of the regime had been held and tortured.

Yet the Dark Side of the Egyptian Uprising was evident in Egypt on March 8 when groups of reactionary men confronted brave women in their demonstration on International Woman's Day and told them to return to their houses. Egypt had long been plagued with a patriarchal society where women were sexually harassed on a daily basis and considered inferior,[39] and it appeared

---

38   See also Gardner (2011, 193ff).

39   The brutalization and rape of CBS reporter Lara Logan in the celebrations after Mubarak's resignation is one of the horrors of the Egyptian revolution. Logan was separated from her crew and brutally assaulted and raped until rescued by Egyptian women and soldiers (CBS News, 2011). On the out-of-control sexual harassment of women in Egyptian society see Drogin (2011). There were also widespread reports that women protestors were subjected to virginity tests (Fisher 2011). On the general problem of sexual harassment of women in Egypt see the illuminating essays by Al Aswany (2011).

that the struggle between women and men would be a protracted one. On the same day at night, fights broke out between Christian Coptics protesting the burning of a church and Muslim Thugs who clashed with them, leaving more than 11 dead (Stack 2011).[40] The next day, there were pictures on Al-Jazeera and other networks of Mubarak thugs attacking peaceful demonstrators in Cairo with knives, machetes, and whips, a horrific aftermath of Mubarak's Thug Regime, which still lived on in brutal men who had assimilated its aggressive and violent tendencies, and would continue to harass protestors in the months to come.

Tunisia, by contrast, was making swifter progress toward regime change and democratic rule. On March 7, The Associated Press (2011) released a report, indicating that Tunisia both named a new government and was the first country in the region to close down its much hated secret police unit and State Security Department. Shortly thereafter, it was announced that former dictator Ben Ali's party had been dissolved, although interviews with Tunisian citizens that day on Al-Jazeera indicated that many people had seen no real changes in their lives.

Graham Usher (2011) argues, however, that after the initial Uprising that drove Ben Ali and his family out of the country and began the tumult of Arab Uprisings, there was a second grass-roots movement in Tunisia that laid siege from January 14 when Ben Ali fled into March, assembling in Tunis's Casbah Square and elsewhere in the country "to protest any and all attempts by the ancient regime to steal back the revolution. Having refused to open fire on demonstrators in the first revolution, Tunisia's 30,000-strong army kept to its constitutional role in the second: it guarded public spaces, but allowed the struggle to play out between serial interim governments and what became known as the Casbah coalition" (ibid.).

Usher argues that continued demonstrations and clashes with interim governments forced the resignation of Ben Ali appointed governors in the provinces; the dissolution of his political RCD party; the disbanding of the state security apparatus and dissolution of the hated secret police, and the legalization of parties previously banned. The struggles culiminated, in Usher's view, with the interim government bowing to the democratic forces key demand for elections to a Constituent Assembly that would be empowered to write a new constitution and prepare parliamentary elections. Usher acknowledges emerging divisions within the Tunisian democratic forces and serious problems that they face in moving forward, including economic disparities and lack of jobs, but sees significant advances since the overthrow of the Ben Ali regime.

---

40   On the situation of the Christian Copts in Egypt see Al Aswany (2011).

Hence, Egypt and Tunisia appeared to be moving forward slowly but surely, with unpredictable consequences through the summer and into the fall. Yet after 18 days of the Libya Uprising against Qaddafi and his family and cronies, a stalemate appeared to have been reached in Libya, with rebel forces controlling the East and Qaddafi's forces controlling much of the West. In Egypt and Tunisia, by contrast, the people were attempting to come to terms with the oppression and crimes of their authoritarian states, and were beginning the slow and often tumultuous process of rebuilding their societies. Questions emerged concerning whether the Egyptian people would have genuine input into the building of democracy and whether new institutions and forms of power could be built.

Impressively, the people of Egypt and Tunisia had both overthrown corrupt dictators and non-violent demonstrations had expressed their will for change and yearnings for democracy, freedom, social justice and dignity. As Slavoj Zizek argued, the Egyptian (and arguably Tunisian) revolutions had been secular, with demonstrators combing calls for democracy and freedom with demands for social justice Žižek, 2011; see also Roy 2011). The Uprisings exemplified the 'People Power' movements of the 1960s, as well as the model of the 'multitude' seizing power developed by Michael Hardt and Antonio Negri. As Hardt and Negri argued in a widely-circulated article on the Arab Uprisings:

> One challenge facing observers of the uprisings spreading across north Africa and the Middle East is to read them as not so many repetitions of the past but as original experiments that open new political possibilities, relevant well beyond the region, for freedom and democracy. Indeed, our hope is that through this cycle of struggles the Arab world becomes for the next decade what Latin America was for the last – that is, a laboratory of political experimentation between powerful social movements and progressive governments from Argentina to Venezuela, and from Brazil to Bolivia.
>
> HARDT and NEGRI 2011

Hardt and Negri do not mention here the role of charismatic Latin American leaders who galvanized social movements to win state power in democratic elections. In his documentary South of the Border (2010), Oliver Stone focuses on several presidents in Latin America who have led movements to produce left and center-left regimes. While Stone arguably exaggerates the role of the charismatic Latin American leaders that he interviews in his film, and downplays the role of social movements, it is likely that the Latin American left had evolved a progressive agenda with a combination of charismatic leaders and progressive political parties aligned with social movements.

The question emerges from the Egyptian and Tunisian revolutions, however, whether movements and masses without charismatic leaders and progressive parties can construct a genuinely democratic society, without violence. Their challenge is also to generate political leaders and groups who nurture democratic institutions and social relations without developing oppressive modes of power and reverting to the old mode of authoritarian government and repression.[41]

Yet, as the Arab Spring passed into a hot and turbulent Arab Summer and then Fall and Winter, there continued to be intense political repression in Egypt. Six days of demonstrations in Tahrir Square from November 25 into December left at least 41 dead and over 1,000 injured in what protestors were calling a 'second Egyptian revolution'. An uneasy peace ensued, and the first phase of planned elections for a People's Assembly that would create a constitutional government took place as scheduled with an extremely high turnout. The Muslim Brotherhood and more radical Islamic Salafis party won about 50% and 25% of the first round of voting, creating fears that elections may provide the road for an Islamic state, or a coup d'etat by the military to prevent such an occurrence (see Kirkpatrick 2011).

More violence broke out during the second round of elections in Egypt, and 2011 was coming to an end with very tense relations between the Egyptian military who continued to wield power, the emerging political parties, and the Egyptian public. In Tunisia, by contrast, a moderate Islamic party Ennahda had earlier won 41% of the seats in the constitutional assembly in a national election and formed a transitional government with liberal and secular parties. Hence, just as the Arab Uprisings had multiple causes, so too did they have multiple and highly unpredictable consequences that will be played out in the years to come.

Concluding Comments

During the Arab Uprisings, powerful new images of Arabs and their political awakening and uprisings were circulating through the global media, subverting notions that the Arab people were passive, or an irrational mass

---

41   The Occupy movements present other examples of leaderless movements, perhaps a defining feature of the Uprisings of 2011 when anyone can participate and create their own parts in the spectacle they choose.

periodically exploding in rages of anger with no constructive effects. From a global perspective, the Arab Spring of 2011 represents the beginning of a turbulent uprising of the Arab people against a series of authoritarian, dictatorial, and corrupt regimes that emerged from a long period of colonialism in the second half of the 20th century. Anti-colonialist revolts in the Arab world took the form of military coups, nationalist uprisings and struggles, or their combination, which in North Africa and throughout the Middle East resulted in authoritarian regimes that had become family dictatorships, corrupted by nepotism, cronyism, kleptocracy, and repressive state regimes of prison, torture, and murder to preserve absolute state power. While the uprisings in Tunisia and Egypt displayed relatively non-violent protest movements that drove dictators to flee the country, not surprisingly, violent state responses and repression took place in Libya, Yemen, Syria, and other countries which in turn generate intense political struggles, still ongoing in these countries.

As I have argued, the Arab Uprisings were global, circulating via broadcasting, new media and social networking, and word of mouth as similar tactics of struggle were used in proximate countries during the Arab Spring, generating media spectacles that inaugurated an era with similar democratic revolts and uprisings throughout the world. In this paper, I have suggested that media spectacle can serve as a major category for explaining contemporary culture and politics, used to orchestrate war, terrorist events, political elections, and now political insurgencies and revolution. I have attempted to explicate my concept of media spectacle, differentiate it from Guy Debord's society of the spectacle, and to present the spectacle as a contested terrain. I have illustrated my concept of media spectacle through analysis of the North African Arab Uprisings of 2011, and my analysis suggests that media spectacle is now becoming a major feature of political opposition and resistance and a major force against repressive regimes.

In a global media and Internet era, the state and corporations no longer controls all of the means of communication, and the Internet provides a forum for political discourse of every spectrum. To be sure, the Internet and media spectacle alone do not produce social change, but mobilized and radicalized groups of people can use the Internet and social networking for informing, organizing and mobilizing political movements and struggle, and the communication and messages from mass protest movements can be themselves a significant force of social change in the contemporary era.

Quite possibly, the media spectacles of the North African Arab Uprisings of 2011, followed by the Occupy movements, could be transformative events that should cheer advocates of a freer and more just world everywhere and that could inaugurate a new era in history. From the time of the 9/11 terror attacks, I have argued that we have been in a period that I call Terror War, in which spectacles of terror and fear of terrorism have driven media spectacle and shaped the imaginary of political regimes in the West (Kellner 2003b). Part of the reason why the West, and in particular the U.S. government and intelligence services, did not anticipate the growing dissatisfaction and explosive uprisings in North Africa is that U.S. foreign policy and the imaginary of the Western media have been obsessed with fear of Islamic-inspired terrorism and have failed to see how masses of people living under dictatorship have been expressing their political opinions, mobilizing new groups and forces, and preparing to struggle against dictatorships and corrupt regimes.

Indeed, with the North African Arab Uprisings and Occupy movements of 2011, we may be entering a new phase of history in which people and new technologies become major driving forces of history, and revolution is once more on the historical agenda. In this emergent period, youth could have roles in political struggle, such as were exhibited in North African Arab Uprisings of 2011 and Occupy movements, as new thinking and political strategies are emerging to strengthen democracy and promote democratic social transformation in the contemporary era. On the other hand, reactionary and counterrevolutionary forces are confronting the democratic insurgent movements, creating the conditions for a highly turbulent and unpredictable future.

References

Agha, Hussein and Robert Malley. 2011. Post-Mubarak Egypt, the Rebirth of the Arab World. *Washington Post*, February 11, A01.

Al Aswany, Alaa. 2011. *On the State of Egypt. What Made the Revolution Inevitable*. New York: Vintage Books.

Associated Press. 2011. Tunisia Scraps Hated Police Unit. March 7. http://www.nytimes.com/aponline/2011/03/07/world/africa/AP-AF-Tunisia.html?ref=world (accessed on March 8, 2011).

Ayish, Muhammad I. 2008. *The New Arab Public Sphere*. Berlin: Frsank & Timme.

Anderson, Kevin. 2011. Arab Revolutions at the Crossroads. *The International Marxist-Humanist* April 2. http://www.usmarxisthumanists.org/articles/arab-revolutions crossroads-kevin-anderson/.

Aouragh, Miriyam and Anne Alexander. 2011. The Egyptian Experience: Sense and Nonsense of the Internet Revolution. *International Journal of Communication* 5: 1344–1358,

Ash, Timothy Garton. 1993. *The Magic Lantern: The Revolution of '89 Witnessed in Warsaw, Budapest, Berlin and Prague*. New York: Vintage.

Barkho, Leon. 2011. The Role of Internal Guidelines in Shaping News Narratives: Ethnographic Insights into the Discursive Rhetoric of Middle East Reporting by the BBC and Al Jazeera English. *Critical Discourse Studies* 8 (4): 297–309.

Benin, Joel. 2011. "Egypt's Workers Rise Up," *The Nation*, March 7/14, 2011: 8–9 (accessed on-line at http://www.thenation.com/article/158680/egypts-workers-rise, March 9.

Best, Steven and Douglas Kellner. 1997. *The Postmodern Turn*. New York and London: Guilford Press and Routledge.

Best, Steven and Douglas Kellner. 2001. *The Postmodern Adventure. Science Technology, and Cultural Studies at the Third Millennium*. New York and London: Guilford and Routledge.

Callinicos, Alex. 2011. Tunisia: Patterns of Revolt. *Socialist Worker* 2236 (January 25). http://www.socialistworker.co.uk/art.php?id=23670.

Cole, Shahin and Juan Cole. 2011. Tomgram: Shahin and Juan Cole, The Women's Movement in the Middle East. *TomDipsatch*, April 26. http://www.tomdispatch.com/post/175384/tomgram%3A_shahin_and_juan_cole%2C_the_women%27s_movement_in_the_middle_east_/#more (accessed May 15, 2011).

Debord, Guy. 1967. *The Society of the Spectacle*. Detroit: Black and Red Press.

Dickinson, Elizabeth. 2011. The First WikiLeaks Revolution. *ForeignPolicy*, January 13.http://wikileaks.foreignpolicy.com/posts/2011/01/13/wikileaks_and_the_tunisia_protests (accessed March 10, 2011).

Drogin, Bob. 2011. Egypt's Women Face Growing Sexual Harassment. *Los Angles Times*, February 23 http://articles.latimes.com/2011/feb/23/world/la-fg-egypt-women-abuse20110223 (accessed February 25, 2011).

Elaasar, Aladdin. 2009. The Last Pharaoh. Mubarek and the Uncertain Future of Egypt in the Volatile Mid East. Missoula: Beacon Press.

El Amrani, Issandr 2011. A Strong Islamist Showing in Egypt's Election Need Not be Cause For Panic. *The Guardian*, December 5. http://www.theguardian.com/commentisfree/2011/dec/05/islamist-egypt-election (accessed December 9, 2011).

El Dahshan, Mohamed. 2011. The 'Demubarakization' of Egypt. *New York Times*, March 1. http://opinionator.blogs.nytimes.com/2011/03/01/the-demubarakization-of-egypt/ (accessed March 5, 2011).

El-Kikhia, Mansour O. 1997. *Libya's Qaddafi: The Politics of Contradiction*. Gainsville: Florida University Press.

El-Madhi, Rabab and Philip Marfleet, eds. 2009. *Egypt: The Moment of Change*. London and New York: Zed Books.

El Rashidi, Yasmine. 2011. 'This is Who Egyptians Are'. *New York Review of Books*, February 11. http://www.nybooks.com/blogs/nyrblog/2011/feb/11/this-is-the-truth-of-whoegyptians-are/ (accessed February 25, 2011).

El Rashidi Yasmine. 2011. 'Freedom'. *New York Review of Books*, February 12. http://www.nybooks.com/blogs/nyrblog/2011/feb/12/freedom/ (accessed February 25, 2011).

Fisher, William. 2011. Egypt: 'Virginity Tests' For Women Protesters? *The Public Record*, March 24. http://pubrecord.org/world/9133/egypt-virginity-tests-protesters-women/ (accessed March 31, 2011).

Fukuyama, Francis. 1992. *The End of History and the Last Man*. New York: The Free Press.

Gardner, Lloyd C. 2011. *The Road to Tahrir Square: Egypt and the United States from the Rise of Nasser to the Fall of Mubarak*. New York: The New Press.

Ghobrial, Gamil. 2011. Personal communication, February 14.

Goodman, J. David. 2011. Friday Prayers Again Lead to Protests in Mideast. *New York Times*, March 4. http://www.nytimes.com/2011/03/05/world/middleeast/05unrest.html?hp=&pagewantedprint (accessed March 5, 2011).

Hall, Colby. 2011. Hillary Clinton: 'America Is Losing' an Information War that 'Al Jazeera is Winning'. *Mediaite*, March 2. http://www.mediaite.com/tv/hillary-clinton-claims-al-jazeera-is-winning-an-information-war-that-america-is-losing/ (accessed December 22, 2011).

Hardt, Michael and Antonio Negri, 2011. Arabs are Democracy's New Pioneers. *The Guardian*, February 24. http://www.guardian.co.uk/commentisfree/2011/feb/24/arabs-democracy-latin-america (accessed on March 5, 2011).

Herrera, Linda. 2011. Egypt's Revolution 2.0: The Facebook Factor. *Jadaliyya*, February 12. http://www.jadaliyya.com/pages/index/612/egypts-revolution-2.0_the-facebook-factor (accessed December 8, 2011).

Horkheimer, Max and Teodor W. Adorno. 1972. *Dialectic of Enlightenment*. Boston: Continuum.

Kahn, Richard and Douglas Kellner. 2005. Oppositional Politics and the Internet: A Critical/Reconstructive Approach. *Cultural Politics* 1 (1): 75–100.

Kaufmann, Vincent. 2006. *Guy Debord: Revolution in the Service of Poetry*. Minneapolis: University of Minnesota Press.

Kellner, Douglas. 1984. *Herbert Marcuse and the Crisis of Marxism*. Berkeley: University of California Press.

Kellner, Douglas. 1989. *Critical Theory, Marxism, and Modernity*. Cambridge, UK and Baltimore, Md.: Polity Press and John Hopkins University Press.

Kellner, Douglas. 1990. *Television and the Crisis of Democracy*. Boulder: Westview Press.

Kellner, Douglas. 1992. *The Persian Gulf TV War*. Boulder: Westview Press.

Kellner, Douglas. 1995. *Media Culture*. London and New York: Routledge.

Kellner, Douglas. 2001. *Grand Theft 2000. Media Spectacle and a Stolen Election*. Lanham: Rowman and Littlefield.

Kellner, Douglas. 2002. Theorizing Globalization. *Sociological Theory* 20 (3): 285–305.

Kellner, Douglas. 2003a. *Media Spectacle*. London and New York: Routledge.

Kellner, Douglas. 2003b. *From September 11 to Terror War: The Dangers of the Bush Legacy*. Lanham: Rowman and Littlefield.

Kellner, Douglas. 2005. *Media Spectacle and the Crisis of Democracy*. Boulder: Paradigm Press.

Kellner, Douglas. 2007. Bushspeak and the Politics of Lying: Presidential Rhetoric in the 'War on Terror. *Presidential Studies Quarterly* 37 (4): 622–645.

Kellner, Douglas. 2008. *Guys and Guns Amok: Domestic Terrorism and School Shootings from the Oklahoma City Bombings to the Virginia Tech Massacre*. Bouler: Paradigm Press.

Kellner, Douglas. 2009. Barack Obama and Celebrity Spectacle. *International Journal of Communication* 3: 1–20.

Kellner, Douglas. 2010a. *Cinema Wars: Hollywood Film and Politics in the Bush/Cheney Era*. Malden: Blackwell.

Kellner, Douglas. 2010b. Barack Obama, the Power Elite, and Media Spectacle. *American Study Institute* 11: 25–70. Seoul: Seoul National University.

Kellner, Douglas. 2012. *Media Spectacle and Insurrection, 2011: From the Arab Uprisings to Occupy Everywhere*. London: Bloomsbury.

Kirkpatrick, David. D. 2011. Military Flexes Its Muscles as Islamists Gain in Egypt. *New York Times*, December 7. http://www.nytimes.com/2011/12/08/world/middleeast/egyptiangeneral-mukhtar-al-mulla-asserts-continuing-control-despiteelections.html?pagewanted=all (accessed December 9, 2011).

Kirkpatrick, David D. and David E. Sanger. 2011. A Tunisian-Egyptian Link That Shook Arab History. *New York Times*, February 13. http://www.nytimes.com/2011/02/14/world/middleeast/14egypt-tunisia-protests.html?pagewanted=all (accessed February 13, 2011).

Le Monde. 2011. Revivez les Évènements de Vendredi en Tunisie. January 14 http://www.lemonde.fr/afrique/article/2011/01/14/suivez-en-direct-la-situation-en-tunisie_1465727_3212.html#ens_id=1245377 (accessed May 14, 2011).

Lynch, Marc. 2006. *Voices of the New Arab Public Sphere: Iraq, Al-Jazeera, and Middle East Politics Today*. New York: Columbia University Press.

Mackey, Robert. 2011. Video that Set Off Tunisia's Uprising. *New York Times*, January 22. http://thelede.blogs.nytimes.com/2011/01/22/video-that-triggered-tunisias-uprising/ (accessed January 22, 2011).

Marcus, Greil. 1990. *Lipstick Traces: A Secret History of the Twentieth Century*. Harvard: Harvard University Press.

Marcuse, Herbert. 1964. *One-Dimensional Man*. Boston: Beacon Press.

Marzouki, Nadia. 2011. Tunisia's Wall Has Fallen. *Middle East Research and Information Project*, January 19. http://www.merip.org/mero/mero011911 (accessed January 19, 2011).

McDonough, Tom, ed. 2002, *Guy Debord and the Situationist International*. Cambridge: MIT Press.

Miles, Hugh. (2005. *Al-Jazeera: The Inside Story of the Arab News Channel that is Challenging the West*. New York: Grove Press.

Morgan, Andy. 2011a. From Fear to Fury: How the Arab World Found its Voice. *The Observer*, February 27. http://www.guardian.co.uk/music/2011/feb/27/egypt -tunisia-music-protests (accessed May 14, 2011).

Morgan, Robin. 2011b. Women of the Arab Spring. *Ms. Magazine*, Spring. http://www .msmagazine.com/spring2011/womenofthearabspring.asp (accessed May 14, 2011).

Mortada, Leil Zahra. 2011. Women of Egypt. *Facebook Album*. http://www.facebook .com/media/set/?set=a.493689677675.268523.586357675 (accessed May 18, 2011).

Pargeter, Alison. 2010. *The Muslim Brotherhood: The Burden of Tradition*. London: Saqi Books.

Parker, Ned. 2011. Crowd's Swell as Protest Seeks a Leader. *Los Angeles Times*, February 9 http://articles.latimes.com/2011/feb/09/world/la-fg-egypt-google-20110209 (accessed February 9, 2011).

Penny, Laurie. 2011. Cyberactivism From Egypt to Occupy Wall Street. *The Nation*, October 31. http://www.thenation.com/article/163922/cyberactivism-egypt-occupy -wall-street (accessed November 7, 2011).

Phelps, Timothy, 2011. Where Egypt's Unrest Took Root. *Los Angeles Times*, February 9, A1.

Poster, Mark. 1995. *The Second Media Age*. Cambridge: Polity Press.

Rogers, Tony. 2011. How Reporters Led their Stories on a Historic Day in Egypt. *About. com*, February 11. http://journalism.about.com/b/2011/02/11/how-reporters-led -their-stories-on-a-historic-day-in-egypt.htm (accessed November 11, 2011).

Roy, Olivier. 2011. This is Not an Islamic Revolution. *New Statesman*, February 15, 2011. http://www.newstatesman.com/religion/2011/02/egypt-arab-tunisia-islamic (accessed on September 12, 2011).

Stack, Liam, 2011. Christians and Muslims in Fatal Clash Near Cairo. *New York Times*, March 9. http://www.nytimes.com/2011/03/10/world/africa/10egypt.html?hp=&adx nnl=1&adxnnx=1299693623-ibuMuLXN5ZXBFctH7S8DuQ&pagewanted=print (accessed March 9, 2011).

The Guardian. 2011. Tunisia Crisis: As it Happened. January 14. http://www.guardian .co.uk/global/blog/2011/jan/14/tunisia-wikileaks (accessed May 14, 2011).

Ulysses. 2011. Hip Hop Revolution. *Open Democracy* December http://www .opendemocracy.net/ulysses/hip-hop-revolution (accessed December 22, 2011).

Usher, Graham. 2011. That Other Tunisia. *The Nation*, September 12. http://www .thenation.com/article/162966/other-tunisia (accessed September 12, 2011).

Wall, Melissa and Sahar El Zahed. 2011. 'I'll be Waiting for You Guys': A YouTube Call to Action in the Egyptian Revolution. *International Journal of Communication* 5: 1333–1343.

Wark, McKenzie. 2008. *50 Years of Recuperation of the Situationist International*. New York: Princeton Architectural Press.

Warrick, Joby. 2011. In Mubarak's Final Hours, Defiance Surprises U.S. and Threatens to Unleash Chaos. *Washington Post*, February 12. http://www.washingtonpost.com/wpdyn/content/article/2011/02/11/AR2011021106690.html (accessed September 12, 2011).

Wirth, Robert. 2011. How a Single Match Can Ignite a Revolution. *New York Times*, January 21. www.nytimes.com/2011/01/23/weekinreview/23worth.htm (accessed January 21, 2011).

Wolman, David, 2011a. The Techie Dissidents Who Showed Egyptians How to Organize Online. *The Atlantic*, February 3. http://www.theatlantic.com/technology/archive/2011/02/the-techie-dissidents-who-showed-egyptians-how-to-organize-online/70734/ (accessed December 8, 2011).

Wolman, David. 2011b. *The Instigators*. Brooklyn: Atavist.

Xan Rice, Katherine Marsh, Tom Finn, Harriet Sherwood, Angelique Chrisafis, and Robert Booth. 2011. Women Have Emerged as Key Players in the Arab Spring. *The Guardian*, April 22. http://www.guardian.co.uk/world/2011/apr/22/women-arab-spring (accessed May 18, 2011).

Zayani, Mohamed, ed. 2005. *The Al-Jazeera Phenomenon*. Boulder: Paradigm.

Žižek, Slavoj. 2011. For Egypt, this is the miracle of Tahrir Square. *The Guardian*, February 10. http://www.guardian.co.uk/global/2011/feb/10/egypt-miracle-tahrir-square/print (accessed March 5, 2011).

60 Minutes. 2011. CBS News' Lara Logan Assaulted During Egypt Protests. CBS News, February 16. http://www.cbsnews.com/stories/2011/02/15/60minutes/main20032070.shtml (accessed March 11, 2011).

CHAPTER 11

Turkey's 'War and Peace'
The Kurdish Question and the Media

Savaş Çoban

There are many minority groups living in Turkey today, and the country
has been home to many cultures and nations throughout history. Among
these minorities, a great many have been made, or have become, Turkish
as a result of cultural assimilation. They have stopped using their own
mother tongue and started using Turkish as the official language. One
major reason for this, is the repressive language policies. Languages of
minorities that were not accepted officially as minority groups were
prohibited – this damaging policy was in use until recently and the effects
of this repression (or the operations of the repressive mentality) still
continue.

During the establishment of the Turkish Republic, the Treaty of Lausanne
was seen as the most important international agreement. In the agreement
there were civil and political rights that were not granted to minorities as,
under this agreement, they were not recognised as being minority groups.
In this respect, the provisions of Lausanne are not adequate in terms of social
life and international agreement policies. The 39th Provision of the Treaty of
Lausanne is as follows:

> Turkish nationals belonging to non-Moslem minorities will enjoy the
> same civil and political rights as Moslems.
>
> All the inhabitants of Turkey, without distinction of religion, shall be
> equal before the law.
>
> Differences of religion, creed or confession shall not prejudice any
> Turkish national in matters relating to the enjoyment of civil or political
> rights, as, for instance, admission to public employments, functions and
> honours, or the exercise of professions and industries.
>
> No restrictions shall be imposed on the free use by any Turkish national
> of any language in private intercourse, in commerce, religion, in the
> press, or in publications of any kind or at public meetings.
>
> Notwithstanding the existence of the official language, adequate facili-
> ties shall be given to Turkish nationals of non-Turkish speech for the oral
> use of their own language before the Courts.

After signing this treaty, the minority issue was shelved. 'It is important to note that Turkish Authorities insisted on applying the rights only to the Armenian, Greek and Jewish minorities as they were the accepted ones in the Treaty of Lausanne' (Kirişçi and Winrow, 1997, 48). The other, non-Moslem, minorities did not derive benefit from any of the rights which were given to these three groups. As such, after the treaty, no cultural or linguistic rights were granted to the non-Moslem minorities – this policy has been applied extensively, for many years, without any change constitutionally.

The Turkish nation-state considered all Moslem minorities as Turkish, and put into practice policies aimed at assimilating them.

It appears that Kemalism in the 1920s and the 1930s offered three definitions of the Turkish nation. The first of them was territorial, an idea embodied in the Turkish Constitution of 1924, which registered all inhabitants of Turkey as Turks. This act promised to accommodate the Kurds, the Armenians, and all others as equal citizens of the Republic. The second definition, less inclusive than the first, was religious. As a legacy of the millet system, the Kemalists saw all Muslims in Turkey as Turks. This was best demonstrated by the overall tone of the Kemalist immigration regime that facilitated the immigration of Ottoman Muslims in the Balkans. This definition had an internal conflict: although all Turks were Muslims, not all Muslims were Turkish-speaking. The third, and least inclusive, definition was ethno-religious. First, Kemalists saw only ethnic Turks, determined by their mother tongue, as Turkish. Second, they used religion to classify the non-Turks into two hierarchical categories as Muslims and non-Muslims. They favored the former over the latter. Ethnic Turks were not a solid majority in Turkey. If the Kurds and the other Muslims assimilated, they could enhance the Turkish population. For this reason, helped by the legacy of the millet system, the Kemalists were willing to accept the Kurds as Turks if they adopted the Turkish language, albeit without forgetting that they were not in reality ethnically Turkish. Accordingly, Kemalists carefully screened them to prevent their number from increasing and their national identity from blossoming. Paradoxically, such moves may have strengthened the Kurds' national identity (Cagaptay 2006, 77).

The 'one language, one nation' policy was considered the most effective tool for promoting such solidarity among people of different ethnic backgrounds and advancing their assimilation into a Turkish national identity.

The Turkish Republic with its strong centralized state tradition had from its foundation the means to disseminate a unified identity. On the historiographical level this has been expressed by the Turkish Historical Thesis and the Sun Language Theory, according to which the Turkish language is the source for all existing languages in the world (Hirschler 2001, 147).

Turkey has no constitutional arrangement concerning minorities. There are no sections concerning minorities in the 1921, 1924, 1961 and 1981 constitutional charters. Turkey's domestic policy concerning international conventions aims to give rights only to those minorities which are non-Moslem. As shown in the example of 'The Framework Contract about the Protection of National Minorities', if the contract especially concerns the rights of minorities, then the policy is not to sign it.

The authorities in Ankara put forward persistently that the policy concerning the minorities is based on the provisions of the Treaty of Lausanne. So, there are no national or ethnic minorities only religious minorities in Turkey, according to them. The leading anxiety of the Turkish authorities is to protect the unity and unitary system of the state and the nation. It seems there is a common belief in official areas that when an accepted ethnic or national minority receives any certain rights, it is inevitable that this will lead to the rights of nations to self-determination or demanding separation eventually (Kirişçi and Winrow, 1997, 48).

The nations which were not accepted officially as minorities in the Treaty of Lausanne did not have the right to teach or learn their own language until recently, so they could not transfer their mother-tongue into writing. Those, especially at education age, speaking two languages still have difficulty reading and writing in their mother tongue. For this reason, some municipalities in Kurdish-inhabited cities have started to make items like bills and street signs bilingual, so that people can learn to read and write their mother tongue – but Kurdish citizens who want to receive their education in their mother tongue are accused of being dividers and demanding separation. In contrast to the Treaty of Lausanne, many international treaties, such as the UN Convention on the Rights of the Child and minorities, mention the educational rights of children in their mother tongue.

Turkey is, historically, rooted in a pluralist social, cultural and historical structure. The two most important sources of pluralism were the commonwealth of the Ottoman Empire and the multicultural system of Anatolia. The Turkish Republic, however, has disregarded difference from the day it was established and has aimed, instead, to lessen the social and cultural traces and effects that result from differences – as opposed to the religiously, linguistically and ethnically pluralist political structures that came from the Ottoman Empire and Anatolia.

During the first few years of the Republic, in the 1921 constitutional charter, 'being from Turkey' was emphasized as the primary identity – but in later years, through the construction of the nation-state, the minority problem began with the application of 'one nation, one language' and with the emphasis on 'being Turkish'. The process has come to a point now, however, where there is a wish, among some, to be in accordance with the EU and the modern world, where there is a need to change rapidly as multiculturalism and multilingualism in Europe and America have become associated with the idea of prosperity. Even so, those municipalities in Turkey which have tried to start bilingual applications are yet to encounter any reward legally. In fact, they often meet with severe criticism and even attempts to take them to court in order to stop their work. Many arguments take place concerning this matter – but both the party in power and the opposition party still see multilingualism as a separation or an end to the country.

The insular and nationalistic construction of the Turkish state, in the 1930s, has limited the ability of contemporary politicians to respond to the present-day challenges posed by Kurdish activities, except through the use of force. However, the military approach, as we have seen, does not provide any long-term solutions. Experiences around the Kurdish uprisings during the founding of the Republic, and more recently in the 1980s and 1990s have shown that this problem cannot be solved with violence. Coercive measures, such as collective detentions, can easily be seen as steps towards deadlock rather than steps towards a solution.

The Kurdish

The Kurdish are a large national group, of around 20 million, living in the mountainous region of Kurdistan, in the heart of the Middle East. Mehrdad Izady describes the region in the following way:

> Kurdistan, or the land of the Kurds, is a strategic area located in the geographic heart of the Middle East. Today it comprises important parts of Turkey, Iran, Iraq, Syria, and Azerbaijan. Since it was, and still is, denied independence, most scholars describe Kurdistan as the area in which Kurds constitute an ethnic majority.
>
> Kurdistan was first divided in 1514 between the Ottoman and Persian empires. Four centuries later, Britain and France further altered the political contours of Kurdistan by dividing the Ottoman Kurdistan into three main parts. Iranian Kurdistan stayed where it was. The area thus partitioned consisted of about 190,000 square miles divided as follows: Turkey (43 percent), Iran (31 percent), Iraq (18 percent), Syria (6 percent), and the former Soviet Union (2 percent), Izady (1992, 3).

The Kurdish question is a central problem for Turkey. Throughout the Ottoman Empire, the Turkish Republic and to the modern day, it has been one of the most important issues and poses an ever greater problem over time. Discussions around the issue have been going on for years, and a low-intensity war has been waged for years, but a serious approach to the problem has yet to be taken. It is now the most crucial question facing Turkey, at home and abroad.

Evolution of the conflict (at armed level and at general level) has taken place in multiple directions and dimensions up to present time. The amelioration in the situation of Kurds in Turkey is highlighted by local and international observers. Legal or de facto changes have taken place in Turkey reducing discrimination and open violence (e.g. lifting of the state of emergency; reduction in human rights violations, such as torture; lifting of some restrictions on linguistic rights; establishment of a state TV channel with 24 hours in Kurdish). However, many restrictions for the development and implementation of the Kurdish identity and their well-being (e.g. restrictions in linguistic rights, including prohibition of public education in mother tongue and access to health services in Kurdish; socio- economic inequalities; difficulties for political engagement at formal level, including difficulties linked to the electoral threshold and the legal provisions for dissolution of political parties; restrictions to media in Kurdish) as well as the continuation of direct violence implies that the Kurdish question remains as a main challenge for Turkey to address (Villellas 2011, 6).

However, approaches to the Kurds, it is important to note, were quite different before the republic was established:

> In his first speech to the newly gathered parliament in April 1920, Mustafa Kemal argued that the parliament was not composed of the representative of Turks, Kurds, Circassians and the Laz, but rather the representatives of a strongly unified Islamic Community. Kemal had even envisaged, according to some accounts of his speeches and conversations with journalists, that where Kurds were in a majority they would govern themselves autonomously. Kemal and his rebellious forces, facing shortages of men and material, could not afford to alienate the Kurds: They needed Kurdish cooperation to carry out the war against the foreign invaders. The Kurds claim that they gave their support on the understanding that a common Muslim cause existed against Western interventionists, and that a future Turkish – Kurdish common multiethnic state would emerge. Still, some Kurds did revolt against Kemal: Among those revolts, that of the Kocgiri in 1920 was the most significant, as it forced Kemal to divert troops from the main theater of

war to deal with what could potentially have led to a serious division within Turkish/Kurdish ranks.

BARKEY and FULLER 1998, 9

Since the early years of the republic, however, the Kurds have been disregarded and attempts have been made to prove that they are actually Turkish – in 1936, the Governor of Tunceli (Dersim) General Abdullah Alpdoğan claimed that the Kurds were actually 'mountain Turks' (Kirişçi and Winrow, 1997:108). He was criticising why these people were called Kurds and why they were acting as if they had been a different race.

Use of the term Kurdistan, and Kurd, to describe the region and people began in the 20th century – the word Kurd deriving from the sound, 'kart, kurt', of taking steps in the snow. Mustafa Kemal Ataturk used the word Kurdistan for the region until he founded the Turkish Republic. However, it is considered a crime now to say 'Kurdistan' in Turkey – it is seen as having connotations of separatism.

Presentation and Perception Internationally

The Kurdish situation was explained, in the 1950s, to the then British Foreign Secretary, Anthony Eden, in the following way:

> The government has tried to assimilate the Kurdish people for years, oppressing them, banning publications in Kurdish, persecuting those who speak Kurdish, forcibly deporting people from fertile parts of Kurdistan for uncultivated areas of Anatolia where many have perished. The prisons are full of non-combatants, intellectuals are shot, hanged or exiled to remote places. Three million Kurds, demand to live in freedom and peace in their own country.
>
> MCDOWALL, 2004:208

The Kurdish issue has long been of importance, and has been followed, in the international arena. It is important to look to the three, recently unclassified, CIA reports on the Kurdish question: Kurdish Minority Problem, 1948; Kurdish Problem in Perspective, 1979; and The Kurds, Rising Expectations, Old Frustrations 1991.

In the 1948 report, which was dominated by concerns with the issue in relation to the Soviet Union, it was stated that the Kurds faced great difficulties in their ability to build a state and that the cause of this was the internal disagreements and conflicts of interests of the tribal constitution. The report also looks into the general features and constitution of the Kurdish people. It investigates and evaluates the Republic of Turkey's efforts to assimilate the Kurds:

> Since 1937 the Turkish Government has kept a strict watch over the Kurdish areas and, while doing so, has worked assiduously to assimilate the Kurds. Turkish policy is based on the concept that 'there is no Kurdish problem, and there are no Kurds'. In official usage, the Kurds are 'mountain Turks' who theoretically possess all the privileges which are the constitutional birthright of every Turkish national. The teaching of Kurdish is prohibited, and primary schools are being set up in which Kurdish children are taught to speak Turkish. Roads and railroads have been constructed in Kurdish areas, not only to facilitate administration and military control, but in an honest effort to raise the Kurdish standard of living; the major railroad construction currently in progress in Turkey is on a line which will eventually run through the heart of Turkish 'Kurdistan', from Elazig eastward to Qutur in Iran, by way of Muş and Lake Van. Kurds who resist assimilation have been transported to the western, non-Kurdish provinces and resettled, a few at a time, in widely scattered villages. At the same time, Turks from western Anatolia, and more particularly immigrant Moslem Turks, are encouraged to settle Kurdish' territory.
>
> CIA 1948, 12

These assimilation policies, aiming at strengthening the construction of the nation- state, did meet with successes in subsuming the cultures of various minorities. However, the Kurdish people persisted in their efforts to preserve a national identity.

In the second report, of 1979, it was again stated that tribal constitution and competing political groups were the biggest barrier to Kurdish national unity. When all the regions (Iran, Iraq, Syria and Turkey) were analysed in turn, an interesting observation was made about the Northern Kurdistan region in the south-east part of Turkey. It was stated, although kept secret, that 'the ruling power in Ankara may permit freedom of expression in broader sense rather than giving them political autonomy'. The report also looks into the relation between revolutionary organisations and Kurds:

> In the past several years, several overt 'cultural associations' and covert liberation groups have formed to promote the idea of Kurdish autonomy

and independence. The appearance of these groups broadly parallels the growth of Turkish radical leftist student groups that appeared in the late 1960s. These radicals often included demands for greater Kurdish autonomy in their programs, and until the Kurds began to form their own associations, Kurds were prominent in these organizations. Mahir Cayan, the most prominent martyr of the Turkish left after he was killed by government forces in 1972, was a Kurd. Because avowedly Kurdish organizations are still illegal, the overt radical groups feature non-ethnic names such as the Revolutionary Democratic Cultural Association and Revolutionary People's Liberation Association. They insist that they are interested mainly in social progress and Turkish recognition of long-denied Kurdish cultural rights.

CIA 1979, 20–21

The report suffers from inaccuracies here, however – Mahir Cayan, for instance, was not a Kurd but from the Black Sea region, and the report also omits mention of those organisations interested not only in social progress but also in a free, socialist Kurdistan.

The 1991 report, though in some parts still censored, explains and assesses in detail the political situation of the Kurds in Iran, Iraq, Syria and Turkey. The parts concerning US interests stand out especially:

The growing Kurdish insurgency in Turkey will place greater strains on the US–Turkish partnership, especially if Ankara escalates its military campaign against the Kurdistan Workers' Party or cracks down even harder on the Kurdish insurgents in the southeast and expects US support in these efforts.

CIA 1991, 59

American intelligence states that building a united and independent Kurdish state is difficult but possible. In this respect, they are correct:

If a serious Pan-Kurdish independence movement develops – which we deem unlikely – the west may be pressed to change its longstanding policy and facilitate the peaceful emergence of a new ethnic state, while trying to preserve its strategic interests in the existing states.

IBID., 5

The attention that is given to the Kurdish problem in these reports by the CIA, and in other international studies, reveals the importance that is placed on the

Kurds within the region. The geographical position and the value of the under-ground resources in Kurdistan is one indicator as to why the region is consid-ered to be so important. That they are such a large and concentrated population without any unifying state, along with historical relationships with the Western world, is also of importance.

Presentation and Perception in the Turkish Media

Perceptions of the Kurdish have changed and adapted over time, shaped, in a large part, by media presentation and representation. There is a political and ideological language surrounding debates and discussions on the Kurdish issue that the public have acquired through the media and through education. The Turkish public are divided over the issue, as we can see in the report Public Perception of the Kurdish Question:

> The survey's results indicate that society seems to be divided into two as far as political representation, claims and hidden intentions of Kurds are concerned, which is a dramatic mix-up of perception and reality. Social or collective political perceptions work differently than those perceptions based on daily experience. This difference might prove to be an opportu-nity if managed effectively; otherwise, it can result in serious problems. Such a reality denotes the responsibilities of public opinion makers and political actors in dealing with these socially significant issues.
>
> ÖZHAN ET AL. 2009, 61

The report is based on a Turkey-wide survey (see Figures 11.1 and 11.2). It shows us that the media plays an important role in Turkey and has strong influence on daily life. The research shows that the media is considered by the people of Turkey to play an important role in resolving the Kurdish problem – but the media has also played a large part in shaping these opinions of the relative importance of these different institutions in the settlement.

Those journalists in the media who are the voice of the war (of course, local journalists whose articles are shaped by editors should be excepted from this), have made great efforts to polarise public opinion on the question, creating a gulf between the two sides. The Kurdish issue has been presented in many dif-ferent ways, which have compounded the quite different public understand-ings and opinions on the question. It is unhelpful, however, to present the issue, as is often done, only in terms of security and terrorism. A recent report on the question considered:

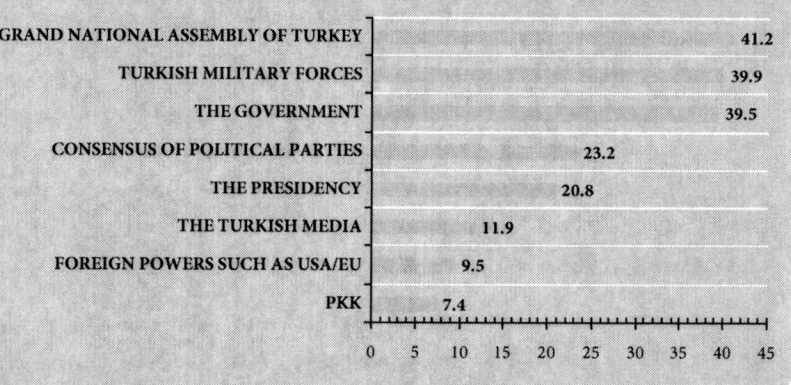

FIGURE 11.1 *Perceptions of the Kurdish question.*
REPRODUCED FROM TAHA ÖZHAN, IBRAHIM DALMIŞ, HATEM EFE ET AL., PUBLIC
PERCEPTION OF THE KURDISH QUESTION (ISTANBUL: SETA AND POLLMARK, 2009), P. 33

In your opinion, which of the below will be the most effective in the
process of settlement of the Kurdish question?
Ethnic Distribution

	TURKS %	KURDS %
THE GRAN DNATIONAL ASSEMBLY OF TURKEY	39.4	50.7
TURKISH MILITARY FORCES	43.8	21.2
THE GOVERNMENT	38.4	45.4
CONSENSUS OF POLITICAL PARTIES	23.0	25.2
THE PRESIDENCY	19.3	28.3
THE TURKISH MEDIA	11.8	11.5
FOREIGN POWERS SUCH AS USA/EU	8.9	12.9
PKK	5.2	18.8

FIGURE 11.2 *Perceptions of the Kurdish question, by ethnic distribution.*
REPRODUCED FROM TAHA ÖZHAN, IBRAHIM DALMIŞ, HATEM EFE ET AL., PUBLIC
PERCEPTION OF THE KURDISH QUESTION (ISTANBUL: SETA AND POLLMARK, 2009), P. 33

The Kurdish Question is not a mere 'terrorism problem', but rather an issue with ethnic, cultural, legal, political, social, economic, and psychological dimensions. It was there before the PKK existed; even if the PKK were to be completely eliminated, the problems and demands of the Kurds would persist. The era of armed conflict has inflicted heavy material and emotional losses on the region and Kurds in particular, and on the entire society in general. The state's failure to pursue policies during non-violent periods in favor of restoring permanent peace has caused it to miss very important opportunities to find a solution, and has created among Kurds a feeling of distrust towards the state. The Kurdish Question, which has so far been a political issue between Kurds and the state, increasingly risks rapid transformation into a clash between the Turks and the Kurds.

ENSAROĞLU VE KURBAN 2008, 5

The relationship between the Kurds and the state is understood by Kurds in different ways across different areas. The state policy of assimilation, and its failures, are understood, lived and resisted by Kurdish people in their everyday lives in specific ways. However, the experience of resisting the assimilation of their national identity by the dominant nation-state is held in common, and there are demands which can be shared:

Despite the fact that different segments of Kurdish society may have highly varied demands, the majority of Kurds, particularly those living in the region, do share similar demands on issues such as linguistic, political, and cultural rights, village guards, landmines, and affirmative action. There is also a group that believes a solution to Kurdish Question requires a general political amnesty, ending the isolation of Abdullah Öcalan on Imrali Island, and providing PKK members a secure place in society.

ENSAROĞLU and KURBAN, 2008, 5

The demands of the Kurdish people may appear to some as unacceptable but it is often a question of empathy and representation, which can make these demands appear less extreme. The media role is very important in this representation of Kurdish demands.

Despite the fact that most Kurds do not want to set up a new state, it very often claimed otherwise – the media has had a big influence on public opinion here, the word 'Kurd', for instance, very rarely appears in the news without being followed by the word 'seperatist'. In another part of the Public Perception of the Kurdish Question report, the distinct perceptions of Kurdish and Turkish respondents on the idea of setting up a new state are explored. The response to the question, 'In your opinion, do the Kurds want to have a separate state?', is very illuminating:

> The results reveal the dominant and widely held perceptions in Turkey on the issues under discussion: 64.4% of the respondents believe that the Kurds want to establish an independent state; 24%, on the other hand, do not share this view. Of the Turkish respondents, 71.3% state that the Kurds want to have a separate state while only 30.3% of the Kurdish respondents share the same view. Of the Kurdish respondents, 59% think that Kurds have no demand for a separate state.
>
> ÖZHAN ET AL. 2009, 61

The question evaluates the extent to which the public perceives a secret agenda behind the demands of the Kurds – and given the response, here, it is evident that much of the Turkish public do believe there is a secret agenda in the Kurdish demands. This perception constitutes one of the greatest psychological barriers to the process of democratic reform of the Kurdish situation.

The Turkish media has consistently failed to have a positive impact on the resolution of the Kurdish issue. Turkey's mainstream media has acted as a spokesperson for the dominant state discourse, espousing civic or assimilationist attitudes regarding the Kurdish question. US analysts Barkey and Fuller have looked critically at the role of the Turkish press:

> The Turkish press is one of the most open in the Middle East today, embracing a wide spectrum of views from far left to fundamentalist Islamist and proto-fascist nationalist. Yet this relatively free press has not been so open when it comes to the Kurdish issue, or indeed any issue that directly touches on the national security. It appeared as if most of the press took its guidance on national security issues from the official bulletins of the government, the military, and the National Security Council. Most coverage of fighting was contained in relatively brief stories about the number of PKK terrorists who were captured or killed the day before, or about terrorist incidents carried out by the PKK. Since there was no formal national debate in Parliament or elsewhere about the Kurds, there was no serious debate in the press either, even though this is not, strictly speaking, a government-controlled press. With the exception of columnists, the press finds it safer to avoid probing discussions of the problem; most journalists describe it as 'self-censorship', which can often be more stifling on a specific issue than review by a state censorship board.
>
> BARKEY and FULLER 1998, 121–122

The mainstream Turkish media has played a substantial role in the 'securitisa-tion' of the Kurdish issue in public discourse. There has also been a prevalence of discriminatory, racist and 'hate' language and representation in the visual and print media.

> Media coverage of the Kurds, the largest minority in the country (approx-imately 15 million), is weak and mostly one sided. Kurds are mostly asso-ciated with terrorism (the PKK), and are portrayed as divisive and as putting forth unreasonable demands. Scholarly research also confirms the nationalistic coverage of the mainstream press, tending to define the nation via perceived internal and external threats. The coverage of the mainstream press treats Kurds as enemy others, belittling and discredit-ing their existence and cultural values. The choice of words and pictures to describe Kurds is mostly biased. While news coverage is expected to build bridges between different cultures, the mainstream press continues to reaffirm and reproduce prejudices.
>
> TUNC 2008, 195

This all serves to give a very negative impression of the Turkish understanding of Kurds and their struggle. The media, as the voice of the state and the medium of war, has contributed greatly to this lack of understanding – it has played its part as a villain in the problems of the Kurdish people.

The Kurdish Media

The Kurdish are, however, also represented in their own media and journalism. An important example of this is the 'Free Press Tradition' newspapers and magazines: Halkın Gerçegi (Public Truth, 1990), Yeni Ülke (New Country, 1991), Özgür Gündem (Free Agenda, 1993), Özgür Ülke (Free Country, 1994), Yeni Politika (New Politics, 1995), Özgür Yasam (Free Life, 1996), Demokrasi (Democracy, 1996), Ülkede Gündem (Agenda in the Country, 1997), Özgür Bakıs (Free View, 1999), 2000'de Yeni Gündem (New Agenda, 2000), Yedinci Gündem (Seventh Agenda, 2001), Yeniden Özgür Gündem (Free Agenda Again, 2003) and Ülkede Özgur Gündem (Free Agenda in the Country, 2004).

Huseyin Aykol, a Kurdish journalist, described the situation of the Kurdish media as follows:

> Our newspapers were published with the aim of covering the develop-ments of the Kurdish problem in Turkey. The reporting we did in an

environment where there was absolutely no tolerance for the word 'Kurd' had to survive and then to be improved under deadly attacks. We lost some thirty journalist and distributor friends. Tens of friends were imprisoned. Moreover, hundreds of friends had to flee to Europe to escape years of prison sentences. Among the media organs, which utilize very high technology and which embrace the ideological arguments of the state, we were usually seen as the agents of a rival country. Although we had the support of some democratic Turks who believed in the peaceful solution of the Kurdish problem, we were usually left by ourselves.

AYKOL 2007, 102–103

Kurdish journalists have paid an enormous price for the extent to which the existence of the Kurds in Turkey is recognised today. The Kurdish have also tried to represent themselves through the media form of television. The first television network broadcasting for Kurds in Turkey, Med TV, was set up by Kurds in Europe – it was forced to close down, however, through international pressure from the Turkish Republic. The Kurds are represented now through the Roj TV network, and it has become an important institution in Turkey, filling a space that has been ignored by the Turkish state for years. It has an important role in broadcasting political news and discussions, but it also runs daily programming around women, children, culture, art, entertainment, and so on. It is followed not only by Kurds in Turkey, but also by Kurds in the neighbouring countries of Iran, Iraq and Syria – it broadcasts segments in Syriac, Arabic, Turkish, Armenian, Persian and English, along with all the Kurdish dialects. Despite some demonisation in the West, Roj TV also now features noted academics, writers, authors and journalists. It is, according to many independent research institutions, the most watched TV channel by Kurds in the region.

Organisers of Roj TV have shown interest in extended the broadcast of their programs throughout Turkey. This could hint at the role that both the Kurdish and Turkish media could play in helping to foster understanding and bringing together the people of both nations and bringing them closer to a settlement of the Kurdish question. However, clearly, this scenario is very far away from the picture today.

Roj TV has come under continuous pressure from the Turkish state, with attempts made to close it down or to interrupt its broadcasting to Kurdish villages. Recently, however, the state has tried to respond in a different way through the setting up of a rival channel, TRT 6, to compete against Roj TV. Previously, the state has rejected the idea of setting up a Kurdish TV channel and, over the past 60 years, has treated broadcasting in Turkish as obligatory, but there is now a recognition that this approach is not getting results.

TRT broadcasting a channel in Kurdish is a sign that domestic and international pressure on the Kurdish issue is having at least some results. The setting up of a TV channel, broadcasting in Kurdish, by the Turkish state could be seen as an important landmark, especially when we consider that in the past the Kurdish people were not even recognised as having a distinct identity, and that a person could be arrested for something as simple as listening to a Kurdish record.

Conclusion

The Kurdish problem, as we have discussed, is the most important and critical problem facing Turkey. Those who have worked for democratic reforms and a democratic settlement to the issue face the possibility of suppression, silencing, inquiries and detention. This acts as a pressure influencing those who work in the media. The Turkish public, in turn, are influenced in their opinions and understandings by the mainstream, pro-government media – and there is no demand for more accurate or alternative reporting. Pressure that is placed on the news and on reporters by the state is generally believed to be legitimate, and there is consent from the public to this process.

The dominant media in Turkey continue in their violent discourse, but then it is impossible to imagine them advancing a different perspective, one which could positively change the public understanding and perception of the Kurdish issue – outside of the public, themselves, actually demanding accurate reporting and alternative, oppositional, perspectives.

References

Aykol, Huseyin. 2007. It is Not Easy to be a Pioneer! In *Another Communication is Possible*, ed. Sevilay Celenk, 102–103. İstanbul: BIA Yayinlari.

Barkey, Henri J. and Graham E. Fuller. 1998. *Turkey's Kurdish Question*. New York: Rowman & Littlefield.

Cagaptay, Soner. 2006. Passage to Turkishness: Immigration and Religion in Modern Turkey. In *Citizenship and Ethnic Conflict Challenging the Nation-State*, ed. Haldun Gulalp, 86–111. New York: Routledge.

CIA. 1948. *Kurdish Minority Problem*. USA: US Government Printing Office.

CIA. 1979. *The Kurdish Problem in Perspective*. USA: National Foreign Assessment Center.

CIA. 1991. *The Kurds, Rising Expectations, Old Frustrations*. USA: National Intelligence Estimate.

Ensaroğlu, Yılmazve Dilek Kurban. 2008. *A Roadmap for a Solution to the Kurdish Question: Policy Proposals from the Region for the Government.* İstanbul: Tesev.

Hirschler, K. 2001. Defining the Kurdish Historiography in Turkey in the 1990s. *Middle Eastern Studies* 37 (3): 145–166.

Izady, Mehrdad, 1992. *The Kurds: A Concise Handbook.* Washington: Taylor & Francis.

Kirisci, Kemal and Gareth M. Winrow. 1997. *Kürt Sorunu.* İstanbul: Tarih Vakfı Yurt Yayinlari.

McDowall, David. 2004. *A Modern History of the Kurds.* London: I.B. Tauris.

Özhan, Taha, İbrahim Dalmış, and Hatem Efe. 2009. *Public Perception of the Kurdish Question,* İstanbul: Seta and Pollmark.

Tunc, Asli. 2008. Turkey. In *KAS Democracy Report 2008 – Media and Democracy Vol II,* ed. Konrad-Adenauer-Stiftung e.V., 189–198. Berlin: Konrad-Adenauer-Stiftung.

Villellas, Ana. 2011. *Turkey and the Kurdish Question: Reflecting on Peacebuilding (Escola de Cultura de Pau -School for a Culture of Peace).* Barcelona: Agència Catalana de Cooperació al Desenvolupament.

Epilogue
'The Left' as Needed Ideology 100

Mandy Tröger

This book is yet another important attempt to bring together critical voices across national boundaries to engage with the "all-encompassing and all-powerful impact of capitalism on mass communication" (Lent 1995, 4). John Lent used this phrase in 1995 when writing about the life and work of critical communication scholars such as Dallas Smythe, Herbert Schiller or Kaarle Nordenstreng. Having taken a 'different road' these scholars have used the academic and public arena to express their restless indignation with how global capitalism affects the "information have and have nots" (Schiller 1984, 8). This book stands in their tradition.

Books like this are the essence of life for young critical media scholars like myself. They dismantle what Robert McChesney calls the "insularity" (1993, 98) that critical scholars in the u.s. and around the globe experience when working within and against pro-market ideologies. Such books make us again realize that the struggles we are facing as individuals around the world are not unique, exclusive or even more difficult than anyone else's. Instead, they are placeholders for deeply rooted institutionalized inequalities whose effects are felt across cultural and political divides, academic disciplines and socio-political orientations. However, these kinds of inequities have by no means been saved for the current moment, more importantly though, neither has the fight for liberation and emancipation. This book then is part of an ever growing body of work that seriously challenges current systems of failure.

Several scholars included in this volume have been my intellectual companions for years; their books are the ones I assign for class, and their ideas are the ones I refer to in discussions with students, friends and colleagues. These scholars fill a void in a world that offers few intellectual voices who speak up against the very institutional structure of which they are part. They might well be considered central figures of 'the (academic) Left'. But, of course, 'the Left' is a social construct. It is word that signifies a potential space for identity which in itself is fragmented. Such labels, therefore, are illuminating our understanding of social reality only in that they simplify its complexity.

The academic Left might best have been described by u.s. sociologist C. Wright Mills who, in 1959, referred to it as "a very small minority in an intellectual community that is itself a minority" (Mills et al. 2000, 277). Mills defined those "few of a few" as intellectuals who question the "nationalist smugness and political complacency among the [very] dominant intellectual circles" that, to him, exercise their research in a "truly deep apathy about politics in general and about the larger problems of the world today" (ibid., 277). Forty years later, Richard Maxwell pointed out that "becoming a critical thinker" inside this ideological mindset "depends on one's ability to escape the strictures of that enterprise" (2003, 22). Maxwell described Herbert Schiller's quest for academic integrity but his words relate to anyone who seeks knowledge outside of the reference frames conveniently offered. Here 'the Left' can serve as an ideology that offers alternatives. It provides different sets of theoretical tools, methodological approaches and intellectual histories. Though fragmented within and across national boundaries while conveying different meanings and forms, 'the Left' contains the hope for resistance. It serves as a platform for dissenting voices and their visions of academic and social reality.

Thus, the authors' overall concern with the political economy of media and communication does not aim to offer an all-inclusive account of leftist voices in media and communications studies in general or claim exclusivity for the 'critical' perspective in particular. Instead, the contributions to this edition have convincingly shown that with a largely unchallenged international capitalism, it is this global institutional critique that gains urgency, popularity, and validity. Whether or not one agrees with specific arguments of their authors is therefore of secondary importance. What deserves emphasis is their continued struggle against, and critique of, the complex and increasing force fields that currently shape the social and academic realities many of us aim to resist. Of course, this should not lead us to fetishize their names or idolize their work. Instead, it is their quest that might guide our own when we again realize that it is not an accomplishment to feel indifferent about the inequalities in the world today. In such a world it needs uncompromising, articulate dissent. This is an important reminder for young scholars whose prospect is to labor as adjunct faculty, who "are encouraged to sacrifice integrity and ingenuity to careerism that does not reward [us] with a career" (Kendzior, 2014). It gives hope that these issues will become increasingly part of public debates outside of academic circles. Still, when academic "publishing is a strategic enterprise" (ibid., 2014) then remaining honest in one's critical stance, and not to give in to the market forces of the academy, is hard to do.

A central theme of this book has been to urge the reintroduction of a sense of history in the analysis of the contemporary conditions of society. Hanno Hardt states that "[history] is the key to identity and understanding" (1992, 8) and the historical dimension "remains a necessary condition for mapping a course of action" (ibid., 9). Put differently, an understanding of history is vital to fully grasp the complexities of current arguments and their informed critique.

On the one hand, scholars from various disciplines joining an interest in communication and information technology (ICT) need a historical understanding of the origin and purpose of reoccurring arguments in general, and for system development in particular. Not without reason does Dan Schiller remind us that "the emergence of the Internet had nothing to do with free-market forces and everything to do with the Cold War military-industrial complex" (1999, 8). What we currently understand as 'the internet' or ICTs did not simply emerge out of the blue but are instead outcome of U.S. government regulations that privileged certain interests and left out others. These political economic interests shaped and, indeed, are 'inherent' in the very network systems that are now put into broader use. This, of course, does not exclude possibilities of (re)adaptation. However, current international communication systems cannot be understood without looking at the interlocking agendas of economic, political and military elites during the Cold War and, more importantly, the crucial role social scientists played in this complex. The latter offered the theoretical foundation for U.S. centered communication strategies while simultaneously providing its tools and methods (Simpson 1994).

This relates to the history of the field and our place within. Communication and media research inheres, as Smythe calls it, a "dialectic political consequence" (in Lent, 1995, 48). In spite of the "naïve notion of science's apoliticalness" (ibid., 48) communication research has always been a highly politicized enterprise and the myopic dogma of 'neutrality' served as its guiding ideology. Thus, for critical communications researchers the dialecticism of the field lies in the fact that their critique is exercised within an academic space that acquired its legitimacy not for its censuring of dominant socioeconomic power structures but precisely for the opposite. The intention of such accentuation is not to be apologetic about the current problems young critical scholars are facing. Instead, only understanding the current moment as a historical one allows us to put our struggles into their proper dimension, and to recognize that surrendering is not good enough. The aim for democratic participatory change has never been easy. It has 'always' been a struggle against a status quo that compromised what might be best for many for that what simply work for a few.

One does not need to be 'a Marxist' to disagree with the ways in which the access to, and distribution of information greatly depends on one's ability to pay. The common assumption that this is how Western capitalist societies work falls short in that we are still promoting democracy, which 'depends' on the ability of 'all' its citizens to make informed choices. These choices relate to all aspects of life. Why is it that my students have no problem identifying as 'consumers' but 'citizen' has become an abstract term used by politicians and academics only? Also citizenry is expressed in everyday life, we simply have become alienated from it. Still, there is a growing political awareness of (and resistance to) issues of surveillance, corporate media and the privatization of information, which cuts across political and ideological camps. The authors in this edition offered their interpretation (and application) of Marx' work. By doing so, they make available theoretical tools that are useful for 'anyone' who thinks about institutionalized oppression, and who realizes that capitalism is not simply an economic system but a 'social' system. Again, following Mills who stated that "I happen never to have been what is called 'a Marxist,' but I believe Karl Marx to be one of the most astute students of modern civilization" (Mills et al. 2000, 23), the aim must be to stay away from the dogmatism we are trying to oppose. Dogmatism simply narrows the ways in which we try to make sense of social reality. Marx helps us to understand the dialectic nature of power relations embodied in institutions (and technology), which is fundamental to any critical analysis of media and communication in the twenty-first century.

I admit that writing about Marx from within the u.s. American context where 'Academic Capitalism' (Slaughter and Rhoades 2004) is at its height is challenging at best. This is not simply because of the material and institutional realities young critical scholars around me encounter. More so, and in spite of the overall claim that 'Marx is back' (Fuchs and Mosco 2012), it is because of the ways in which Marxism is still simplified and instrumentalized to delegitimize visions of structural change. Ironically, I was born in socialist East Germany where 'the Left' was 'the Right' and Marxism, as an alienated and distorted (sinnentfremdet) ideology, fulfilled the same purpose of muting dissent. With the fall of the Berlin Wall, Marxism was dead – anti-Marxism wasn't. Western Marxism that had for years survived in little 'radical' niches nowadays experiences a revival not simply as an analytical lens though which to understand and analyze societies but also in popular discourse. Still, this does not make the institutional and intellectual boundaries of academic capitalism less burdensome, or the poignant critique of Marxism more informed. By the end of the day, it takes patience and constant battles to break with long-held assumptions and fears. This takes time and energy we are told we do not have by those who think of their careers first. After all, critical scholars also need to be attractive for the market if we are not blessed with an Engels to help us out.

If we are lucky, we get to work with faculty members who are discerning, interested and supportive; it is those rare few who have not forgotten that finding one's own voice in the face of pro-market academia is a worthwhile if difficult pursuit. Those without such mentors have books like this one to offer intellectual guidance. These sources of inspiration make us realize again that research should matter. It is not us but the institutional environment that requires change. After all, asking challenging questions is the essence of intellectual life, it needs to be nourished rather then suppressed in order to formulate the next phase of a long-standing critical tradition.

References

Fuchs, Christian and Vincent Mosco. 2012. Introduction: Marx is Back – The Importance of Marxist Theory and Research for Critical Communication Studies Today. *tripleC: Communication, Capitalism & Critique* 10 (2): 127–140.

Hardt, Hanno. 1992. *Critical Communication Studies. Communication, History and Theory in America*. London: Routledge.

Kendzior, Sarah. 2014., What's the Point of Academic Publishing? *Chroniclevitae*, January 24 https://chroniclevitae.com/news/291-what-s-the-point-of-academic-publishing?cid=VTEVPMSED1 (accessed January 31, 2014).

Lent, John A., ed. 1995. *A Different Road Taken*. Boulder: WestviewPress.

Maxwell, Richard. 2003. *Herbert Schiller*. Lanham: Rowman & Littlefield.

McChesney, Robert W. 1993. Critical Communication Research at the Crossroad. *Journal of Communication* 43: 98–111.

Mills, C. Wright, Kathryn Mills, and Pamela Mills. 2000. *Letters and Autobiographical Writings*. Berkeley: University of California Press.

Schiller, Herbert. 1984. *Information and the Crisis Economy*. Norwood: Ablex.

Schiller, Dan. 1999. *Digital Capitalism: Networking the Global Market System*. Cambridge: MIT Press.

Slaughter, Sheila and Gary Rhoades. 2004. *Academic Capitalism and the New Economy: Markets, State, and Higher Education*. Baltimore: Johns Hopkins University Press.

Simpson, Christopher. 1994. *Science of Coercion: Communication Research and Psychological Warfare, 1945–1960*. New York: Oxford University Press.

Index

ABC   140, 141, 142, 144, 146, 159, 193

Al-Jazeera   191, 199, 201, 203, 204, 206, 208, 212, 214–216, 218–222

Althusser, Louis   47, 49–51, 56, 134, 136
  Althusserianism   50

American Dream   123

Anarchism   111, 114

Arab Uprising   3, 190–192, 194, 198–203, 208, 214–216, 220, 222–226
  Arab Spring   67, 113, 199, 200, 203, 220, 224, 225

Autonomy   6, 24, 47, 106, 238, 239

Bagdikian, Ben   122

Baran, Paul A.   68–76, 78, 81–94, 96, 97, 99

BBC   49, 68, 87, 94, 96, 105, 109, 110, 154, 214–216, 218

Benjamin, Walter   75, 76, 87, 88, 93

Bourgeois   2, 5, 7, 37, 46, 50, 56, 63, 73–75

Brecht   74–76, 79, 86, 87, 89, 93
  Brecht on Theatre   93

Cable channels   162

Cain, Herman   115

Candidates   115–121, 129, 144

Capitalism   1–3, 5–7, 11–15, 18, 27, 35, 38, 41, 54, 59, 62, 63, 68, 69, 72–74, 77, 78, 81, 82, 84, 85, 88–93, 96, 99, 100, 105, 107, 108, 113, 134, 136, 138, 148, 162, 173, 190, 198, 249, 250, 252

Cayan, Mahir   239

CBS   121, 140–144, 146, 149, 159, 160, 193, 221

China   5, 12, 60, 133, 148, 158, 166, 181, 182

Chomsky   67, 151, 152, 174

CNN   136, 140, 145–149, 153–155, 157, 167, 199, 214–216, 218

Cold War   104, 113, 132, 251

Commodification   73, 106, 108, 137, 179, 196

Communication   2, 3, 15–33, 35, 37, 39, 41, 47, 52, 59, 62, 67–77, 79–86, 91, 92, 94–100, 104, 106, 107, 111, 113, 123, 133, 135–138, 141, 143, 144, 148, 152, 159, 166, 168–170, 173–175, 177, 180, 183, 190, 193, 214, 225, 249–252

Communications (Williams)   2, 94, 95, 97

Corporate Social Responsibility   166
  CSR   166–172, 175–177, 180–184

Critical discourse analysis   15

Critical work   16, 33, 37, 38, 39, 41
  Critical workers   37, 39

Cultural Apparatus   71–84, 87–89, 91–94, 96, 99
  of Monopoly Capitalism   73, 74, 77, 82, 84, 85, 88, 89, 91–93, 96, 100

Culture   3, 8, 13, 14, 19, 21–26, 30, 32–34, 37, 38, 41, 43, 47, 48, 51, 54, 55, 67, 68, 70–74, 76, 78–83, 85, 87, 91–93, 96–98, 100, 105, 108–110, 112, 124, 126–130, 132–135, 137, 157, 159, 169, 170, 174, 182, 192–197, 199, 203, 207, 212, 217, 225, 232, 238, 244, 245
  Cultural Theory   65, 125, 130, 131, 185
  Cultural work   15, 21, 23, 24, 32, 35, 37, 39, 75, 79
  Physical cultural work   23, 24

Das Kapital   5, 6, 8, 11, 13, 14

Debates   45, 60, 61, 115–117, 120, 122, 123, 240, 250

Debord, Guy   107, 190, 192, 194–198, 225

Democracy   3, 6, 10, 11, 13, 14, 52, 57, 60, 63, 82, 91, 95, 97, 104–108, 110, 132, 134, 150, 199, 202, 208–212, 220, 221, 223, 226, 244, 251

Dialectics   29, 72, 132, 167, 172, 183

Douglas, Mary   125–129

Eagleton, Terry   34, 52, 54

Egypt   191, 193, 199–201, 203, 204, 208–214, 216–226

Engels   20, 22, 55, 56, 88, 252

Ethics   7, 38, 154, 170, 171

Exploitation   12, 18, 33–35, 75, 77, 168, 174, 180, 182, 197

Facebook   111, 122, 136, 179, 193, 201, 206, 207, 209–214, 217

Federal Communications
  Commission   84, 86, 135
  FCC   84, 85, 98, 135, 141, 144, 148, 158

Fox News 122, 145, 147–150, 154, 193
Fox TV 49, 136
Frankfurt School 72, 73, 76, 78, 79, 82, 96, 196, 197
Fromm, Erich 72–74, 76–78, 89, 93

Garnham, Nicholas 96–98, 173, 174
Gingrich, Newt 116–121
Google 156, 166, 175, 178–180, 182, 183, 211, 213, 217
Gramsci 39, 42, 50, 51
Greece 6, 11, 151
Grid-Group Theory 125, 127, 128

Habermas, Jürgen 15–18, 21, 97
Hall, Stuart 45–52, 56–58
Hegel, Georg Wilhelm Friedrich 16, 18, 22, 31, 74, 183
Hegemonial Ideological Domination 124, 125
Herman 67, 151, 152, 173, 174
  Herman and McChesney 173
Hollywood 5, 132, 141, 153, 160, 193
Holzkamp, Klaus 15, 16, 19–21, 36, 37
Horkheimer 72–74, 76–78, 82, 89, 93, 174, 197
Huberman, Leo 82, 84–87, 90–93

Ideology 1–4, 15, 25, 33–41, 44, 46–54, 56, 57, 62, 63, 88, 106, 107, 124, 132, 135, 136, 148, 249–252
  Ideological effect 15, 44, 46, 54
  Ideological work 35, 36, 38, 39, 41
  Ideological workers 37, 39, 41
Information work 23, 24, 30, 31, 41

Journalism 3, 9, 10, 67, 104, 106, 107, 122, 137, 156, 160, 170–172, 193, 194, 211, 244

Kafka 87, 88
Kellner, Douglas 3, 107, 146, 151–153, 190–192, 194–200, 202, 203, 206, 215, 226
Kemal, Mustafa 236, 237
  Kemalists 233
Keynesianism 12
Kurds 233, 235–245
  Kurdish 3, 234–246
  Kurdish media 244
  Kurdistan 235, 237–240

Labour (Labor) 3, 4, 6, 8, 9, 12, 14–17, 22, 25, 26, 28, 32, 33, 39, 41, 42, 55, 59, 61, 80, 84, 88, 90, 105, 109, 110, 133, 137, 139, 148, 174, 181, 182, 187, 196, 205, 209, 211, 250
  Labour (Labor) Party 68, 69, 85, 92, 94–96
  Labour Rights 181
Liberal media 9, 148, 162
Libya 190, 191, 199–201, 203, 216, 220, 223, 225

Mainstream media 58–60, 111, 134, 135, 148, 156, 193, 243
  MSM 134, 137
Marcuse 71, 72, 74, 77, 82, 88–91, 93, 97, 197, 199
Marx, Karl 1, 5, 6, 8, 9, 11–16, 18, 20–22, 24, 25, 27, 31, 40, 41, 46, 51–53, 55, 56, 67, 90, 93, 101, 173, 183, 184, 202, 252
  Marxian 74, 90, 173, 197, 198
  Marxism and Literature 21, 93, 124
  Marxist(s) 3, 6, 15, 21, 26, 31, 32, 41, 44, 54, 56, 68, 71, 79, 80, 90, 93, 111, 173, 251, 252
McQuail 123, 171, 174
Media
  Media Conglomerates 121, 122, 161
  Media Consolidation 122
  Media Effects 45, 123
  Media ethics 171
  Media spectacle 190–195, 197–201, 203, 205, 216, 225, 226
MI5 46, 49, 61
Microsoft 149, 160, 166, 175–177, 182, 183
Miliband 56, 71, 88, 93, 97
Mills 71, 74, 78–80, 88, 91–93, 96, 97, 249, 252
Minorities 80, 147, 232–234, 238
Monopoly Capital 67–74, 81, 89–91, 100
Monopoly Capitalism 68, 73, 74, 77, 82, 84, 85, 88, 89, 91–93, 96, 100
Monthly Review 68, 70, 71, 73, 74, 76, 78, 82–85, 87–89, 91–93
Mosco 2, 3, 173, 252
MSNBC 140, 147, 149, 150, 154, 157, 193
Murdoch, Rupert 6, 7, 8, 110, 121, 122, 136, 147
  Murdock and Golding 173–175
Muslims 233

NBC 121, 135, 140–142, 144, 146, 149, 150, 159
Neoliberalism 8, 98, 106, 112, 113, 132, 192, 193
New Left 52, 71, 80, 96
New World Information and Communication Order 97, 133
New York Times 86, 117, 123, 135, 162
News of the World 7, 9, 10
Non-Muslims 233
NSA 179

Obama, Barack 116–118, 120, 121, 124, 130, 148, 179, 190, 198, 219
Occupy Wall Street 124, 137
One-Dimensional Man 89, 90, 91
Orwell, George 104–106
Ottoman 233–236

Perry, Rick 115, 118, 119
PKK 241–244
Political Economy of media and communication 173, 250
Presidential 3, 115, 130, 190, 191, 200, 214, 219
Primary 115, 117, 198
Privatism 124
Proletarianisation 6
Propaganda 5, 13, 18, 48, 57, 63, 132, 133, 135, 136, 138, 151

Republican 115–124, 130, 147–150, 162, 198, 205
Responsibility to Socialize Corporations (RSC) 183
Roj TV 245
Romney, Mitt 115–121, 123, 130
Rossi-Landi, Ferruccio 3, 16, 26, 27, 30, 33, 41
Ruling ideas 1, 44, 53, 56, 63

Santorum, Rick 116, 119–121
Schiller, Herbert 26, 47, 67, 68, 151, 174, 249–251
Semiosis 28–30, 35
Semiotics 3, 16, 26, 46, 196
Situationist International 195

Smythe, Dallas 67, 68, 174, 249, 251
Social irresponsibility 172
Society of the Spectacle 107, 194–198, 225
Soft diplomacy 132
Software patents 176, 182
Soviet Union 5, 90, 132, 148, 201, 202, 235, 237
Super PACS 116–118
Surveillance 161, 179, 182, 252
Sweezy, Paul M. 68–74, 76, 78, 81–94, 96, 97, 99
Systemic Propaganda 136

Tea Party 118, 124
Telecommunications Act of 1996 136
Terrestrial channels 139, 141, 142, 148, 150, 159, 160, 162
The Cultural Apparatus 71, 72, 74–81, 83, 84, 87, 88, 91, 92, 94, 96, 99
The cultural industries 22, 82
The Guardian 8, 9, 176, 179, 207
The Walt Disney Company 166, 175, 180–182
Thompson, E.P. 51, 71, 78, 80, 81, 93, 96
Treaty of Lausanne 232–234
Tunisia 191, 193, 199–201, 203–208, 210, 212–214, 217, 220, 222–225
Turkey 3, 232–241, 243–246
Turkish media 3, 240, 241, 243–245
Turkish 3, 232–246
Twitter 111, 122, 193, 201, 213, 214

UK 5–11, 14, 34, 44, 45, 57–62, 104, 109, 111, 180, 190
US 3, 9, 60, 139, 140, 143, 144, 146, 147, 149, 151–158, 161, 162, 179, 239, 241

Wildavsky, Aaron 125–129
Williams, Raymond 1–3, 15, 21, 22, 24, 25, 41, 54, 71, 73, 78, 80, 81, 88, 91, 93–99, 124
Work 3, 13, 15–27, 30–39, 41, 44, 46, 50, 56, 63, 67–69, 71–79, 83, 84, 88–94, 97–100, 105, 111, 119, 123, 125, 126, 151, 153, 171, 181, 190, 194, 195, 197, 203, 235, 240, 246, 249, 250, 251, 252
Working Conditions 15, 170, 181